NO

The Noble Dwellings of
IRELAND

The Noble Dwellings of
IRELAND

John FitzMaurice Mills

with 158 illustrations,

77 in color

THAMES AND HUDSON

Dedication

Appreciation and gratitude are
expressed for the encouragement
and inspiration received from
'Cilla of Hamilton House
and
Charlotte, once of Castle Caldwell

*(frontispiece) Marcus Aurelius on a proud
charger, both in white marble, stands guard
by the principal window in the splendid
Gothic Revival ballroom in Slane Castle.*

© 1987 John FitzMaurice Mills

All paintings and drawings of the houses
and grounds are by the Author
© 1987 John FitzMaurice Mills

First published in the United States in 1987
by Thames and Hudson Inc.,
500 Fifth Avenue,
New York, New York 10110

Library of Congress Catalog Card Number
86–50970
0 500 24129 5.

Printed and bound in Hong Kong

Contents

Introduction

7

Afterword

216

Further Reading

220

Acknowledgments

220

Index

221

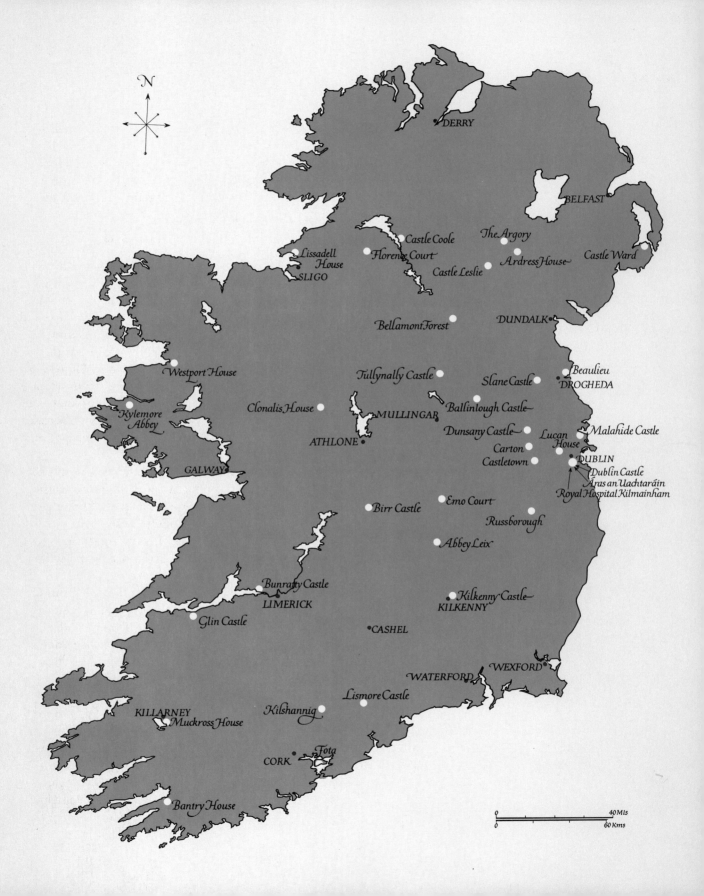

N

DERRY

BELFAST

Castle Coole The Argory
Lissadell Florence Court Ardress House Castle Ward
House Castle Leslie
SLIGO

BellamontForest DUNDALK

Westport House Tullynally Castle Slane Castle Beaulieu
DROGHEDA
Clonalis House Ballinlough Castle Malahide Castle
Kylemore MULLINGAR Dunsany Castle Lucan
Abbey ATHLONE Carton House
Castletown DUBLIN
GALWAY Dublin Castle
Áras an Uachtaráin
Royal Hospital Kilmainham

Birr Castle Emo Court
Russborough
Abbey Leix

Bunratty Castle Kilkenny Castle
LIMERICK KILKENNY

Glin Castle CASHEL

WEXFORD
WATERFORD

Lismore Castle
KILLARNEY Kilshannig
Muckross House

Fota
CORK

Bantry House

0   40 Mls
0   60 Kms

Introduction

Visual and mental surprise are both becoming scarce items in this media-saturated world of package tours, jumbo flights and whistle-stop travelling. The Châteaux of the Loire, the German Schloss, the British Stately Homes, even the temples of the East, the Pyramids, the Aztec sites, have become familiar; and familiarity is the great leveller. Over-exposure hacks off the highlights; repetitive gabbling can degrade even the finest work to something mundane – dismissed in a few brief sentences as the blasé traveller seeks something, almost anything, as long as it is new.

Ireland is not a large country, yet worldwide it is well connected by air and sea travel, and its sons and daughters have peopled many places. It has had great influence from the days of the Dark Ages and before, when Irish men of saintly dedication long-legged it right across the map of Europe and since then have turned up all over the globe. Yet strangely little is known about many facets of the home-life; this is a private area not only to the visitor but also at times to the Irishman himself. Ask the man in Sligo what he thinks of Fota and it is short odds he will feel that you are trying to take the rise out of him, or that you are talking about some native potentate. In many ways this attitude is a survival of the tribal kingdoms, whose borders must stay intact, even if today there are no visible signs of such constraint, only wraith-whispers from the past.

But there is this phenomenon: ask at Bunratty for Mount Ievers, just six miles away – blank look; ask in Newmarket Fergus for Urlanmore Castle, a bare half mile away, and again a negative. Is it that these great stone things have become so much a part of the landscape that they are no longer recognized for what they are? Perhaps they have joined the mystical, legendary, fairy world that wraps itself around the soul of everyone with a drop of the right blood.

If you coast slowly across the Clare landscape, you become conscious of several layers of living. Over the top there is the glittering and at times brash veneer of CIE coaches crammed with visitors from Detroit and Massachusetts, from Birmingham and Poitiers, from Cologne and Sydney; the next layer is young Ireland on the trot, bustling and executive. Then below these come those who are slowly walking the fields, or leaning gently against the old homes, or seeking a bit of the shade from a wind-bent tree; here is the parent, the fellow, the man who begins it all and holds it all together. But is that all? No! In Clare, especially, there's something else, the slow momentum of the primordial. Here is an almost silent place – pause and there will be a soft sibilance from the wandering breeze that every now and then picks up a minute speck of Clare and steals it away. Come to think of it, the great-grandfather of that breeze must have helped remove part of its 225 castles, built so long ago to make it safe for certain people to live there.

Great places in other countries have to a degree become part of the vocabulary. But who could name even a few of these noble dwellings of Ireland?

What is a noble dwelling? A dictionary reels off a string of phrases that include references to social and political status, feudal ancestors, dignity, grand and imposing. Could another inference be added to these – that to a high degree very often it is those who have lived in, loved in, fought for, crippled their finances to maintain these places, who have truly made such castles, houses and mansions noble?

For many people, one of the most attractive features must be that the noble dwellings are in very many cases remote. Remote not just in the sense that they may be a league away from a railhead or grade one motor road, but also hidden away in a delightful, fey country that secretly glories in the traditions of the past, whether they are built from the great heroics of the fabulous kings and queens, or from beautiful, sad legends. Yet, traveller, step warily: for this country that – as a popular song calls out – 'was powdered with silver', has produced more wise heads per acre than most, and has a fascinating upside-down logic which, when penetrated, can be rewardingly invigorating.

Thumb through a directory of properties for the country and it can be discouraging to discover how many seem to have fallen during the years: neglect, fire, Cromwellian gunpowder have had their terrible effect; the remains stand around the map jagged and often further destroyed by those who have sought building stone for themselves. But dig deeper, explore the smaller places, tackle the bog roads and reward will be there. Thirty-five examples have been selected, to all of which can be applied one or other of the qualifications mentioned earlier for the title of noble; some of them are also dwellings which have harboured their families half a millennium or more. Please come with a free mind. These dwellings are greatly varied – the people who raised them were in themselves ingredients from disturbed times, with roots very often trailing across the Irish Sea or St George's Channel. The early ones of Ireland themselves would have already absorbed the rich, persuasive cultures from Neuchâtel and also no doubt a generous draught of the no-fear blood of the longboat warriors.

The people who built these noble dwellings – whether home-grown or immigrants – managed to create their places in an astonishing variety of manners and styles. For many, an overriding need seems to have been to enclose land with as strong and high a wall as could be managed, and to combine this with long, long drives that wind their way through dark pine forests or across bare boulder-strewn landscapes. Some can truly be described as labyrinthine, and finding them a joy of accomplishment. Track down an old road, potholed and swathed in dust, and suddenly come face-

Russsborough – a rampant and well-weathered lion, one of a pair that challenge the visitor to the main entrance.

to-face with a Palladian façade that would grace with distinction a ducal palace in Italy. Push westwards, thread with the narrow road through passes between the Twelve Pins, and emerge from the seclusion of a giant rhododendron-skirted lane, and there across the blue waters of a lough stands a Neo-Gothic fortress complete with an extraordinary array of turrets and battlements. Or walk just a few yards from the speedily moving centre of Dublin to find a Georgian town house of exquisite proportions.

The noble dwellings of Ireland will surprise, reward, and delight all who seek to understand them.

Abbey Leix
Abbey Leix, Co. Laois

Abbey Leix – the garden front that breasts on to a layout that owes its genesis to the Palace of Aloupka, near Yalta, in the Crimea.

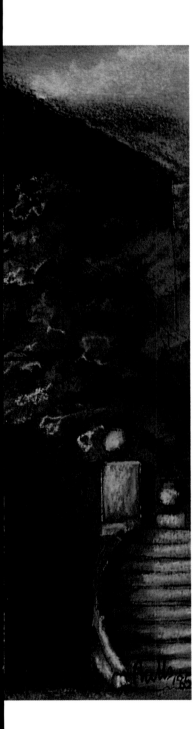

The market town that laps the demesne lies on the site of an early Cistercian Abbey entitled Clonkyne Leix or De Lege Dei, probably founded around 600. Of this first abbey there are no recognizable traces and there is no further mention of it until 1183, when it was refounded and dedicated in honour of the Blessed Virgin Mary by Conogher or Corcheger O'More, Prince of Leix; the first monks were brought from Baltinglass.

The de Vesci family have been in Ireland for a considerable period and can trace their origins back to the eighth-century King of Denmark, Herioldus; then through nine generations to Robert Tete d'Arne de Vassy, father of Robert de Vesci (1066–85), and on to Eustace de Vesci who was one of the signatories of the Magna Carta in 1215. Possession of Abbey Leix came through a marriage into the family of the Marquess of Ormonde.

Abbey Leix demesne is entered by a long drive that begins about a mile outside the town and bores its way through one of those delightful woods that seem to grow and flourish only in Ireland. Long-standing timbers are jostled by lesser and more recent growths, shrubs fill in where they can find a rooting, an age-old lily pond stands motionless with the round leaves afloat and small green weeds cluster the edge. A first visit to such a place is always a moment of expectation. When will the house appear – how will it look – what will be the setting? Eventually the woods clear and lush pastures are fenced off from the drive by the type of timber poles and uprights that bespeaks bloodstock.

Then the silver-grey façade comes into sight, a graceful and satisfying building that has composed itself into the landscape with a harmony not always found with other noble mansions. It was Thomas Vesey, 2nd Lord Knapton and afterwards 1st Viscount de Vesci who had Abbey Leix built as a wedding present for his future wife, Selina Brooke. The family had occupied an earlier house which stood to the north-east, but of this there are no remains today. The architect selected for the present building was Sir William Chambers and construction started in 1773. The elevation that fronts on to the drive has seven bays with a three-bay breakfront, and the entrance door is framed by coupled Doric columns with an entablature. The garden front has five bays with a three-bay breakfront.

During the nineteenth and early twentieth centuries various alterations and additions were made by succeeding generations of de Vescis. The elevations were made more ornate, with balustraded balconies added to some first-floor windows and entablatures placed over them. The roof parapet was given an all-round balustrade, and a wing for domestic and other offices was added in the early nineteenth century. The graceful terraces on the garden side were also added around this time by Emma, daughter of the 11th Earl of Pembroke, who married the 3rd Viscount de

Vesci. This part of the garden emanates a certain atmosphere of mystery. The layout of the flower-beds, the planting of the ornamental shrubs, the green pillars of the yews – it all seems somehow not quite native to the country. Other gardens undoubtedly reveal traces of French influence, with touches of the ornate beloved by the nobles who frequented the courts of the French kings. But the gardens at Abbey Leix have a quality of their own, and the reason is that the general layout is likely to have been influenced by that wondrous place Aloupka, near Yalta in the Crimea. This was the home of Emma's grandfather, the Prince of Woronzow. Sit on a stone slab seat and let the eye wander down the various flights of steps, past the ornamental urns with their flashes of bright blue lobelia (that pretty little plant that takes its name from the Flemish botanist Matthias de Lobel, 1538–1616), between the tight-clipped hedges down to the lowest of the well-kempt lawns. Here the sinuous curves of a curiously formed gate hint at that far-away Aloupka – which, incidentally, has been restored and brought back to life to become a much-visited noble dwelling out there in the Crimea.

The interior of Abbey Leix carries across its walls a parade of fine and interesting portraits of the family. The hall is dominated by a screen of columns with Ionic capitals. Beyond it, the largest of the reception rooms, the White Drawing-Room, has a restrained and lovely plaster ceiling, designed by James Wyatt and regilt in the 1960s; there is more of Wyatt's refined plasterwork in other rooms. In the White Drawing-Room there are a number of outstanding objects: an unusual chandelier with globular forms reputedly from Russia, an immaculate inlaid desk with ceramic plaques of Sèvres of a very high order, and a marble fireplace that perfectly complements the work of Wyatt. The Blue Drawing-Room is rich with the original William Morris warm blue, lightly patterned wallpaper.

The large windows of both fronts make Abbey Leix essentially an outside house, as light pours into the rooms – these are windows that beg to be looked out of towards the distant Kilkenny Hills which act as a backcloth to the vista of the Russian garden and down to the river Nore, where the old pack-horse bridge has flat-topped arches; although built of stone, the bridge has always been known as 'the Wooden Bridge'.

In the King's Garden there is an old wall with a large alcove in which stands the stone tomb of Malachy O'More, the last King of Leix. The time-battered stone carries the inscription: 'Malachias O'More Lassie Princeps. Requiescat in Pace Amen. MCCCCLXXXVI.' The other tombstone here is almost certainly that of William O'Kelly, one of the early abbots of the Abbey.

In 1902 a collection of rare and beautiful plants was lost when one of those fabulous storms that become a part of local lore totally destroyed a large conservatory attached to one side of the house. The conservatory has been replaced by a wing containing a new dining-room.

One of the beautifully proportioned stone vases and urns that decorate the terrace on the garden front; they have weathered to a harmonious surface that blends with the rich mixture of plants and shrubs.

A detail of inlay with various coloured woods that presents almost a three-dimensional effect; just one example in the house of the cabinet-maker's skill.

The de Vesci family are held in high repute by those who live in the town and round about, for they have done much good work locally. One feature of the demesne which may strike the visitor as unusual is the absence of any high stone wall to keep out the unwelcome; there are just hedges, fences and some low walling. Traditionally this was because the owners did not feel apart from the people and thus saw no need for what in many other cases amounted almost to a fortification. In the nineteenth century Lord de Vesci erected a schoolhouse for the parochial school and Lady de Vesci maintained an almshouse for poor widows. But the whole appearance of the town owes much to an earlier Lord de Vesci who had most of the old town razed and then rebuilt to a more open plan. The result today is that, although the main road from Dublin to Waterford passes through the centre, the generously wide street eases the burden for traffic and pedestrian alike – not least in dissipating the thundering roar of the multi-wheeled mastodons.

But back once more to the environs of the house. Step through a legion of very friendly pheasants whose real joy in life seems to be the discomfiture of one medium large cat; turn slightly to pass down the left-hand side of the house and lift the latch of a charming and delicately wrought open-ironwork gate. Spare a glance for the tiny winged heads in the pattern of the gate, weatherworn, stained, but still with something rather special about them. Down the front of the garden side stands a line of small children in stone, some chipped, some disarmed, all dressed with a spattering of grey-green lichen. Walk down past the house and note on the left a small drinking bowl surmounted by a charming little lead figure. . . . But there is a much more important function to the grounds here than just small, pretty, delightful things which echo the charm of Aloupka or late-nineteenth-century sentimentality.

Abbey Leix is mentioned by H. M. Fitzpatrick in his *Forests of Ireland* as being among the first estates in the country to practise commercial sylviculture. There are notable examples of true hardwoods in the old forest, as well as such trees as the sessile oak and common beech which were introduced into England by the Romans. For the specialist there are specimen examples: a Lucombe oak down by the Dairy Pond and on the far side a tulip tree; down through the lime avenue and there appears a weeping beech and, on the opposite side, an Oriental plane tree. The pinetum contains a catalogue of species that would fill a whole page with examples from the Caucasus, Himalayas, California, Japan, Siberia . . .

The grand old monarch of all these must be a marvellously gnarled and curved, rock-hard body of wood: 'The Old Oak', said on good report to be the oldest of its kind in Ireland, mentioned by the naturalist Evelyn as being just that. Experts guess that the elderly gentleman may have seen at least a thousand summers.

Áras an Uachtaráin Phoenix Park, Dublin

Áras an Uachtaráin – the elegant building that was originally the Viceregal Lodge. In 1938 all links with its original title and purpose were severed and it became The House of the President. (left) Detail of the back of a settee showing skilled carving to some considerable depth; the wood has then been covered with a coat of gesso and finally gold leaf applied and finished with an agate burnisher.

Green turf can be the very breath of a great city. Dublin has its share of garden squares but it also has much more: out on the west side it has Phoenix Park, which is the largest public park in Europe. The debt for the provision of this fine area is owed to the seventeenth-century Duke of Ormonde who, more from selfish motives than public service, requisitioned almost two thousand acres consisting mainly of the confiscated demesne of the Knights Hospitallers of Kilmainham. (The Duke did, however, allocate some 250 acres on the south side of the Liffey for the construction of the Royal Hospital, at Kilmainham, for aged war veterans.) The park then measured some seven miles all round and the nearest entrance is not much more than a mile from the city centre. But the Duke's intention was to provide a great deer park for the enjoyment of the Viceroy and his friends.

Phoenix Park derives its name from an anglicized corruption of the Gaelic *Fion-uisce*, meaning literally 'spring water'. One of the beauties of the park is that, apart from a few ventures into ornamental gardening and artificial waters, it has been left very much as a natural landscape; and its great size enables it to house a whole crowd of objects and activities. By the Knockmaroon Gate there is an example of a megalithic tomb, probably unsuspected by many who visit the park. A fine monument erected by Lord Chesterfield, with a dignified Corinthian column and capital surmounted by the figure of a phoenix, leads many to think that the park was named after this rather than a spring of clear water. Overshadowing the entrance coming in from the Quays is a gigantic obelisk set on a platform of slanting steps. Rearing up all of two hundred feet high, this massive statement in granite, the Wellington Monument, was erected by public subscription to commemorate the warlike prowess of this Irishman – who was born in Mornington House, Upper Merrion Street, Dublin. It was originally intended that the Monument should be placed in St Stephen's Green – what a disaster that would have been. But out here it can provide a sometimes welcome indication of where one is heading. Just over the main drive from the Monument are the Zoological Gardens; founded in 1830, they are the second oldest such establishment. Then there is the Phoenix Park Racecourse, and the residence of the United States ambassador, and down on the left-hand side of the Kingsbridge-to-Castleknock Gate drive, the so-called 'fifteen acres'. This hallowed spot was the site for the magnificent altar at which hundreds of thousands from all parts of the world worshipped during the thirty-first Eucharistic Congress in 1932 and it was here that one of the greatest congregations ever seen in Ireland celebrated with Pope John Paul II when he visited the country in September 1979 – a giant cross more than ninety feet high stands as a reminder. There is also the former residence of the Papal Nuncio and the Ordnance Survey building, pitches for soccer and Gaelic football, and wandering around quite happily a large herd of very fine deer.

But besides all this out here in the Park there is the official residence of the President of Ireland – Áras an Uachtaráin. The story of this house started when Nathaniel Clements, Member of Parliament, banker, developer and amateur architect, built a simple, plain-brick dwelling, with two storeys, five bays wide, and curved curtain walls on either side terminating in single-storey pavilions all in the Palladian style. This was probably around 1751–52. With its land it became a private demesne within the huge public demesne. Clements took to himself the title of Park Ranger and Master of the Game. For a number of years he worked with Luke Gardiner, Deputy Vice-Treasurer and Deputy Paymaster of Ireland, on the development of the impressive Georgian streets and squares in the city; he employed or worked alongside Edward Lovett Pearce and Richard Castle, although probably his major contribution came from his business as a contractor. One way and another he must have made a lot of money very quickly.

In 1782 the house was purchased by the British Government for the use of the Lord Lieutenant as a country residence – his official one was Dublin Castle. So the Chief Ranger's Lodge became the Viceregal Lodge after some considerable work was done on it. Apparently at this time it had fallen into such disrepair that – so rumour had it – when it was offered to Henry Grattan he refused it and accepted instead Tinnahinch House in Co. Wicklow as a gift from the people of Ireland. It was not only the house that had deteriorated but also the grounds; in fact the well-ordered park to be seen today was in sad condition – ill-drained and a place often used for duelling by insulted noblemen and for other skulduggery.

In 1787 Michael Stapleton, the Dublin master stuccodore, is known to have put in some work on the Lodge and it is possible that he created the delightful Aesop ceiling in the dining-room – the details have remarkable accuracy and the story, unfolded and picked out in gold above the heads of the diners, must have drawn many eyes upwards.

The maturing of the Lodge was a gradual process and several hands were involved. One who probably did more than the others was the architect Francis Johnston. In 1808 a second storey had been added to the wings, and also a single-storey Doric portico to the entrance. Johnston then went to work and extended the garden front by five bays on either side and made the two end bays project forwards; at the same time he added a truly impressive portico: four large, well-proportioned Ionic columns with finely carved capitals supporting a great pediment. Johnston, who at this time was working as a Board of Works architect, is also credited with the addition of the first wings to the building. Another new wing was erected to one end of the garden front for Queen Victoria's visit in 1849.

A few years previously the gate lodges and the formal gardens were brought into being to the designs of Decimus Burton. How well he foresaw how the gardens would mature. The yew bushes have grown dense and strong under the shears of generations of topiarists; they stand proud on the crisply mown lawns, their large, almost ninepin shapes framing a variety of views of the garden front.

In 1908 electric light was installed and shortly afterwards in 1911 the west bedroom wing was completed in time for the visit of King George V. In 1922, after the Anglo-Irish Treaty, the Lodge was handed over to the first Governor General of Saorstát Éireánn; his successor was to reside there also, after which the noble building was empty for some years.

In 1938 the Viceregal Lodge severed all links with its original title and purpose, and became truly Áras an Uachtaráin – 'The House of the President'. In that year Dr Douglas Hyde, the first President, came to this pleasant and dignified white building, maybe often to stand under the portico and look past the giant columns towards the gathering golden lights of a summer sunset across the mountains. Dr Hyde was followed by Seán Tomás Ó Ceallaigh in 1945 and then came Eamon de Valera. He was followed by Erskine Hamilton Childers in 1973 and barely eighteen months later by Cearbhall Ó Dálaigh, and then Dr Pádraig Ó hIrighile.

The interior of the house has a number of fine rooms displaying examples of skilled craftsmanship: fine cabinet-making and glass chandeliers, magnificent Irish carpets, the modelling of the heads of past presidents. In the dining-room there is not only the Aesop ceiling but also a remarkably fine heavily carved and gilt Irish mirror that is full of dynamic imagery.

Improvements and slight alterations have continued: in 1946–47 the west wing was reconstructed. In 1952 the stewardship of the house came under the supervision of Raymond McGrath, the chief State architect, and in that year, with the encouragement of Dr C. P. Curran, the leading authority on Irish plasterwork, the ceiling from Mespil House was installed, the house itself having been demolished by the Pembroke estate; the scene represented is the composition of Jupiter and the elements. This was a new glory for the President's House. It was also Dr Curran who had casts made of the Francini plasterwork at Riverstown House, Co. Cork, and put up in the ballroom and the adjoining corridor at Phoenix Park; the ballroom itself doubles on state occasions as the reception room where the President receives diplomatic envoys and other personages of high rank.

There is one last feature of this dignified and pleasant house, and that is the colour schemes that have been used throughout – they have been selected with a quite outstanding application of refined taste. The pale blues merge with pastel shades of ecru, warm creams with variants, as one moves from one area to another. Never once does the harmony falter.

Outside the muted grumble of the city traffic may perhaps be heard if the wind is from an easterly direction – but there is peace in plenty in the gardens that lap almost to the feet of the walls, while overhead on its tall spar of white the Tricolour of Ireland flaps gently to a breeze.

Ardress House   Co. Armagh

The name Ardress in Gaelic is Ard Dreasa, literally 'Height of the Brambles', which sets the imagination working on just what kind of a building will appear when the rather fine iron gates are entered and the short drive opens out. The instant impression is of Dutch influence, indeed of even farther away down on the Cape where white, smooth-faced houses with similar parapet treatment and simple fenestration warm themselves in the sunshine. But here in Co. Armagh the more varied climate gives to this rather delightful building unique qualities – indeed, what stands today is the result not only of a marriage between a talented architect, George Ensor from Dublin, and the heiress to the property, Miss Sarah Clarke, in 1760; but also a marriage of the perceptive vision of an architect with an already existing building and site.

Ardress stands a few miles to the east of Moy, a delightful, almost private village that was laid out by James Caulfield, Earl of Charlemont, on the plan of the Lombardy town of Marengo. To the south stand some ruins of what was once Charlemont Fort, which was built in 1602 and burnt down in 1922. The outer defences were once said to have been the best in Ulster; now only a gateway with the Caulfield arms survives. Travel south for about five miles from Ardress and there is Loughgall, known today as a centre for the cultivation of fruit trees and for a tablet on a house which marks the founding of the first Orange Lodge in 1795 after the battle of Diamond. The bloodied cape of history has trailed across the scene but has not paused to bring any great destruction; rather has it threatened as it passed and then left a fertile backwater for the fruit growers, the villagers of Moy and the quiet delight of Ardress House.

The original house on the site belonged to the Clarke family and was destroyed during the civil war of 1641–42; a second house was put up on the same site in 1660 and this is the one which supplied George Ensor with the skeleton on which to work. Basically it was a two-storeyed, five-bay, gable-ended house, a seventeenth-century farmhouse set in one hundred acres of pleasantly wooded grounds.

George Ensor's family came originally from Warwickshire and had a connection with the Armagh district as early as 1612 through the marriage of a John Ensor of Willingcote to Athlanta O'Neill, daughter of Ferdoragh O'Neill; but after this time there is no further mention of Ensors in the district until George's marriage to Sarah Clarke. George and his brother John appear to have arrived in Dublin during the 1730s intending to work as architects. John apparently worked as an assistant to the celebrated German-born architect Richard Castle. George was for a time clerk of works to the Surveyor-General, Arthur Jones Neville, in the Ordnance Department at Dublin Castle, possibly between 1744 and 1751; and he may

Ardress House – the cool, almost severe façade shows some Dutch influence, particularly of houses on the Cape; but fortified by the quality of the northern light.

well have worked not only on the castle but also on other public buildings in Dublin. He is also credited with the design of the Seven Houses in Armagh, but after coming to Ardress and his work there he does not seem to have practised as an architect again.

Some subconscious force must have taken him to Ardress. It was a land that must have given him the rooting quality he needed; Sarah brought him the house to work on and what he did there was an act of personal satisfaction rather than the commission of a patron. Thus the building we enjoy today is a reflection of George's own taste and creation and to walk through it is to experience a privileged visit to a private house.

The outside of the house is largely a matter of extensions: on the front Ensor added a new wing to the north and a screen wall with false windows to the south side. The front door was given some prominence by a porch of Tuscan columns made from local limestone, with a pediment to produce a form of portico. Low parapets carried curved coping stones with carved stone urns on either wing and a centrally positioned Coade stone urn; the extremities of the wings were finished with quoin stones.

The most unusual feature of the rear or garden front is a curving screen wall round the south side, its surface pierced by semi-circular niches in which are marble busts said to have come from the Winter Garden at Downhill. In the centre of the gravelled forecourt stands another of the urns made from Coade stone. The sweeping curve of the screen wall, concave on one side and convex on the other, has a fascinating effect. Looked at from the edge of the woodlands by evening light, the long arm appears to beckon, to welcome, to propose an embrace; the deepening shadows almost suggest a movement towards the viewer, the plain stuccoed surface of the wall acting as a theatrical cyclorama.

Enter from the main door and entrance hall into the inner hall, which was the dining-room in the original house, and the atmosphere is of a homely house, a place where happiness has been found through the years. The gently worn paving slabs are cut from Armagh marble, the fireplace from white marble, the simple staircase from well-seasoned oak. The fixtures and furniture of doors and other pieces are worth examination: the front door has a fine 300-year-old brass and mahogany lock and catch. With one exception this area speaks of a relaxed, simple way of life, the exception being the drawing-room, which could almost have been lifted from another house – a sophisticated city dwelling of the late eighteenth century.

Here is a room on a totally different scale from the simple, almost 'farmhouse' chambers of the rest of Ardress. It measures 27 feet long by 20 feet wide by 13 feet high. The illusion of being somewhere else, perhaps in one of Dublin's stately Georgian houses, is compounded by the superb plasterwork on the ceiling and walls executed by Michael Stapleton, the justly famed Dublin stuccodore. The designs include oval and circular plaques showing figures from classical mythology: arranged symmetrically

The rear or garden front has the unusual feature of a curving screen wall round the south side, the surface of which is pierced by semi-circular niches; in them are white marble busts that are said to have come from the Winter Garden at Downhill. The subjects range from classical figures to what could be portraits contemporary with the building of the house.

on each wall, they are festooned with decorative husk chains that make wide sweeps up and down and across the walls. The ceiling is a true *tour de force* by Stapleton, its centre a robustly modelled figure and chariot with rearing winged horses representing the Chariot of the Dawn. The inspiration may possibly have been drawn from the Bartolozzi engraving from a painting by Angelica Kauffmann. From this centrepiece radiates a sunburst of thin, low modelled ridges to connect with two further circles featuring arcs of trailing leaves and other motifs that echo the manner of Adam, whose influence was starting to spread to Ireland. The cornice is also notable and altogether Stapleton has produced a work of quite outstanding quality so brilliant that it outshines the rest of Ardress. The National Trust has here and in other parts of the house conducted some magnificent restoration work, seeking to conserve and applying decorative treatments that would have been in sympathy with the work of the original craftsmen.

Michael Stapleton was a Kilkenny man who in the opinion of many matched and at times excelled the craft of the Francini brothers, certainly in refinement if not in Baroque bravura. He was much in demand and his work included the frieze in the Examination Hall at Trinity College, Dublin in 1777; four years later he carried out fine decorations in Powerscourt House, and his work may also be seen at 16 and 17 St Stephen's Green, Áras an Uachtaráin, Lucan House and houses in Mountjoy Square. His son George followed his father's profession and among his commissions was the decoration of the Gothic Revival Chapel Royal at Dublin Castle where he worked with Francis Johnston, the Armagh-born architect.

In the west wing at Ardress there is the picture gallery which was originally the dining-room and was reconstructed at the end of the last century – possibly it may once have carried decoration equal to the drawing-room. Here hang some fine canvases which come from Stuart Hall, near Stewartstown, and are now on permanent loan to the Trust from the Earl of Castlestewart. Much of the furniture in the drawing-room has been added by the Trust but it has been carefully selected.

At the back of the house the atmosphere and history of the craft of farming has been preserved in the stables, period byres, a tackle or harness room and a smithy with many of its original tools, including a huge bellows. There are bits of equipment that will need some identifying: a strange gadget called a Kent gapper, and a Wallace scarifier which turns out just to be a tool for loosening the soil.

The grounds include a terraced garden sloping down towards the river Tall, and there are woodland walks where the only watching eyes may be those of grey squirrels peering round a tree trunk. A picnic site is thoughtfully provided and a play area with swings safely hung from stout branches. Herein lies much of the real charm of Ardress House: it is quite without pretension, and this pleasant feeling spreads out from the house into the gardens and grounds.

The Argory Co. Armagh

The Argory – the somewhat strange name is said to be derived from the Gaelic 'Ard Garraidhe', meaning 'The Hill of the Garden'.

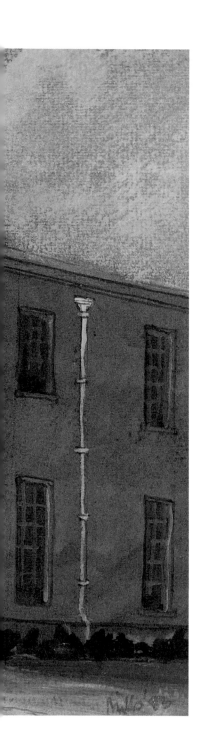

The estate of some 315 acres lies just to the north of the Derrycaw road near Moy in Co. Armagh. The name Argory is thought to be derived from the Gaelic 'Ard Garraidhe', meaning 'The Hill of the Garden'; the house itself stands firm-set on a slight hill looking down across the Blackwater river. The land is cut roughly in half by the Derrycaw road; the area to the south, which is not open to the public, contains the so-called Argory Mosses, a bog of some ecological importance. On the farmland meadows may be noted some strange cattle. These are survivors of a rare breed of Irish beasts known as Moillies that the National Trust has saved from extinction and has been breeding since the early 1980s. They are reddish-brown and white hornless cattle with an odd distinctive feature: a white stripe goes down their backs and round their bellies up to their throats, more or less dividing them in half – in the stock world a beast so marked is said to be 'ring-straked'.

Formal gardens are laid out to the north of the house – neatly clipped box hedges safeguard lovely old roses that still have sweet perfumes lingering in their petals. Here also is the Sun Dial garden, brought into being during the 1830s; the dial in the centre, made by Lynch and Sons of Dublin, is dated 1820 and carries the inscription, 'Here Reader Mark the Silent Steps of Never Ending Time'. To the north of the outbuildings and offices an area known as the Pleasure Ground stretches almost down to the Blackwater. Two garden pavilions which were built at the same time as the house and of similar materials stand at the extremities of a retaining wall: these are the Garden House and the Pump House. Yews have been trained to form two arbours in geometric patterns – an unusual use of topiary. Wild rhododendrons give splashes of rich colour in their season; hornbeams and oaks are plentiful. Specimen trees include a tulip, and presiding in majesty is a fine cedar of Lebanon, reaching upward with its dark green layers of foliage.

The history of the immediate area shows it to have been of some importance during the reign of Elizabeth I. One of the chief crossings of the Blackwater was situated hereabouts and the river was an important transport link: vessels up to one hundred tons burden could make passage with cargoes of corn, coal, iron, slate, timber and salt. There must have been extensive bleach-greens for the use of the linen weavers. The Earl of Charlemont built a commodious market-house in Moy and alongside it a spacious market-place which could accommodate the popular and well-attended horse fairs. The lands to the west of the Blackwater are fertile and productive, and limestone was quarried in abundance for fertilizer.

In the eighteenth century estates in the vicinity included The Grange, where lived a Miss Thompson, and Grange Park, belonging to a Mr

Handcock; but the largest was the Derrycaw estate, which during the 1740s came into the hands of Joshua McGeough (spelt MacGeough by later members of the family). On his passing in 1756 his principal house and estate at Drumsill went to his son William, who was married to an heiress by the name of Elizabeth Bond. In 1817 matters became a little complicated: William's grandson Walter and his three sisters inherited Drumsill but there was a proviso that Walter could not occupy Drumsill while two of his three sisters remained unmarried and in residence – and so they remained, eventually dying in the house as rich spinsters. With few other options open to him, Walter decided to build himself a new house on land inherited by him from the Derrycaw estate, so he commissioned the brothers Arthur and John Williamson to set to work around 1820. One or both of the brothers had worked in the office of Francis Johnston.

What evolved was an impressive, somewhat squat building verging towards the classic in style. It was faced with ashlar and the main entrance is on the garden front. This has seven bays with a breakfront centre bay incorporating a striking porch: two baseless Doric columns flank the entrance itself and a flattened arch above carries at its centre a bravely carved lion's head with bulging eyes and a tongue in the form of an acanthus leaf. Overhead is a Wyatt window surmounted by a shallow pediment with acroteria. Around 1834 a porch was added to the opposite, east, front, as the weather for much of the year made the original entrance uncomfortable. Between 1824 and 1834 a wing was added on the north side; this was the same height as the main block but set back from it, and culminated in a three-sided bow with a chimney stack in the centre. After a serious fire in 1898 this part was rebuilt. An odd fenestration detail can be noted, particularly on the south front where – apparently at the request of the owner – the centre windows of both storeys were given an extra pane, so lowering their sills below the line of those on either side.

During these years Walter McGeough assumed the additional surname of Bond and the arms of his paternal grandmother's family. The matter of names becomes yet more complicated as Walter's eldest son Joshua Walter inherited Drumsill and The Argory went to his second son Ralph Shelton McGeough Bond, who then in 1873 reversed his names, desiring to be known as Captain Ralph Bond Shelton. This gentleman was responsible for some considerable alterations, since when the building has remained largely unchanged. In 1916 the Captain died and his nephew Sir Walter Adrian MacGeough Bond, who already owned Drumsill, inherited The Argory. Much of the contents of Drumsill were moved over and Drumsill house itself was sold. To bring the saga up to date, his son, Walter Albert Nevill MacGeough Bond, in 1979 gave the house and most of its contents plus the estate to the National Trust.

Walk round the shingle path to the garden front and enter under the intimidating glare of the lion into the west hall, and almost at once you will

Clock tower in the stable yard.

The large cabinet barrel organ on the first-floor landing was installed by Walter McGeough, the builder of the house, and was made by James Bishop. Sadly, only three of the original barrels survive; the remainder may have been destroyed by fire in 1898.

notice something unusual about The Argory, something unlikely to be met in any other of these noble dwellings. Most have chandeliers, decorative light fittings, using either electric bulbs or sometimes candles. But up here in Co. Armagh this delightful place is still lit by its own acetylene gas plant – one of the few surviving examples. The equipment was installed by the Sunbeam Acetylene Gas Company of Belfast in 1906 and still works.

In the west hall there is another seeming anachronism: beside the staircase is a massive cast-iron stove dating from 1821 when the architects made a drawing for it and the descending flue; it is surmounted by a replica of the Warwick vase. Probably when this mass of metal was heated through, it performed its intended task very well, rather in the manner of the large cast-iron fire surround in the dining-room at Bantry House away to the south. Overhead hangs a nineteenth-century Colza oil lamp that has been adapted for gas. The cantilevered staircase has some fine brass banister supports – a fashion seemingly popular in Ireland: they can also be seen at Castletown, Co. Kildare and in Fota House, Co. Cork. The court of the hall is amply guarded by a truly powerful, almost life-size bronze cast of a mastiff, one of two bronzes of dogs, the other being of a greyhound. They date from 1835 and are the work of the French *animalier*, Charles Fratin.

Turn to the right from the west hall, enter the drawing-room and the mystery of the extra pane for the centre windows is explained: extra light. The furniture reflects the taste of well-to-do Irish householders of the nineteenth century – on the heavy side, well upholstered, but undoubtedly comfortable. Over the door is the family coat of arms with their motto: *Nemo me impune lacessit* ('No one provokes me with impunity').

On the other side of the west hall is the dining-room, much of the furniture for which came from Scotland in 1827 from the firm of James Whyte and Son of Glasgow – the long table of good workmanship will seat twelve. Accessories include a warming cabinet to the left of the fireplace and also a pair of those most necessary items, brass-banded plate buckets. The other two main rooms on the ground floor, reached from a central corridor, are the billiard room, as essential then as a swimming pool seems to be today, and the study. Here there is much family history, notably a powerful portrait of Walter McGeough by Sir Francis Grant – the character is evident from the slight cant forward of the head and the drooping eyelids.

But return to the west hall and mount the stairs to the Organ Lobby. This houses a piece which is probably unique – a very large cabinet barrel organ which stands firmly fixed between floor and ceiling. It was Walter McGeough, the builder of The Argory, who had this instrument made by James Bishop. There are letters between Walter and Samuel Wesley which show a shared concern for the quality of the music that should be included on the barrels. Sadly, only three of the original barrels survive – the other three may have been destroyed in the fire of 1898.

The outside buildings reflect the same quality as the house – indeed, some features are more impressive. Through a proud entrance with monumental arch surmounted by a large urn and across the yard, the stable block has a breakfront entrance with pediment, atop this a stylish cupola with a handsome weather-vane. The clock is an eight-day striker by Waugh and Son of Dublin. In this area also are the laundry yard, which was at first intended as a poultry yard, the fold yard, a dairy, a churning room, the coach yard and the bullock yard.

The Argory has preserved within its boundaries a way of life that gives a vivid impression of the era between its building and the First World War. The memory will take away with it an impression of sturdy comfort, of careful taste, nothing exuberant or fanciful but the choice of people who could be relied on and who are very much part of the story of nineteenth- and twentieth-century Ulster.

(opposite) The life-size dark patinated bronze mastiff guards the entrance hall. Overhead hangs one of the acetylene gas light fittings – the Sunbeam Acetylene Gas Company of Belfast equipment was installed in 1906 and it still works.

Ballinlough Castle *Clonmellon, Co. Westmeath*

Co. Westmeath, once the main roads are left behind, can be a maze of a place in which to find anywhere – for some this can be an added insecurity, since there is nothing like having to ask the way several times in as many minutes to become almost irretrievably lost. The trouble is that each fresh guide will either get the left and right mixed up, or will know one great house and think that is what is wanted. The area out here is well castled, from the immensity of Trim to the numerous remains of mottes with and without ruins, and the places that have incorporated earlier fortifications into themselves.

Ireland has a recognizable total of over 2,900 castles, although all that remains of the large majority of these is just a jumble of stonework, a mutilated motte or a record on a map or in a document. Most of these would have been built during the century following the arrival of Strongbow in 1170. Apart from neglect, weather and the slighting that went on – particularly by Cromwell's troops – what really signalled the end of the stone castles was the introduction of gunpowder and siege guns. The first mention of the use of firearms seems to be 1487, when an O'Donnell shot an O'Rorke, and in 1488 there is a record of a piece of artillery at the siege of the castle of Balrath in Westmeath.

A fair number of the Norman-built or -inspired castles survive either as great chunks of hard masonry incorporated into later buildings, or with much of their earlier exteriors more or less intact and interiors extensively remodelled to provide a comfortable living. Such a one is Ballinlough.

The Nugents of Ballinlough can cause a little confusion historically as they are really O'Reillys – the name Nugent was assumed as a surname in 1812 in order to claim a legacy. The family is Catholic Celtic-Irish and unlike most of this tradition has continued to live in the castle rather than build a mansion close by. The roots of the O'Reilly sept can be traced very far back and it is a matter of debate whether the oldest ancestor is Eochaidh Moighamheadhoin, who is recorded as King of Ireland around 366, or the fourth Milesian King Brian whose sons were reputed to have been baptised by St Patrick. What is in little doubt is that a number of Irish families have the longest pedigrees of any in Western Europe – another example is the O'Conors of Clonalis. Records of the early history of the castle and its links with the O'Reillys are scarce. Over the front door, high up and in line with the second-storey windows, is a coat of arms with the date 1614 underneath. It is unlikely that this refers to the structure itself: probably it marks the date when the estate came to the O'Reillys as part of the dowry of Elizabeth Plunkett.

It is likely that around 1730 quite major reconstructions took place, with results very much in line with what we see today. The building would have

Detail of carving from the frieze that runs along underneath the delightful bridge-gallery in the entrance hall. It was probably worked from pine and displays a lively bravura imagination with the use of grotesque masks and sinuous plant forms.

been a two-storey affair with seven bays, three of these being incorporated in a breakfront section with a segmental pediment over the front door, the windows tending to be tall and on the narrow side in the centre.

Later in the eighteenth century, possibly about 1780, Hugh O'Reilly, afterwards to become the 1st Baronet, organized a considerable amount of work. This included an additional range at right angles to the front, with two somewhat thin round towers at the corners. The centre breakfront was heightened by another storey just in the centre and then Irish crow-stepped battlements were added. This treatment of the towers gives the house a slight similarity to certain views of Malahide Castle, the home of Sir Hugh's brother-in-law, which had been reconstructed a few years earlier.

But what a delight it is to approach Ballinlough from the path that runs round the lake. The waters in the late autumn were attracting wildfowl that skittered down on to the surface, raising slight slashes of spray as they lost momentum, came to a stop, ruffled and adjusted their feathers before seeking out friends and beginning an excited gossip. The sun was warm and numerous large dragonflies flew low among the reeds, their iridescent wings glistening as the strange insects made sharp turns, hovered and darted before settling momentarily with wings still outspread. The thickly packed reeds ranged in colour from dark steel-green to hints of warm purple and ash-grey where some had withered. The castle from here is sited on a raised shoulder of bright gleaming grass with a backcloth of varying deep foliage. There are no signs of twentieth-century mechanical devices or other clues to period or time, and from a distance the eighteenth-century windows are vague: one might well be back in the sixteenth century or earlier still. Watchful sentries with cocked crossbows might be manning the embrasures as concealed knights and pikemen work their way through the twisting rides of the woods. Or the sheer peace of the sylvan scene could speak of romance and the stuff of the ballad singers.

It is not absolutely certain who was responsible for the design of the reconstructions: some would point to the amateur architect Thomas Wogan Browne, others to the influence, if not the actual hand, of James Wyatt. Documentation is scarce, and Ballinlough, like many other houses, keeps the secrets of its progressive growth to itself.

Enter through the front door and the hall will spring a surprise. It is a lofty place two storeys high; the staircase rises at the back, pauses for a landing halfway up and then leads on to a delightful bridge-gallery – an unexpected feature for the period. The balusters along the front of the bridge have simple, squared heads and feet and, set close together, present an attractive contrast to the richly carved frieze that runs along underneath them. The carving here, probably in pine like other examples in the hall, displays a lively bravura imagination, with plant forms and sinuous stems and masks that leer and grimace.

The drawing-room and dining-room both have some plasterwork of exceptional quality. The basic designs are clearly Gothic Revival, but a version with an individuality of its own that can be associated with the romantic influence of Batty Langley. The cornice treatment in the drawing-room is particularly effective and fresh, with small decorated Gothic arch tops underneath the rigid fluting. The marble chimneypiece reflects the design of Wyatt and is similar to one at Curraghmore, Co. Waterford that is certainly by him.

The placing of the downstairs windows makes for pleasant vistas when the communicating door is opened between the two principal rooms. No trees grow near the castle on the two sides involved so that the sunlight pours in, animating the immaculate white plasterwork with reflected light and producing areas of deep shadow that give a great sense of substance and atmosphere to the two rooms. The chandelier in the drawing-room is a beauty, with well-cut drops and sparkling glass – a jewel set in an elegant room which also contains fine furniture and examples of the Meissen manufactory: two very unwarlike cherubs contrast happily with the heavy muzzled cannon.

The fibres of these noble places are not really the stones and mortar, the timbers from which they are built, but rather those who have manned their history. Through most family trees can be discerned that extra quality that every now and then lifts one figure above the rest – gentleman or lady, warrior or politician, cleric or writer, or more simply one with courage, enough eccentricity and sheer bravura to engender a legend.

Along the walls at Ballinlough hang a number of portraits of the family, including Sir Hugh O'Reilly, who was made a baronet in 1795 and changed his name to Nugent in 1812. The likeness by Gilbert shows a man of determination, with straightforward honest eyes, who wears his uniform with ease, the gleaming gorget high on his chest, a remnant of the days when the gorget was a full collar-like strip of steel to protect the throat. Yet it is not Sir Hugh who most excites the imagination: rather it is Andrew O'Reilly, who to judge by his portrait was a very different character from Sir Hugh. Of slighter build, he has a look of the intellectual, but he was one for often outrageous adventure, in line with some of those gentlemen from Glin Castle or Castle Caldwell who dearly loved to follow if not to lead the action. Early in his life he set his cap at a Bohemian heiress, the Countess Wuyrlena, got himself arrested for planning a duel, escaped to answer the challenge to honour, and did for his opponent. With a taste for more excitement Andrew next fought against the French at Marengo in 1800, and succoured the Austrians from almost certain destruction at Austerlitz. When Napoleon attacked Vienna in 1809 Andrew was the governor. Honours and rank came his way from grateful people. He was promoted to general,

(opposite, above) Ballinlough Castle – the appearance of the ideal romantic castle has evolved through the years. The earliest part probably dates from the 14th century or possibly earlier. Various reconstructions, notably around 1739, have produced this pleasant place sitting on a small plateau beside a placid lake ringed with reeds and bushes that echo to the gabbling conversation of flights of waterfowl.

(opposite, below) Formal heavy iron gates hung between massive rusticated columns protect the private depths of the demesne.

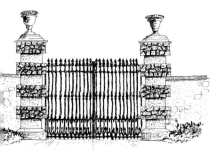

created a Count of the Holy Roman Empire and lived on in Vienna where he died at the age of 92.

Sir Hugh Nugent succeeded to the title in 1927 only to find that the estate was an empty promise; by the rulings of the Wyndham Land Act the lands had been broken up and the castle had been taken over by the Land Commission who had it marked down for demolition. But Sir Hugh managed to recover the castle and the demesne, made extensive restorations and in the early 1930s undertook much replanting of the woods. The joy of these woods may be experienced by turning off the side road through the iron ornamental gates hanging on their heavily rusticated stone pillars.

Bantry House   *Bantry, Co. Cork*

On 21 December 1796, as the shades of evening drew across the south-west of the country, a great concourse of ships dropped their anchors at the mouth of Bantry Bay – that enticing deep-water anchorage lying between Dursey Head and Sheep's Head. This long reach of water could be likened to the cavernous jaws of some great shark – one which was soon to take its toll from the assembling vessels.

It is likely that with the coming of the dawn next morning the good folk of Bantry were shaken from their sleepy awakening by sharp cries of horror, fear and disbelief as the word was passed from house to house that men-of-war and troop transports without ensigns or marking had assembled at the mouth of their bay. Yet this affront was to end well, with the ennoblement of their respected citizen, Richard White.

A Richard White had settled on Whiddy Island in the Bay in the seventeenth century. He obtained from the Earl of Anglesey much of the land of today's demesne.

At the head of the Bay, on the southern arm, the Hutchinson family had built about 1750 a square, three-storey house with five bays. Richard White, the son of the foregoing Richard, was a well-set-up lawyer who had left full-time practice to become a farmer on Whiddy Island. Looking towards the east, he could cast a covetous eye on the great house which lay back into the hill behind it and enjoyed a superlative view including not only the rich, blue waters of the bay (upon which legend has it that the man St Patrick had sailed), but also the islands, with the mauve and warm grey heights of the Caha mountains behind them. Legal acquisition was arranged, and sometime around 1770 Richard White began the alteration and expansion of the house which had first been called Blackrock, then Seafield and, finally, Bantry House. A wing was added at the same height as the original building, but of only two storeys; it had a curved bow at the front and back, and a six-bay elevation at the side. Richard White had a son Simon, who married and had a son christened yet again Richard; the latter eventually continued the acquisition of land. Into the now more superior residence, surrounded by a large estate, Richard settled, and might have gently progressed on his way if that mysterious fleet had not suddenly arrived.

Attempted invasion was no novelty – in 1689 the French had needled away at the idea; in 1697 troops supporting William of Orange had been landed there. Soon word confirmed that this new fleet was again bringing the French, but this time their intentions were different. Another factor had come into the plan. Wolfe Tone, a young Dublin Protestant, with the Society of United Irishmen, had seen a great chance to strike at England by collaborating with the new France emerging from the trauma of the

A formal dressed stone archway and gatehouse marks the beginning of the drive that leads up to Bantry House. The quay, like others at, for instance, Westport on the west coast of Ireland, gives evidence of past prosperous ventures – an exhausted pilchard fishery, butter markets, old and derelict mines for copper and lead. Bantry town today is a happy place, maybe not so wealthy but still able to afford the hour for an exchange of chat.

Revolution of 1789. At the same time, the French had seen that they could profitably use the activities of the Irish also to strike at England. Wolfe Tone had journeyed to Paris and, after much planning and many frustrations, he had been instrumental in organizing a fleet. Exact figures are difficult to calculate since sources differ, but the total must have been around 35 to 40 vessels, which would have included 17 ships-of-the-line, sundry frigates and corvettes, and 15 large transports crammed with some 15,000 troops mostly conquest-hardened from their triumphs across Europe. This collection of ships was under the command of the highly favoured General Hoche, and Wolfe Tone himself, wearing a personally designed naval uniform, took passage in the *Indomptable*. Sailing in three groups, the fleet cleared Brest on 17 December. The last weeks before the sailing had been disturbed by postponements, haphazard planning and arguments. Shortly before the departure, the Directory decided to cancel the whole idea. They sent a messenger posthaste, but a wheel came off his carriage and he arrived to see the ships hull down on the horizon.

Out in the Atlantic, the fleet ran into assorted winter weather that ranged from fog and calm to heaving gales. The groups lost contact with each other and individual commanders opened sealed contingency orders. These stated that the target should be Bantry Bay, rather than the area much farther to the north which Wolfe Tone had hoped for. It had not gone unnoticed by the French command that there had recently been opened a new coach road to Cork; they reasoned that they would be able to reach Cork in a day and surprise the garrison; then, using the large landlocked harbour and city as a base to take over the rest of Ireland, they would be in a position to strangle the English.

So it was that 14 ships, including the *Indomptable*, dropped their anchors at the mouth of the Bay, off Bear Island. The troops, weakened by days of heavy rolling, might yet be effective if they could be thrown ashore with their artillery. But doubts assailed the individual commanders – General Hoche was still somewhere out at sea; rations were running low, mainly because Wolfe Tone had assured the French that there would be plentiful supplies when they landed. Now the weather again took a heavy hand: a strong wind blew down the bay and made movement towards the head shores almost impossible. The anchors had to remain down. A calm came, and with it an all-obscuring fog. The hours passed. Richard White organized the local yeomanry and sent a rider with a warning to the garrison at Cork; the distance was 52 miles and the man made it in four hours. More French ships arrived at the anchorage, but there was still no sign of Hoche. The English Admiralty was sceptical about the news; indeed, one senior member is on record as saying that he would eat his hat if the

The rear of Bantry House viewed from the top of a mighty range of stone steps that climbs the steeply sloping hill. Creepers are taking over and some warm brick pilasters appear to hang in space shorn of their lower parts. (opposite, above) The anchorage that would have been used by the French on that fateful day in December 1796 – it lies at the mouth of Bantry Bay strewn with hard knuckled rock reefs. (opposite, below) The front entrance side of the house; in the foreground a monumental archway obtained by the Earl.

French fleet was really in Bantry Bay. Local militia stationed in Bantry would have been badly outnumbered, but they made a brave face by lining up along the shore to give the impression that they were the vanguard of a large army. Yet more French ships arrived, though still no move could be made. Richard White placed his house at the disposal of General Burgoyne, who had arrived with further troops. Here occurred what seems to have been the sole contact between the French and the English. A French lieutenant, who had been trying to cross from one ship to another, had been swept away and washed ashore near Glengarriff; he was brought for interrogation by the General's staff.

Again the weather took the side of Albion. The winds became gales, and the great wooden ships rolled and dragged at their anchors until the commanders took council and decided to leave this tumultuous place. Those who could not free their anchors cut their hawsers and headed back to France to tend to the storm damage and plan another attempt at the back-door of England. The only evidence of their presence in recent memories has come when fishermen working down over the French anchorage have torn their nets on the firmly embedded anchors which the fleet left behind. But for Richard White the affair marked a beginning of some importance for the family. In 1800 he was created a viscount and in 1816 the Court Notice announced his elevation to the earldom of Bantry.

The house received considerable additions in 1845 from Viscount Berehaven, son of the 1st Earl of Bantry. This gentleman, also Richard, was very different from his father, who had preferred a peaceful and quiet life after his brief encounter with the excitements of international intrigue. On his accession as 2nd Earl, Richard largely worked up the alterations from his own designs and plans. He systematically travelled across Europe, buying, dealing and acquiring an impressive amount of fine art and antiques: his coach became known to the needy with things to sell in France, where he purchased many priceless objects, perhaps with the thought in mind that it was some retribution for the insolence of the earlier men-of-war in daring to enter his beloved waters in and around Bantry Bay. Other beautiful things were found in Bohemia, Flanders, Germany, Italy, Poland and even as far afield as Russia.

Somewhere along the way, the 2nd Earl must have become impressed with the Baroque palaces and great houses of southern Germany. He added a long, fourteen-bay front, with huge red-brick pilasters whose bases and Corinthian capitals were cast from the attractive cream-coloured Coade stone, the windows being surrounded also with red brick and the intervening areas filled with a grey stucco; further brick pilasters and capitals adorned other walls and the complete house was given a well-modelled and pleasantly balustraded roof parapet.

Entry to the demesne is from the quay in the town of Bantry, a restful place which has an air of happiness despite the evidence of ventures that

One of the herons, the crest for the coat of arms of the earls of Bantry, that stand argent-beaked and robed in the same thick white paint that covers other sundry figures, architectural urns and balustrades. The heron is a watchful bird and no doubt these on the terrace at Bantry will be ready to loose their raucous shriek at the first sign of any future invaders.

have failed – woollen mills; nearby derelict copper, barytes and lead mines; butter markets; the pilchard fishery that became exhausted, leaving only fish warehouses as reminders of what might have been. Turn left off the quay, through a quite impressive cut-stone archway and up a well-kept tarmac drive, past flowering shrubs and shiny laurels, and after a few hundred yards the romantic image of the house suddenly comes into view.

On the west side, wide, open, green, close-cut turf leads down to white-painted balustrades – scattered around are large urns and some classical figures, also white-painted, and close to the house stand sentinel herons, argent beaked, representing the crest of the coat of arms of the earls of Bantry. The old house today is a harmonious place, seemingly growing out of – or is it sinking into? – the luxurious landscape. The trees, the shrubs, the grasses are a vivid green, while, as one sits on the lawns near the house and looks to the west, the impression is that the waters of the bay must be almost lapping the white balustrade.

Behind the house is a wonderful confusion of growths; flowering creepers reach up with gentle fingers to the walls, ebullient shrubs swell out and engulf the paths. In the middle is a fancy area with an Italian feel that sports a delicate fountain and round pond, the fine jets on sunlit days producing quavering rainbows as delicate as gossamer. From here, for those with determination, starts a long climb: a noble set of stone steps, with uncomfortably high risers, leads towards one of the great views in Ireland. Persevere and try not to look round until the top is reached. Then swing round quickly and there will lie a horizontal tapestry of a beauty which will hook itself into the mind and stay: if it is a grey day, it will still be something, a monochrome of soft, grey greens; but if the sky is clear and the sun shines down with that special golden light that can powder gild, the scene will repay those who record the myriad palette of exquisite colours nature has provided for this corner of Ireland. The view is given another dimension by the fact that the top step provides a platform for an unusual aspect of the house: here the eye is looking down onto the roofs and the balustrade appears almost as a collar of lace, while the multitudinous chimney-pots are fretted against the surface of the waters.

To enter the house, you approach across the gravelled drive, pass through a conservatory and into the main hall, stepping on four mosaic panels picked up by the great collecting Earl when he visited Pompeii in 1828. Overhead can be noted details from the arms of Bantry and Thomond. On a sturdy side-table stand mutely white marble busts by John Hogan of Cork of Richard and Mary, 2nd Earl and Countess of Bantry. Tucked away to the left of the wide-mouthed fireplace is an off-beat object – a box with a glazed front, it is a Russian household shrine containing a large array of fifteenth- and sixteenth-century icons. Other oddities which point to the wanderings of the family include a mosque lamp from Damascus; a Japanese inlaid chest; a seventeenth-century Flemish overmantel; and the original

The Rose drawing-room is rich with the finest that France could produce during the 18th century. Delicate tables, desks intricate with inlays, stand prettily around the room displaying the curves of their cabriole legs. On the walls tapestry in large expanses – one at least from Aubusson made for Marie Antoinette on her marriage to the Dauphin. In a neighbouring Gobelins room the central features are other tapestries designed by that master of escapist pleasures at the French court, François Boucher. One can hardly wonder at the huge number of French visitors who come here to see those things that were walked over, looked at and worked at by their ancestors before they mounted the tumbrels that wheeled them away for a meeting with Madame Guillotine.

standard of the Bantry Cavalry, raised about 1780 to defend the area against invasion and to uphold law and order.

Leave the hall and wander through the Rose and the Gobelins drawing-rooms, and you could be for just a moment walking through a scaled-down Versailles, or one of those charming royal châteaux. Is it to be wondered that an appreciable proportion of the visitors from overseas come from France to see the things that once were sat on, worked at, looked at by the famous before tumbrels trundled them away for ever? Four panels of Aubusson tapestry, made for Marie Antoinette on her marriage to the Dauphin, grace the walls of the Rose drawing-room. The main subject is *fêtes champêtres*, with insets designed by the painter François Boucher and decorative surrounds by Tessier. In the Gobelins room are two large tapestries from this workshop, reputed to have been the property of Louis Philippe, Duc d'Orléans, cousin of Louis XV and grandfather of Louis Philippe, King of France, at whose sale they were bought in 1850 – subjects include *The Nuptials of Venus and Mars*, and the *Toilet of Venus*.

Pass through into the great dining-room and the scene changes from the gentility of the French influence to a robust Baroque which in some areas bursts into an amazing Rococo, especially in the incredible frames that surround the large portraits of George III and Queen Charlotte from the studio of Allan Ramsay, the court painter. A framemaker's imaginative explosion, a frame cleaner's nightmare, they have flaring palm fronds which reach out from the baseframe in all directions. Heavy, moulded and carved, Germanic-inspired sideboards girdle two sides of the room, and from a bracket high on one wall the gilded likeness of St Patrick looks down.

Inside Bantry House the intimate feeling of a truly inhabited house takes hold. All around on shelves, small tables, desks and other display places are the memorabilia of two centuries and more. It is the small things, whether objects or decorative motifs, that can often tell most about a house and those who have built it, lived in it, loved it, cared for it, wanted it and needed it. Bantry exists quietly; it does not thrust itself on the visitor, but seems to stand shyly waiting for the perceptive eye to be led to its secrets. Then, when the discovery is made, the gentle house can produce almost an act of legerdemain and transport one back through the years. Can the fabric of this precious place withstand the wearing factors of time, the insidious, clammy fingers of damp, the whole process of the passage of years?

Bantry, tucked away as it is down in the south-west corner, is something we all need: a reminder of things from the past, yes; but most of all a place that selflessly offers relaxation, an atmosphere of sheer peace where the wandering prisoners of the twentieth century can find again the freedom which is their true inheritance.

Beaulieu Drogheda, Co. Louth

A place of dignity and infinite charm that stands back from the road a hundred yards or more. A place as far removed from warlike intention as it would be possible to find. A building that was achieved by the work of interested craftsmen. But above all a home that welcomes.

Beaulieu. Its top windows on the south side could have provided a view of the aftermath of tragedy. Eyes peering round the curtains might have seen the frightened stragglers, the wounded who could still walk, trying to find sanctuary somewhere down the shores of the swiftly flowing Boyne, whose waters on that day – in July 1690 – must surely have carried a cruel blush from the efforts of the swordsmen, the musket men and the master gunners farther upstream, as armies met and savaged each other.

Before the present house came into being, a fortress occupied the site of what is now a small wood just on the right as you look out of the doorway on the south side. The top embrasures would have commanded a view of the river Boyne as it starts to widen and approach its estuary by Baltray. This would have been a strategic spot 300-odd years ago but today is a pleasant place with good smooth bathing sands.

Sir Felim O'Neil used the castle as his headquarters when, with an insurgent army of some 20,000 men, he took part in the siege of Drogheda in 1642. The beleaguered town was under the command of Sir Henry Tichborne, one of the Lords Justices of Ireland. The men who followed the Rising were in sympathy with the likes of Rory O'More and Conor Maguire, Baron of Enniskillen, who contrived a plot to seize Dublin Castle on 23 October 1641. An act of treachery foiled the plot but not the spirit behind it: in Ulster there was a general uprising that stood with the standard of Sir Felim. The hollow sadness of the whole matter was that it was brought on by too long a suppression of the native people. Massacres of up to 10,000 decimated the ranks of the planters and for a time most of the province was held by Sir Felim. At Julianstown, north of Drogheda, the Irish won some encouragement with a small victory over Government forces, and the English, to gather breath, sought refuge in garrisons such as Derry, Bandon and Drogheda. But the fires that had smouldered broke into fierce flame – Catholic against Protestant, Old Irish against New English. General Munroe, encouraged by Charles I, landed at Carrickfergus with a large force of Scots. The sands began to pour the other way for the patriots. The siege of Drogheda dissolved and the estate of the Plunkett family was in jeopardy. Charles II granted it to Sir Henry Tichborne in the manner of a purchase rather than the indignity of a confiscation. It was Sir Henry's son, Sir William Tichborne, who built Beaulieu between 1660 and 1667.

Prim white iron railings and gates give access to the house, one of the first country homes to be built in Ireland without fortification, though it

Detail from the large tympanum over the entrance door. It is entirely concerned with martial matters: a decorated suit of armour and a murderous array of swords, daggers and firearms with sundry banners, shields and other devices necessary for the soldier to pursue his craft.

(right) Carved tympanum over one of the doors at the back of the hall at Beaulieu. Various stringed and woodwind instruments can be picked out. The wood used for such carvings was generally pine, which would be given some form of isolation treatment and then painted.

did stand behind a token tall thick hedge which could have been taken as a symbolic palisade. Basically the building is of stone with dressings of brick. The bricks have weathered to a most harmonious subdued orange-pink and have all been set with joints of almost hairline thinness. The areas dressed include the surrounds of the entrance doorway and the windows. The entrance doorway is additionally enriched with Corinthian pilasters and a curved pediment containing a central feature with decorative festoons. The front façade has seven bays, with the two end bays on either side breaking forward, their angles strengthened with settings of slightly protruding fine-dressed blocks. The stone wall surfaces have been rendered. Something which gives much character to the house is the massive wooden modillion cornice, which is echoed to a lesser degree by the quite strong string moulding that goes round the house just above the ground-floor windows. The house that most nearly resembles Beaulieu is probably Eyrecourt in Co. Galway which has a similar cornice but sadly today lies open to destructive forces, a plaything for vandals and the weather. Its magnificent carved oak staircase with cut-through scroll balustrades, gay with flourishes of acanthus leaves and ebullient carved urns of flowers, was ripped out some time in the 1920s and suffered the indignity of storage in the Detroit Institute of Arts; while poor Eyrecourt, yielding with dogged courage to the ravages of the elements, stands like some sightless, soundless, gutted animal.

Enter the front door into the love that pervades Beaulieu and the great hall has a loftiness that reaches up to allow in further light from the first-floor windows. Here are four fine examples of the alliance of the carver's art with the designer's ability satisfactorily to fill space. Over the main door at

Beaulieu – a beautiful place that ignores the passage of time. Built between 1660 and 1667 by Sir William Tichborne, it can lay an honest claim to being the earliest unfortified house to be built in Ireland.

the back is a coat of arms with all the glories of complicated quartering as families intermingle, held in place by two energetic lions and backed by bravura chisel work. To the left and right are tympanums over the side doors; here the subjects are musical, and violins, harps, recorders and many other instruments can be discerned. The wood used was probably pine, which was then treated to accept a top coating of paint.

The decoration of the two principal reception rooms has such a feel of sincerity that it must surely date from the late seventeenth century. The walls carry bolection-moulding (a form of reverse moulding popular at the time) framed panels which pleasingly complement the paintings and other architectural details. Precious and rare are the things of Beaulieu: canvases rich and explosively loaded by the genius hand of Jack Yeats; exquisite miniatures; the skilled carving of a great alabaster pedestal bowl; the refined white marble centrepiece of the fireplace depicting the Roman god of the sea, Neptune – or is he the Greek counterpart Poseidon, trident in hand, riding in a huge scallop shell hauled along by two sea-horses?

Sir Henry Tichborne, 1st (and last) Lord Ferrard, had two sons both of whom met an early end, leaving him with a daughter for an heir. She married William Acton and the couple had one daughter who in her turn married Thomas Tipping. This time three daughters were co-heirs; the second, Sophia Mabella, married the Reverend Robert Montgomery, rector of Monaghan; their issue was Richard Montgomery, on whose passing the property came to his daughter, Mrs Nesbit Waddington.

Behind a hedge and a curtain of trees about half way down the drive on the left-hand side stands a little church, of neat and unpretentious structure; it was built in 1807 with the help of a gift from the late Board of First Fruits (a Church of Ireland organization) of £600. Inside can be found some fine marble monuments to the Montgomery family and one to the Donagh family of Newtown. Leaning against the building outside is a macabre figure of a skeleton in a stone coffin dating some say from around 1117; this kind of subject appears not only in stone and wood but also in paintings – commenting perhaps on the frailty of mortal man.

If there is any direct source for the design of Beaulieu it would seem to be early Dutch – those warm buildings that appear in paintings by seventeenth-century Dutch artists: perhaps it is the lovely tint of those bricks. But for many Beaulieu seems to exude its own influence. It looks at the visitor with a peaceful glance, not a stare but rather a show of welcome which envelops you as you move towards the shingled turn-around. Beaulieu likes to share its past and many an hour could be spent in talk that compasses history – though history has largely avoided Beaulieu, at least keeping its more violent elements outside that guardian hedge. On the journey away, every few steps turn unashamedly round and absorb each detail as it grows smaller with increasing distance – a last sighting by the gates of bars of sunlight and shadow across the lawns.

Bellamont Forest *Cootehill, Co. Cavan*

Architectural delights in Ireland seem so often to be well hidden away from casual eyes. In many cases the demesnes are not only immense but also have in previous centuries built themselves in behind stone and brick walls that are of a height to prevent any sight of what is inside and may travel for miles round some of the larger estates. Signs may be in short supply and word-of-mouth directions divergent.

Come from Dublin on the Cavan road and shortly after leaving the town branch right for Tullyvin and follow through for Cootehill, a straightforward small town that consists mostly of four wide and welcoming streets. A lake or series of large waters border the town and could provide navigation in a suitable craft up to Ballybay in Co. Monaghan. There is also the river Annagh and its tributary the Dromore. It was the Coote family who founded the town. Records show that they came to this part of Co. Cavan around 1660, but there is no mention of where they lived. They had gained possession of confiscated O'Reilly lands during this century. Part of this acquired territory to the north of the town was known as Bellamont Forest, and within this fastness came into being the house known as Bellamont Forest.

Pass down the main street of Cootehill, turn right by the church at the bottom, then quite quickly left, and beg an entrance through a lodge-watched set of gates and railings. Almost at once the drive plunges under the sheltering shade of looming conifers. A bend and the lodge disappears. The wheels squelch through soft patches and still the timber persists. The silver light of the late autumn sky just manages to slip through the thick cover – but now the larger trees thin out and the undergrowth on the right becomes more stunted and a field or so away is a long reach of water. The breeze has dropped and the total surface is without movement – in the distance the colour is almost identical with the soft, cool, leaden clouds overhead and then, as it comes towards the eye, the tint changes to a subtle grey-emerald that deepens to a darker tone as it disappears behind the thorn bushes. It is one of these stretches of water that seem to be found only in Ireland; there is an atmosphere about them that holds a promise of strange things gliding around in their depths, and many an angler will tell of gargantuan struggles with monster pike that may come to a spinner in such waters.

The drive seems to go on endlessly – more fields and trees, then with some twists and a bit of a hill, Bellamont Forest the house comes into sight.

A paean to the person who conceived such perfection – lauded as one of the finest examples of a Palladian villa in Ireland and Britain.

In the mid-1720s Thomas Coote, who became Lord Justice of the King's Bench in Ireland during the 1690s, made a decision to build himself a fine

The great saloon in Bellamont Forest; the architect was Sir Edward Lovett Pearce. Rich in the purity of its design, splendid ceiling, superb proportions reflected in every aspect – doorcases, windows, and moulded framing. The canvas is a copy of the 'Death of Dido' by Guercino, the original of which hangs in the Vatican.

new house, and to do this he turned to his nephew Sir Edward Lovett Pearce, in turn related to Sir John Vanbrugh who produced the majestic splendour of Blenheim Palace for the Duke of Marlborough. Lovett Pearce drew much of his inspiration from Palladio's Villa Rotonda at Vicenza and also his Villa Pisani at Montagnana. Palladio (1508–80) was the Italian architect who absorbed probably more deeply than all others the refinements and details of the classical style – in particular the ancient Roman ideals of symmetrical planning and harmonic proportions. In 1570 he published his treatise *The Four Books on Architecture* and this, with his designs for villas and palaces, profoundly affected domestic architecture in the British Isles. It was Palladio's work that drew Lovett Pearce to Italy for a long period of study, and on his return to Ireland in 1724 he was quick to make an impression. In Dublin his most powerful statement must be the Bank of Ireland opposite Trinity College, which was originally the Irish Parliament House.

What grew out of the hill-top in an open space of the forest was an exercise in purity and sheer excellence. Bellamont Forest is created from fine bricks that have toned to a softness of tint only possible to match with good French pastels, and the ashlar facings are in a soft stone that has withstood

The entrance hall, with circular niches containing bravura busts of persons unknown or unverified. Fine ceiling with a strong cornice – and again every part reflecting Lovett Pearce's search for that elusive quality: architectural purity. (opposite) Bellamont Forest as it sat then and sits today atop a small hill which underlines its claim to being one of the finest Palladian villas in Ireland, or even across the Irish Sea.

the weathering process. The really delightful thing about Bellamont Forest is that it is one of the very few fine places which has managed to preserve its original appearance except for quite minor alterations.

The plan is almost an exact square, with two storeys over a rusticated basement and the addition of a mezzanine at the sides. As in a number of other houses, the main domestic offices – stables, coach houses and estate offices – are some distance away, lying in a hollow to the north and connected to the main house by one of those large tunnels that have ventilation or light-holes every so often; this particular one debouches into the area round the basement, which may have been covered in at one period. The tunnel could have defensive possibilities; it could also have been used as an approach route for any nefarious characters.

The front has five bays and an immaculate portico with sturdy, well-shaped columns with Doric capitals supporting the classic pediment. A flight of wide stone steps leading up to the portico is itself contained by low thick walls and stout squared end stones – all of which gives a sense of power to the entrance but does not in any way diminish the feeling of gentility that is so attractive about this house. The upper storey is treated as an attic above the cornice with the windows square in contrast to the rather high reaches of the ground floor lights.

To mount the steps and to come under the shadow of the classic portico measurably affects the thought and perhaps prepares one for the interior – which has been lovingly restored and cared for by today's owners, in a spirit which Lovett Pearce would surely have approved.

An interesting and unusual carved stone bracket for the sill. Cut from Portland stone, it is an elegant addition to the façade. The bricks, which have toned to a pleasant dark pink, were baked locally from specially built kilns.

Fine plaster ceilings adorn the hall itself, also the great saloon, the dining-room and the library. In the hall there is a high-coved ceiling with a modillion cornice and a use of the keyhole pattern. High up on the walls are roundels containing busts, maybe of the gods of far gone days, though some suggest they may represent members of the Coote family. An extremely fine door with classic pediment and an architrave decorated with carved mouldings leads to the saloon, the dimensions of which give a splendid feeling of space. All the doors leading from it echo the architrave treatment of the main entrance but lack the pediment. The ceiling is coffered and divided into a circular feature with a large rose supporting a glittering chandelier, surrounded by segments to make up a rectangle and then an outer border of small inset squares – the whole carrying bold relief decoration contrasted with sinuous plant-form scrolls in the segments. It is one of the triumphs of conservation that this great weight of plaster has been made safe and can remain in place. At one end of the saloon hangs a very large canvas of the *Death of Dido* by Guercino (real name Giovanni Francesco Barbieri), the Italian painter working in the early part of the seventeenth century; this is a copy of the original which hangs in the Vatican. It seems likely that the canvas was brought to the house when it was built, a not uncommon practice: quite often gentlemen, when embarked on the Grand Tour, would see original paintings that entranced them and would have copies painted.

What makes the saloon so attractive is the colour-scheme used for the decoration. The skirting boards are a tone of deep mulberry, then a white moulding has just a touch of softness to it; the dado comes in a lighter tone than the skirting, then there is another moulding and above this a very subtle, warm ecru grey with just a flick of something else. The combined effect of this with the ceiling, the great painting, the chandelier, the curtains and the soft, light stone colour of the carpets is very successful.

The stairs ascend by easy stages to the first floor. Here all the bedroom doors give on to the landing without leaving any space for windows, yet the area is flooded with soft and generous light. This comes from a large lantern that springs from the centre of the ceiling: oval in shape, it is trimmed with a moulding close to the classic egg and dart. Although these lantern lights became something of a feature of Irish houses, it is thought that Lovett Pearce was the first to incorporate one. The base colour of the flat plaster is an eggshell blue, with just a touch of cerulean, and the white baroque florid mouldings react pleasantly against this.

Bellamont Forest is a house that embodies the sense of a true home, one that has listened to many conversations by past owners, and seen some of the eccentrics who have moved through the years.

Sir Thomas Coote died in 1741 and was succeeded by his son Charles, who died only nine years later leaving his son, another Charles, the owner of what at that time was still called Cootehill House. This Charles became

One of the jewels of Bellamont Forest – the lantern that lights the first floor landing. Here Lovett Pearce was being truly innovative, for this was the first use of such a device in Ireland. After his time it became popular and there is a good example in Russborough. Decorated today in pale cerulean blue, it seems to hang overhead like some private sky, with a wide-winged white eagle clasping the chain for the chandelier.

(below) Detail of the large niche in the entrance hall: a highly decorative design based on a scallop shell and various classical motifs – notably egg and dart, which appears many times throughout the house.

Lord Colooney in 1764 and Earl of Bellamont in 1767, and it may have been he who started to call this noble place Bellamont Forest. By gossip he seems to have been a rather odd character – and a great fan of all things French: apparently when he made his maiden speech in the Irish House of Lords he insisted on speaking French. Another of his pursuits was chasing the ladies and he left an unknown number of illegitimate children. One of these received Bellamont, as the only true heir of his lordship died while travelling in France at the age of twelve. In 1870 the estate was sold to the Dorman Smiths, since renamed O'Gowan. Brigadier Eric O'Gowan was a man of character, who was not a bit afraid to conduct a famous legal duel with Winston Churchill, and he was also a friend and correspondent of Ernest Hemingway. In 1981 the house and adjoining lands were purchased from the O'Gowan family by Mr and Mrs Bryan Mills.

Birr Castle Birr, Co. Offaly

Birr Castle – firm-set in its fine parkland, it is almost but not quite overshadowed by the walls that once carried the 'Leviathan'.

The great wall surrounding the demesne encloses the confluence of the Camcor and Little Brosna rivers and also the boundary line between Offaly and Tipperary counties. The name Birr is derived either from the Abbey of Biorra, which was founded here by St Brendan Luaigneus, or from *bior*, an Irish term for the bank or edge of a river. The ground in this area has witnessed some gory passages of history, as well as some unexpected happenings in later centuries. In 241 a great battle was fought nearby between Cormac, son of Conn of the Hundred Battles, and the people of Munster, and Birr suffered much in 841 and 842 when the Vikings ravaged the district. Neither distance from the coast nor unnavigable rivers nor seclusion offered much protection. Other places the Vikings plundered included Glendalough, Clonmacnoise, Clonfert, Durrow, Ferns and Kells – they seemed to know instinctively where the best loot could be found. The slaughter was horrific and many were carried off into slavery, valuables vanished and books seemed to arouse anger, for they were wantonly destroyed either by fire or 'drowned in water'. In 1154 O'Hedersgool, king of Cathluighe, was cut down at the church door.

With the coming of the Anglo-Normans Henry II granted the area to Philip de Worcester and Theobald Fitzwalter; then it seems that in the

The gatehouse, which in its time served as a meteorological station; its ponderous gates with the Rosse coat of arms were cast by the Countess.

general scramble for land it was sold to William de Braosa and others. Next it was transferred to Hugh de Hose, or Hussey, with whom it stayed until the time of James I. In 1533 Gerald, Earl of Kildare, laid siege to the castle in support of his son-in-law, Ferganainim O'Carroll, but the siege was of short duration as the commander was wounded by one of the garrison. Lord Grey took the castle in 1537 when he was lord-deputy: he seems to have connived with Ferganainim O'Carroll, and a series of outrages were committed which led to his execution. Edward VI received the territory back from the O'Carrolls and then restored it to them, plus a peerage. The succession then became more complicated, for there were a number of sons and claimants, but out of the mêlée Sir Charles O'Carroll emerged as undisputed lord of the territory then known as Ely O'Carroll. On his death in 1620 Birr and its appendages, described as the castle, fort, village and lands of Birr, were assigned to Sir Laurence Parsons, who had been knighted as Attorney General of Munster in 1612. The estate consisted of 1,277 acres of land, wood and bog.

Sir Laurence quickly set to work to bring the castle into some shape for defence. He brought in two English masons, paying them the then quite good wage of two shillings a day. Work was concentrated not on the Black Tower of the O'Carrolls (which has since disappeared), but on the gatehouse and on adding two flankers diagonally at either side which formed the basis of the unusual plan the castle has today. The castle faced not towards the park but, rather in the manner of Kilkenny, into the town of which it was in a sense a part.

Sir Laurence was very much involved with the people of the town: he obtained a licence to hold a market on Tuesdays and two fairs, and later a further licence for another market on Saturdays and two more fairs; and he set up a glass factory. The county assizes were to be held in Birr and from material in the castle archives it seems matters could be a little strict – fines for litter were established and one could be banished for lighting fires in houses without chimneys; the punishment for any woman serving beer as a barmaid was 'to be sett in the stocks by the constable for 3 whole market days'.

After the death of Sir Laurence and his elder son Richard, the estate passed to his younger son William, who was made Governor of Ely O'Carroll and Birr Castle, which he garrisoned with his own tenantry. Came the Rebellion of 1641: for fifteen months the castle was under siege by the Catholic forces, but relief arrived with Sir Charles Coote who apparently managed to get in supplies of food and ammunition for the garrison. The mayhem continued and the castle changed hands first to General Preston, commander of the Confederate Catholics in Leinster, who held it till it was taken by General Ireton in 1650. After the Restoration Birr was back with the Parsons, and Laurence, William's son, who was created a baronet in 1677, did much work inside – particularly on the very fine staircase with its sweeping curves of banisters, the whole made from the wood of yews from the estate.

In 1689 the agent Oxburgh, by devious means, forced a surrender of the castle and accused Sir Laurence of treason against King James. The luckless baronet was incarcerated in the 'haunted room' at the top of the north flanker, until he was eventually rescued by the Williamite forces. In 1690, the year of Boyne, the castle was under siege once more, this time by the Jacobite army led by the Duke of Berwick, Lord Galway and General Sarsfield – traces can still be seen in the park of trenches from which the castle was bombarded. The siege was raised at last by Sir John Lanier for King William and this sorry catalogue of shot, siege, intrigue and general slaughter closed with the castle being used as a hospital for the Williamites.

The eighteenth century brought signs of change for Birr: members of the family turned to more intellectual pursuits – the 2nd Baronet was a friend of Handel. But a wary eye had still to be kept on defence and law and order. Sir William Parsons, 4th Baronet, held the rank of Colonel with the Parsonstown Volunteers, a fact recalled by a large white jug and a teapot carrying the inscriptions: 'Sir William Parsons And the Birr Volunteers – Feby 27 1776.' His son Sir Laurence inherited the earldom of Rosse from his uncle in Co. Longford; he became interested in politics, entered the Irish House of Commons in 1782, and was one of those who studied the possibilities of complete independence from England. Possibly disillusioned after the Act of Union, he turned his energies to Birr Castle. A programme of Gothic treatment in line with the fashion of the times adorned the castle with assorted battlements, most of them crow-foot. And it is to him the credit must go for the beautiful saloon with its elegant vaulting, supported by delicate columns in the shape of bound bundles of rods; his also is the fine Gothic entrance, which symbolizes strength without being oppressive. It is likely that he was largely his own architect but did have some help from a John Johnston (no relation of Francis Johnston).

In the nineteenth century one of the greatest figures of the long line of the Parsons family – William, the 3rd Earl of Rosse – made an impact far outside the little town and the borders of Ireland. He studied at Trinity College, Dublin and then went to Oxford where he graduated in mathematics. Between 1823 and 1834 he was Member of Parliament for King's County as it was then, but resigned his seat to give more time to his burgeoning scientific interests. What particularly fascinated this active mind was the celestial immensity which on clear nights displayed an uncountable array of points of distant light.

Up to this time the largest and most powerful telescope in existence was a reflector with a 49-inch mirror which had been erected at Slough in Buckinghamshire by Sir William Herschel. The 3rd Earl set himself to improve on this. In 1839 he set up a telescope with a 36-inch reflector, and from this moved on to designing and making an absolute giant – a telescope

(overleaf) The gardens and demesne are full of the unusual: (left, above) the greatest and tallest of all box hedges, not just in Ireland but in the world. (left, below) Detail from one of the formal gardens, with well-trained hedges and ornamental urns and other decorative devices. (right) The library, like other chambers in the castle, is full of the trappings of comfort and an elegant way of living.

that would have a 72-inch reflector. This monster was erected in 1845 and was unsurpassed until 1915. Untrained as an engineer or mechanic and with no expert help, he went after the seeming impossible. The mirror, when it was cast, weighed four tons and took four months to cool down in the annealing oven. Mirrors at this time were made not of glass but of an alloy called speculum. The 3rd Earl's recipe for this was four parts of copper and one part of tin. The combination yielded a brilliant reflective power with a high resistance to tarnish.

Brewster's *Edinburgh Journal of Science* for 1928 carried a description of the machine Lord Rosse used for the all-important polishing of the speculum. It imitated the motions made in polishing by hand while the speculum revolved slowly; by shifting two eccentric pins the course of the polisher could be changed from a straight line to an ellipse of very small eccentricity, and a true parabolic figure could thus be obtained. The Giant of Birr had a tube with a diameter of seven feet and a focal length of no less than 54 feet, the whole thing being supported between two sturdy brick walls. The size and method of suspension did, however, constrict its use, for it was only possible to move it a short distance from the meridian and very little to the north of the zenith. And there was one feature Lord Rosse had overlooked: the local weather. Birr is in the same area as the Bog of Allen and for much of the time it is raining, is about to rain or is pervaded by soft woolly mists. Apparently when the Astronomer Royal visited the site he found it 'absolutely repulsive'.

Nevertheless, the immense optical power of the telescope did make possible many valuable observations of nebulae. The 4th Earl succeeded his father and carried on the work, with notable observations of the moon and studies of the radiation of the moon, and a later member of the family published 'Observations of Nebulae and Clusters of Stars made with the 6-foot and 3-foot Reflectors at Birr Castle from 1848 to 1878' in the Scientific Transcriptions of the Royal Dublin Society.

Today in the park a hundred yards or so from the front entrance of the castle there still stand the supports of the Leviathan, as it was nicknamed, looking rather like the beginnings or the ruins of some great cathedral; between its thick walls rests the vast barrel of the telescope – the reflector was removed to the Science Museum in London when the 4th Earl died in 1908. But no one can take away those years of pride for Birr, when the eyes of two brilliant men looked further out towards the infinite than any before them.

The dining-room at Birr is a place of rich carving, brocade paper on the walls of warm crimson red, a ceiling reflecting the tracery of Gothic ideas. Over the fireplace hangs a portrait of Admiral Lord Hawke, the victor of the great battle of Quiberon Bay, and in the hall hangs a large canvas of this battle by Dominique Serres – the 4th Lord Rosse married the Hawke heiress in 1870. To the right of the Admiral hangs the 3rd Earl and with him his very talented wife Mary, who was heiress of the fields of Heaton outside Bradford, which allowed her to contribute to the cost of the Leviathan. Not to be outdone by her husband's casting talents, this charming lady apparently not only designed the gates, with their massive coat of arms, but also cast them. But her real talent lies in a special room deep in the castle – a darkroom, the contents of which and the reason for which remained unknown for long after the Countess's death. What treasure for the archivist and historian lies here is only now being fully explored. The darkroom, set up around 1855, has boxes and boxes of glass plates carrying images of the life of that time, shelves with all the original chemicals, glass jars, dishes, plate-holders, cameras – all the impedimenta of a fully fledged professional photographer. In 1856 Mary Rosse is believed to have become the first lady member of the Dublin Photographic Society and was awarded their silver medal 'For the best paper negative'. She must have been a wonderful partner for the 3rd Earl, helping not only with his work but also rebuilding the fortifications and moats to provide employment for famine relief. She herself had eleven children, the youngest of whom, Charles, added further lustre to the family legend by inventing the steam turbine engine and being the first engineer to be awarded the Order of Merit.

Today part of the glory of Birr lies in its gardens and woodlands. In the latter part of the eighteenth century Sir William Parsons started to improve the landscape of the park with clumps of trees to make the view more exciting; he also dredged the lake. Interest was maintained and the impetus gathered force under the 5th Earl when he inherited in 1908; while his successor, the 6th Earl, became one of the most notable leaders in this field. Expeditions were made abroad – to the Americas, East Asia, notably China, Chile, Mexico, Guatamala, the Himalayas and the Caucasus – and seeds brought back to Birr, some so rare that specimens from them have been sent to the Royal Botanic Gardens at Kew.

In their season these beautiful plants, shrubs and trees give of their best to the heart of Birr – magnolias, cherries, crabapples, azaleas and the celebrated peony Anne Rosse. There is a famous box hedge, which towers up like the reaching nave of some green cathedral, and formal gardens with their patiently trained trunks and branches contrive vistas of a decorative urn or statue. In the background, marvellously tall and feathery dark green against the skies, stand rank on rank of Greek firs, Caucasian firs, Douglas straight trunks stretched to compete in vain with enormous Wellingtonias. There must in all be well over a thousand trees.

It is a remarkable reversal: Birr, which began its days battered and blood-spattered, turned and changed course to become a place of colour, of perfumes of sweet flowers and the heady resins of conifers, the hushing rustle of a million greens, the music of the waters.

Some six miles to the west of Limerick stands probably the best known of all the ancient castles of Ireland, challenging perhaps even the wistful claims of Blarney. If possible, approach it early in the morning when the rising sun is melting away the mists of the night, or make your way to it in the evening as the pastel shades of the approaching quiet time soften crude parts of the landscape and obscure brash building statements that crowd the edges of the road.

The imposing mass stands on what was formerly the island of Tradree, on the northern bank of the Shannon, which by this point has become a wide spate of waters that are engaging themselves with the salty running swells of the Atlantic. It is more than likely that the site was first fortified by the Vikings.

The name Bunratty actually means the mouth of the Raite river, which is now called the O'Garney. Archaeology has yet to substantiate the presence of Bronze or Iron Age settlers.

The great corner towers rear up over the flat waterlogged land defiant as ever they were. The grass grows green round Bunratty today – and well it might, for all the blood that must have drenched the turf during its history as sharpened blade and smoking cannon took their toll of those bent on conquest and defence.

The first serious fortification was probably a timber bretesche – a house stout enough for defence – built in 1251 by a Norman knight called Robert de Muscegros. In 1248 he had been granted 'The Cantred of Tradraighe' by Henry III for an annual rent of thirty pounds; at this same time a licence was given to Bunratty to hold fairs and markets. Records suggest that by the end of the thirteenth century Bunratty was a place of some prominence, a town that boasted two hundred burgesses. After De Muscegros's death Edward I granted the lands to Thomas de Clare, son of the Earl of Gloucester, and he constructed the first stone castle in 1277 – this must have been quite a formidable place as there were also stout defensive walls surrounding the great tower. Thomas was the great-great-grandson of Strongbow and Eva McMurragh, but despite his Irish blood he was resented as a Norman usurper, particularly by the powerful O'Brien sept. In this same year Brian Ruadh O'Brien, deposed as the King of Thomond by his nephew Turlogh Mor O'Brien and uncertain where to turn for aid, appealed to De Clare for assistance. Apparently he was received into the castle as guest of honour at a banquet. A passage in the *Annals of Loughfea* describes what followed: 'After they had poured their blood into the same vessel and after they had pledged Christ's friendship and after they had exchanged mutual vows by the relics, bells and croziers of Munster, de Clare had Brian Ruadh taken outside and torn asunder by horses, his head

Bunratty Castle – a stark statement from the age when cold steel ruled, now peacefully evoked to the strains of the harp and makebelieve medieval wassail.

59

cut off and his body gibbeted to a tall post outside the Castle of Bunratty.'

In 1280 Turlogh Mor O'Brien and his brother Donal, with strong forces of foot and mounted soldiers, assaulted the castle by night; it must have been a bloody business as the attackers forced their way through outer defences and close up to the castle proper – many were the casualties on both sides. Another brave sept took a hand in matters; the McNamaras, whose lands had been ravaged by the Normans, twice fired the building before 1306. Twelve years later, at the battle of Corofin some twenty miles to the north, the combined forces of the Irish inflicted heavy losses on the Normans and killed Richard de Clare, the son of Thomas; on hearing the news his widow gathered her belongings, fired the castle, fled to the Norman ships lying in the river, and made all sail back to England.

Once more the castle was rebuilt, this time probably by Robert de Welle acting for King Edward II. A few short years of apparent calm and then the O'Briens and McNamaras came raging in again and this time totally overran the defences and left the castle an almost total ruin. Another twenty years passed and another attempt was made to restore it, this time by the King's Justiciar, Sir Thomas de Rokeby. But it can hardly have been completed when the Irish once more slammed their way into it and reduced the masonry to rubble.

A deceptive peace came to the west as the English became engaged with such other troubles as the Hundred Years War and the Wars of the Roses. The history of the province lacks reliable records, but it seems that about the middle of the fifteenth century Bunratty Castle was again rebuilt, though on a slightly different site: the earlier buildings stood close to the present site of the Bunratty Castle Hotel. The patron this time was Maccon MacSioda Macconmara, Chief of Clann Cuilein, and the work was completed by his son Sean Finn who died in 1467. The place remained with the McNamaras until about 1500, when either by more bloodshed or by a useful marriage it passed to the O'Briens. Turlogh O'Brien had married Raghnailt McNamara; in 1542 their son Murough made a submission to Henry VIII and in return was created Earl of Thomond. Of the Earl it was recorded that: 'He has dominions among the wild tribes, he has lords and knights upon his estates who pay him tribute . . . he keeps better justice throughout his dominions than any chief in Ireland. Robbers and homicides find no mercy and are executed out of hand. His people are in high order and discipline.'

At the beginning of the Great Rebellion in 1641 the castle was held by Barnabas, the 6th Earl of Thomond, by repute a sly one who could at one and the same time be a Royalist, a Rebel and a Roundhead. In 1646 a Parliamentarian fleet commanded by Sir William Penn and Lieutenant Colonel McAdam anchored within sight of the castle. Meekly Barnabas allowed a strong body of some 700 men to occupy his castle. Not far to the east the Irish Confederates had taken over the city of Limerick and they rightly saw Bunratty in the hands of the Parliamentarians as a menace to shipping coming to and leaving the port of Limerick. A determined siege was laid to the fortification, the Confederates being encouraged by the arrival in their ranks of Cardinal Jean Baptist Rinuccini, who had been dispatched to Ireland by Pope Innocent X and given the rank of Papal Nuncio to the Confederation of Kilkenny. He remained with the forces until the surrender of Bunratty on 13 July 1646. Apparently the Cardinal must have been greatly taken with the castle and surrounding area, for he wrote to his brother: 'I have no hesitation in asserting that Bunratty is the most beautiful spot I have ever seen. In Italy there is nothing like the castle of my Lord Thomond. Nothing like its ponds and parks with its three thousand head of deer.'

The survivors of the English forces under Sir William Penn withdrew, probably taking the wretched Barnabas with them, as it appears that he retired to England and lived there until his death in 1656. (Sir William Penn was the father of the famous Quaker who founded Pennsylvania.)

During the following years the castle seems to have been spared so high a level of bloodthirsty drama and outright mayhem. Records show that in 1709 a Robert Amory took a lease of 'the castle, farm and lands of Bunratty, of 472 acres, with free ingress, egress and regress, for coach or cart through the park of Bunratty to the town of Sixmilebridge'. Next came Thomas Studdert, who took up residence in 1720; his family lived there for some years and then built a mansion in another part of the demesne, allowing the castle to be mangled by the forces of the weather and ivy and other tree growths. Some parts were apparently kept habitable and these were used for a constabulary barracks.

Since 1954, through the combined efforts of Lord Gort, Percy Le Clerc and John Hunt acting with the Office of Public Works, there has been an impressive restoration and refurbishment. The work has now been completed and the result is a worthy recreation of the face and the feel of a great castle of earlier centuries. The rectangular keep must be the finest in the country and the crow-foot battlements which loom up some ninety feet above it make a sure target for the thousands of visitors who annually pour in by coach from Europe or roar down on Shannon airport in a succession of full-bellied jets. One of the first of the true travellers round Ireland was Arthur Young and as he passed by on 8 September 1776 he remarked in his journal: 'Castle of Bunratty, a very large edifice, the seat of the O'Briens, princes of Thomond; it stands on the bank of a river, which falls into the Shannon near it. About this castle, and that of Rosmanagher [another seat of the Earls of Thomond], the land is the best in the county of Clare; it is worth £1.13s. an acre, and fats a bullock per acre in summer, besides winter feed.'

Outside it is plain enough, probably the most unusual feature being the way in which the towers on the north and south sides are linked by broad arches close up on the top storey. Enter the fortress over the drawbridge and there is first a small room, an entrance lobby with a 'murder hole' overhead such as was often used as a defence for the main doors: through it various repellents such as boiling water could be showered down on unwelcome intruders. Thence to the Main Guard, where originally the menials and lower soldiery would have fed and waited – but this is a place of small circumstance compared with what is to be found on the next floor. Climb a spiral staircase (a pretty tight one) and after seemingly endless turns and boot-worn stone steps the Great Hall is reached. Here the Earls of Thomond held their court. It measures 48 feet by 30, and is a quite unexpected 48 feet high. It is furnished today not with items collected by the earls in earlier centuries, but with pieces garnered by the conservators, diverse yet fitting most happily into this evocation of an era. The roof itself is a copy in an enlarged form of one of the few medieval oak roofs left in Ireland, that at Dunsoghly Castle, which dates from the middle of the fifteenth century. There is no chimney and the smoke from the welcome fires would have found its way out through louvres in the roof. The seeking eye here can pick out a late Gothic oak chest, an array of leather blackjacks, a fifteenth-century south German carved figure of St George and the dragon still exhibiting the original gilding. Move round the great room and examine a Brussels tapestry of the mid-sixteenth century telling the story of David and Absalom, and not far away the centre panel of a Spanish triptych by the Lanaja Master showing St Peter enthroned and flanked by four Apostles. Over another tapestry are suspended the antlers of a giant Irish elk, and it is fascinating to note that these animals were known to have inhabited the wetlands of Europe some twelve thousand years before man made his appearance.

After the hall the Lower Chapel, with the richness of its trappings, gives forth an atmosphere of reverence. The paintings include a Swabian altarpiece of the Crucifixion, the deathbed of the Virgin and the decapitation of St Blaise. Climb again and thread the narrow doorways to the Great Solar – the solar in these old castles and houses was essentially a place where the master could find peace and rest. In the centre stands one of the most striking pieces in the castle: the famed Armada Table, which by repute was salvaged from the Armada flagship by one Boethius Clancy, High Sheriff of Clare, and given to his brother-in-law Conor O'Brien of Lemenagh Castle, the ruins of which still stand impressively fretted against the skyline not far from Kilfenora in central Clare. The massive top of this table carries a richly carved frieze and is supported by stout corner legs carved as bravura lions bearing shields. Close by the Great Solar is the earl's private chapel – a small place of sanctity holding some notable treasures: a Spanish silver gilt processional cross which has a small platform halfway down on which are six figures of winged saints standing under Gothic tracery, and a quite superb Hungarian ciborium of enamel and gilt set with

The great hall of Bunratty
with its central burning fire.
The raised dais was for those
to dine who were 'above the
salt'. Objects from the past
adorn the walls, the furniture
is heavy and massive, the
floor of stone flags that ring to
the step. Herein has been
created a quite creditable 'time
capsule'.

precious stones. To the left of the altar is a sixteenth-century carved polychrome figure of St Catherine of Alexandria.

Considerable care has been taken throughout to avoid anachronisms and not to place objects that might be discordant with their surroundings. The final effect is a good one and undoubtedly gives satisfaction to the flow of diners who come to the twice-nightly medieval banquets. In the banquet hall the sound of harps and lilting voices, the guttering candles, the proud words of the herald, the heady beakers of mead and strange dishes offer them a momentary escape to the world of long ago.

Leave the revelry and determinedly climb those winding steps till the topmost battlements are reached. If there is enough of the evening light still showing, the view will be a timeless one – the muddy tidal creeks, the soft green saltings. Take an angle of sight that excludes the buildings of today, which seem to creep up to the walls for shelter. Lift the eyes so that they take in the distant waters of the Shannon, the spectre of the gaunt ruins of Carrigogunnell Castle – and then listen.

Carton *Maynooth, Co. Kildare*

Maynooth is a pleasant small town that stands astride the main road to
Galway about half an hour from Dublin. It is principally one broad street,
with the ruins of the once great castle of the Earls of Kildare and St
Patrick's College at one end and at the other the chief entrance to Carton.
The house stands within one of the most beautiful demesnes in the country:
the lands which originally belonged to the 'Maynooth Estate' of the
FitzGeralds, the Earls of Kildare. There is no evidence of a house there until
the early seventeenth century.

In 1603, William Talbot, Recorder of the City of Dublin, who was
created a baronet in 1623, was given a lease of 'Cartowne' or Carton by the
14th Earl of Kildare. Two of Sir William's sons distinguished themselves:
one became Archbishop of Dublin while the youngest, Richard, was
commander of James II's forces at the Battle of the Boyne, and was
afterwards created Duke of Tyrconnell. Sir William Talbot built the
original house at Carton but no distinct details remain. After the death of
the 3rd Baronet in 1691 the lands were forfeited to the Crown and then in
1703 were sold to Major-General Richard Ingoldsby, Master-general of the
Ordnance and a Lord Justice of Ireland. A painting executed about 1730 by
the Dutchman Johann Van der Hagen shows Carton as it was probably
built by the Talbots in the early part of the seventeenth century – it appears
as a Tudor-style building with flanker towers.

Ingoldsby is credited with adding a two-storey, nine-bay pedimented
front to the earlier house and also wings joined to the main range by curved
sweeps in the popular Palladian style. In 1739 Thomas Ingoldsby sold the
reversion of his lease back to the 19th Earl of Kildare. It is thought that for
a time the Earl did ponder the idea of reconstructing the great castle in
Maynooth but that it was in too bad condition to make the plan feasible, so
he decided that Carton should become his principal seat.

Choice of an architect fell on the versatile genius, the German Richard
Cassels, who had settled in Ireland and anglicized his name to Castle. He
had a fine training under Sir Edward Lovett Pearce, whose practice he to
some degree took over. The great Irish houses he worked on included
Westport, Co. Mayo (1731); Powerscourt, Co. Wicklow (1731);
Russborough, also in Co. Wicklow (begun in 1741); and Leinster House,
Dublin (1745). The commission for Carton was given to Castle in 1739, and
so the magnificent building to be seen today started to come into being. A
perfectionist, Castle insisted on the finest materials – the stones used included
Ardbraccan, blackstone from the Leixslip quarry, Mountmellick flags,
Portland stone, mountain granite, Palmerstown stone and stone from the
Carton, Moygaddy and Maynooth quarries. Castle's preference appears to

have been for the local blackstone or black limestone, while the white limestone from Ardbraccan was used for details.

There are records showing that one shipment of Portland stone from Dorset, worth £41 15s. 1d., was captured in 1739 by some freebooting Spaniards – who must have been somewhat disappointed when they found out just what their loot was. It is also recorded that insurance compensation was given for £39 1s. 8d. Further, the total cost of the rebuilding came to £21,000 – at today's prices three noughts would have to be added to this.

Although since Richard Castle's time other hands have added and subtracted, the overall conception of the original design can be clearly picked out. Carton is a splendid house and is worthily complemented by the magnificent growth of trees and shrubs that surround it. The vistas of arable, grassland and woodland seem to stretch out to the horizon at all points. The demesne was originally entered from many directions. The lime avenue of Maynooth goes straight to the principal lodge-gates, where there are two lodges of two storeys with blind arches and small windows, possibly designed by Thomas Ivory. The main Dublin road entrance has wrought-iron gates to stone pillars, while the lodge is single-storeyed and dates from around 1816. The other entrances are Kellystown Lodge and another lodge on the Dublin road nearer Leixslip, c.1840.

As soon as one enters, one becomes conscious, as in other great places walled in behind their stone barriers, that time loses its place in the calendar and years flick backwards. As you follow the narrow strip of asphalt you come very soon, on the right, to a length of water that started out as a small stream and then was widened. That great traveller of Ireland, Arthur Young, records how on 27 June 1776 he:

Left Lord Harcourt's, and having received an invitation from the Duke of Leinster, passed through Mr Connolly's [Castletown] grounds to his Grace's seat at Carton. The park ranks among the finest in Ireland. It is a vast lawn, which waves over gentle hills, surrounded by plantations of great extent, and which break and divide in places so as to give much variety . . . The park spreads on every side in fine sheets of lawn, kept in the highest order by 1100 sheep, scattered over with rich plantations, and bounded by a large margin of wood, through which is a riding.

Today Mr Young would have to be even more lavish with his praise, for the plantings that he would have been looking at have reached their full prime and the vision of the early planners can now be appreciated in a wonderful statement of what trees can really do: regal oaks, spreading beeches, limes, poplars, cedars of Lebanon and many other specimen and rare timbers with their infinite tints of green. Such must be one of the most soothing sights on earth.

(top) Detail of window treatment on the north side of Carton as carried out by Sir Richard Morrison.

(above) Detail of coupled Doric columns on the garden side, also the work of Morrison.

The rebuilding of Carton under the hand of Castle hid more or less all traces of the earlier building. Yet, something of it must remain – one clue is the unexpected thickness of the interior walls, and there is also the cornice on the entrance front. The position of the four flanker towers of the first house would appear to be related to the Chinese bedroom, the library, the ballroom and the anteroom.

A storey was added and the main part of the house lengthened by the addition of projecting bays at each end. The idea of the curved sweeps of the earlier house was retained but they were replaced by curved colonnades. The pediment over the entrance portico carries the coat of arms of the 19th Earl and his wife Mary O'Brien. An entry in an account book gives the details: 'To carving the familie Arms, by John Houghton and John Kelly, in ye pediment in Ardbraccan stone, with other decorations of boys, Cornucopias etc, £60.' John Houghton was a skilled carver who also worked on fine picture frames and is likely to have made the frame for the portrait of Archbishop Boulter in the Provost's House in Trinity College, Dublin.

Early in the nineteenth century some major alterations were carried out to the designs of Sir Richard Morrison. The curved colonnades were changed to straight links between the pavilions and the main block, colonnaded with coupled Doric columns. Morrison also made a new main entrance on the north side, converting the music room that had been there into a hall, which was a little odd as the room hardly had the grandeur and loftiness which might be expected of a hall for a house the size of Carton.

The 19th Earl died in 1744 and was succeeded by his son James, who was created a Marquess in 1761 and 1st Duke of Leinster in 1766. James did not make any alterations to Carton although the existence of drawings for a plan and elevation by an unknown architect suggest that he did have some idea of doing so. He did however use Richard Castle to build him a town house to the east of Dublin. This was known as Kildare House and was unusual in that the front and rear façades were of equal importance and also that it is one of the few houses with a foundation stone bearing details and the name of the architect; it reads: 'This house, of which this stone is the foundation, James, twentieth Earl of Kildare, caused to be erected in Molesworth Fields, in the year of our Lord, 1745. Hence, learn, whenever, in some unhappy day, you light on the ruins of so great a mansion of what worth he was who built it, and how frail all things are, when such memorials of such men cannot outlive misfortune. Richard Castle, Arch.'

Fortunately one room does survive at Carton from the mid-eighteenth century in more or less its original state. This is the saloon: surely one of the finest of all such rooms in Ireland, it can indeed stand comparison with the great salons of Germany and the French châteaux. On entering the visual effect is truly stupendous – where should the eye look first? Perhaps upwards, where the room rises through two storeys and the ceiling, deeply

Carton – one of the really large ones. The house and offices spread themselves on the garden side in front of lawns and thick hedges that rise and fall with the sensation of an ocean swell. On the north side there are well-raked shingle driveways and in the centre a wonderful gigantic burst of yew and other shrubs.

coved, provides a wonderful setting for the display of Baroque plasterwork by the Francini brothers, Paul and Philip. The Francinis came from the Italian-Swiss border and built up a considerable practice in England and particularly in Ireland, where they worked at Castletown, Russborough and No. 85 St Stephen's Green. Their style relied very largely on gifted freehand modelling as opposed to the more slavish moulding, and they inspired a number of stuccodores among the native Irish craftsmen whose work appears in many houses throughout the country.

Here in the saloon (which was originally the dining-room) the Francinis' work not only adorns the ceiling but spills down the walls with the sheer exuberance of master craftsmen – although much of this last is nineteenth-century work. The main theme for the ceiling is the Courtship of the Gods. The central figures are Bacchus and Ariadne, and other couples include Neptune and Ceres, Pluto and Proserpine, Venus and Mars, Apollo and Daphne, Mercury and Iris – the last lady in a somewhat curious attitude

67

clutching her rainbow. The whole composition spreads round the curved surface of the coving while on the flat of the ceiling above are three squares with sunken frames, two with large rosettes and the third dominated by the figure of Jove on his eagle as he hurls down thunderbolts. On the walls are ovals linked by swags with swinging putti, and busts of classical poets such as Homer, Virgil, Sophocles, Euripides and Ovid. What is more, at one end there is today a further piece of magnificence: a large organ installed in 1857 with an elaborate case designed by Lord Gerald FitzGerald, a son of the 3rd Duke. To add to the splendour of the saloon some highlights have been picked out with gold. It is not known how much of this masterpiece Richard Castle would have seen, since he died at Carton in 1751, apparently while writing a letter to a carpenter.

The interior holds so many rooms of distinction that it is difficult to select or leave out. Certainly the Chinese bedroom cannot be passed by. Like the saloon it remains as it was decorated in the mid-eighteenth century. The basic wall covering is a blue paper on which are fixed five quite large panels and a number of smaller ones. There is also a Chinese Chippendale giltwood overmantel. One of its most famous occupants was Queen Victoria when she made a visit to Ireland and stayed for part of the time at Carton with Prince Albert. It is noted that the little anteroom was fitted out in the Chinese manner specially for her visit. The Queen recorded in her diary how delighted she was with the Irish jigs danced to Irish pipes on the lawn. During her stay she was driven round in the Duke's large jaunting car with which she was so taken that the Duke had a copy specially made and sent to Windsor.

The second splendour of Carton is the dining-room, a reconstruction by Morrison; its measurements alone make it noteworthy – it is 54 feet long, 24 feet wide and 24 high. The ceiling is barrel-vaulted and carries a rich pattern of interlocked circles of oak and vine leaves; at each end are warm red scagliola (artificial marble) columns with intricate Corinthian capitals. Yet at first glance the treatment of the room seems far removed from that normally used by Morrison, who was a perfectionist when it came to handling the motifs and methods of the classic period; here very little use is made of the refinements that he brought, for instance, to the dining-room at Fota House. The large chimneypiece, with paired Siena marble columns, came from Leinster House.

To a more personal and intimate room, the Duke's study in the west wing on the ground floor. Another of the early nineteenth-century reconstructions, it has some fine doorcases which match the pedimented bookcase in mahogany. The best piece here is the chimneypiece, which is early eighteenth century, carved from grey marble and decorated with white rosettes.

Outside once more there are a number of points of interest, one certainly a rather strange looking depression in the side yard. It is roughly circular

*The superlative saloon at
Carton – certainly it ranks
among the finest in Ireland
and, indeed, the work of the
Francinis high up on the
ceiling places it among the
great salons of Germany and
France. The elegant organ
case was designed by Lord
Gerald FitzGerald, a son of
the 3rd Duke of Leinster.*

and has low walls round two sides, and what appear to be low guiding
walls at each end. No, not a dip for sheep or cattle – it is something more
rare, a carriage wash for those beautiful works of art from the coach-
builders, to keep the glitter on the marvellously finished enamelled or
lacquered bodywork.

One of the moving minds behind the reconstruction of Carton was
Emily, wife of the 1st Duke, who with the resources at the disposal of her
husband could encourage the conversion of the demesne into what was in
many ways a private amusement park. It is believed that that master of
landscape creation, Capability Brown, was consulted, but when asked to
come over he apparently replied that he was too busy to come to Ireland.
But the work went on from the middle of the eighteenth until late in the
nineteenth century.

There was a vogue, for a time, for the great lady of the house to have
available places in which to practise some form of husbandry. Thus an
idealized dairy was built for Emily. It had tiled walls with mandatory
marble slabs where the milk could stand waiting to be skimmed, and on a

(above) Detail of the Chinese bedroom with an overall blue paper on which are mounted a number of oriental panels. A Chinese Chippendale giltwood overmantel mirror can be seen to the right-hand side. One of the most celebrated people to occupy this chamber was Queen Victoria when, on a visit to Ireland with Prince Albert, she stayed part of the time at Carton. (left) The small figures echo the exuberant modelling by the Francinis on the saloon ceiling, and the richness of full baroque decorative motifs.

central oval table stood a fluted marble bowl with rams' heads to act as handles. The lady is reputed to have written in a letter: 'Did I ever tell you of my passion for spotted cows? I believe not. You have no notion what a delightful beautiful collection I have got in a very short time, which is owing to my dear Lord Kildare; who, ever since I took this fancy into my head, has bought me every pretty cow he saw. It is really charming to see them grazing on the lawn.'

Another extravagance was the Shell House, which was also started by Emily; her mother, Sarah, 2nd Duchess of Richmond, had a similar construction at Goodwood. It is thought that the mistress of Carton, the 1st Duchess, may herself have decorated the ceiling and chimneypiece wall and other parts may have been worked on by the 3rd Duchess during the 1830s. The interior gives an effect of some three-dimensional collage using all manner of materials: pottery shards, fragments of mother-of-pearl, glass crystal, coral, stones, shells, fir cones and odd shaped pieces of wood. Originally it was thatched but was later reconstructed with a tile roof, romantic Tudor stacks and a verandah supported with cast-iron columns in the shape of tree-trunks – another little place that would have delighted Queen Victoria.

Over the Rye Water was built a bridge to the design of Thomas Ivory, but its original balustrade was replaced with a simple parapet, probably about 1772. Opposite the little Ham Island is a small grotto made from rough worked stones and sheltering iron seats from which the view from the north bank of the river may be admired. One more small folly to seek out – the Bower, an octagonal hut with a timber roof supported by a cast-iron tree-trunk similar to those on the verandah of the Shell House.

In 1883 the Duke owned large tracts of land which at their peak yielded an income of over £55,000 a year. Unfortunately there were a number of quick successions, added expenses for the estate and the Land Acts. The 7th Duke, who was the third son and therefore reckoned that he would never inherit, signed away his expectations to a gentleman known as 'the fifty shilling tailor', Sir Henry Mallaby-Deeley. Sadly, one brother died and the other was killed in the Great War. The 7th Duke may have had his cash and an annuity, but Carton passed over – although Sir Henry and his family never dared to live there in face of the hostility of the locals. In 1949 the house was bought by the late Lord Brocket and then in 1977 by a patron who can and does care for the needs of one of those great places that really should not be allowed to die. Carton still holds on to that private and inspiring sense of the period in which it was built. The work of a talented architect is just as precious as the brushwork of Rembrandt or the modelling of Rodin – who can say which should be most loved and cared for? Each exhibition of talent will find the echo it seeks. So gratitude to those who look after those things that say something about the past which can enrich us all.

Castle Coole

Enniskillen, Co. Fermanagh

Co. Fermanagh lies almost due north-west of Dublin – 106 road miles to Enniskillen, the chief town. Fermanagh is bordered by the counties of Donegal, Tyrone, Monaghan, Cavan and Sligo. One cannot but wonder just why great houses and castles should have been built out here – so far away from centres of business and industry, from towns of any great size. Clearly the older castles, notably those of the Maguire sept, would have been essential for maintaining control over the owners' lands. Yet with the coming of more gentle ways others sought out this spot. The logistics would have been formidable: gathering a work force of skilled artisans and bringing in large amounts of materials that were not native to the area.

Look at a map. To the north and the south of Enniskillen there stretch out the large expanses of Lower and Upper Lough Erne, with all their hundreds of islands, countless secret reaches of still water, tiny loughs with rivulets feeding into the main confluence. This scene starts as far south as Ballinagh, where a little stream that is the beginnings of the River Erne empties into Upper Lough Erne; then away to the north of Lower Lough Erne, just about opposite Castle Caldwell, a well-fed, more robust river Erne pours the excess waters down past Belleek, becomes tidal around Ballyshannon and finally meets the full saltwater flood beside Tullan Strand.

In the eighteenth century and through most of the nineteenth the Loughs of Erne and their surrounds were very much private places: huge areas of totally natural country inhabited largely by wildfowl, by game on land and in the water, by the few humans who could grind a living from the land either as labourers or as independent souls scratching and catching whatever could be found. But there were also the nobles and gentry who discovered here a glorious isolation in the most delightful surroundings. Around the borders of the two loughs could be found: the Earl of Belmore, at Castle Coole; the Marquess of Ely, at Ely Lodge; Sir James Caldwell, at Castle Caldwell; the Earl of Rosse, at Bellisle; the Earl of Enniskillen, at Florence Court; General Mervyn Archdall, at Castle Archdall (later known as Archdale); Colonel Stewart, at Crocknacrieve; J. Irvine Esq., at Rockfield; and the Rev. Irvine, at Cork Hill.

The site of Castle Coole lies a short distance to the south-east of Enniskillen, which takes its name from an island in Lough Erne. It was originally called Inniskillen and early on was mainly a stronghold of the Maguires, who built themselves a castle here. There follows then another saga of blood – take, win and run. The English forces under Sir Richard Bingham took it in 1594; Sir Richard retired from the scene leaving a royal garrison which was promptly besieged by the forces of O'Donnel; the garrison surrendered and was at once butchered, the O'Donnel men saying that they were only paying back in kind what Bingham had done earlier.

Early in the seventeenth century a royal fort was erected there. The town came into importance when James I made a grant of one third of it to William Cole in 1612. Apparently around this time there is mention of the manor of Coole, which is thought to have been the territory of the O'Cassidys, hereditary physicians to the Maguires, being granted to a Captain Roger Atkinson – an Englishman who had come to Ireland towards the end of the sixteenth century. His appointment was as provost marshal of Lough Foyle and of the garrison of Derry. Whether there had been an earlier building on this site is not known but the Captain set to and erected a building beside the lough close to the avenue which leads up to the present house.

A survey report in 1619 by Pynnar records that: 'Captain Roger Atkinson hath one thousand Acres called Coole. Upon this Proportion there is a strong Bawne [walled fortification] of lime and stone sixty Feet Square, with three Flankers. He hath a strong Stone House, in which his Wife, with his Family dwelleth. He hath two Freeholders all resident on the Land. Here are two Water-mills, one for Corn, and another a Tucking-Mill.' In 1643 the Captain submitted that all the above building and estate arrangements had cost him £1,700. What in effect he had erected here was a place similar to other Plantation castles around the area, the common factor being that they should be efficient for defence – 'battlemented at the top, either for ordinance or for any other use of shott, being very defensible'.

In 1640 the estate was sold to an Arthur Champion and the tale of blood resumes. Champion was living in his other castle at Shannock near Clones. In the Rebellion of 1641 he was brutally cut down in front of his own gate by the Maguires, who then burned down the castle as well as the so-called Castle Atkinson. Just after the middle of the century the estate was sold once more, this time to John Corry, merchant and freeman of Belfast and an ancestor of the Earls of Belmore; he had crossed to Ireland from Dumfriesshire some time during the 1640s. Corry set about renovating the remains of Castle Atkinson and brought it up to a high standard. The estate passed to his son James, but then came to grief with the Williamite wars and in 1689 the castle was again burnt. James waited a few years before undertaking more building, but in 1709 he had plans in hand for a new house that would adjoin parts of the old castle that were still habitable. A traveller to Fermanagh in 1718 commented that the castle 'was rebuilt in a stately & costly manner . . . together with many other ornamental buildings and Emprovements as are stables coach houses orchards pleasant trees & quick Setts'.

James Corry died in 1718 and his only son John in 1726; then in 1740 Leslie, John's son, died unmarried and the male line came to an end. Leslie

Castle Coole – surely James Wyatt's ultimate statement in Ireland, proving yet again the power of symmetry when it is well handled.

did, however, have four sisters: Martha, Sarah, Mary and Elizabeth. Sarah in 1733 married Galbraith Lowry of Co. Tyrone. Their son Armar Lowry Corry inherited Castle Coole in 1774 and was successively ennobled: Baron in 1781, Viscount in 1789, and 1st Earl of Belmore in 1797. It was he who on 17 June 1790 laid the foundation of the great house, Castle Coole, that stands today.

From the start it was clear that the master of Castle Coole was set on making his house one of the most impressive in the country. For the architectural historian there survive comprehensive and accurate records of the construction and the costs – on completion in September 1796 the building charges came to £120,000 and the furnishings to £22,000.

It appears that the first architect approached was Richard Johnston; he prepared plans and elevations but James Wyatt got the commission – his basic plan being very similar to Johnston's. Wyatt operated from London and the execution of the work on site was in the hands of a resident builder-architect, Alexander Stewart: such was Wyatt's fame and the trust he inspired. Indeed, it is interesting to note that he visited Ireland only once and this was in 1785 when he went to Slane Castle. Yet, during his heyday he must have been one of the best-known architects and he had a considerable practice in Ireland. Much of Castle Coole was imported from England – not only the designs of the architect but also Joseph Rose, who worked for Adam on the plasterwork at Syon and Kenwood, and Dominic Bartoli, master of the difficult art of scagliola, who had worked at Kedleston. The fabric of the great house was also imported. The finest Portland stone from Dorset was loaded into sailing vessels and then travelled at least half way round Ireland to Ballyshannon, where a special quay had to be constructed to handle the weighty loads. One wonders which way round the ships' masters chose – north up the Irish Sea and then round Rathlin Island and Malin Head and south to Rossan Point and into Donegal Bay, or into the Atlantic for the long haul across to Mizen Head, but keeping well out to clear the Skellig and the Blaskets, then bearing away north by east, rolling along across the huge rollers just in sight of the Cliffs of Moher, out to sea again to clear Slyne Head and Clare Island before making up to Ballyshannon. Either way it would not have been a pretty trip and there must have been some hard words passed around the crews about the gentry and their great houses. From Ballyshannon the last few miles was a matter for sturdy waggons hauled by teams of bullocks.

What emerged as the elevations from Wyatt's drawing-board took concrete form was an example of purity: the architect distilled in his own thought all that he felt was fine from the ways of the Greeks. Enter by the single-storey lodge on the Enniskillen road, through the somewhat massive iron gates, climb slightly through woodland, then after a number of turns the woods are held back and for a moment the drive runs parallel to the rear elevation. It really is a masterpiece of all the arts and subtleties, the strengths and truths of architecture. James Wyatt has added to his vision of Hellenism some of the tenets of Palladio: the central block with wings, colonnaded at the front but not at the rear, the end pavilions, windows in the Venetian manner and the balustraded roof parapet. The great facade commands rather than dominates the parkland that lies in front of it. The centre block has nine bays and is of two storeys. At the front there is a superbly proportioned portico with four towering columns surmounted by Ionic capitals that support a pleasing pediment in line with the parapet. The pediment has slightly more acute angles than are usual on each side; this allows for a flatter apex, which in turn seems to give a more restful appearance. At the rear, on the garden front, Wyatt placed a curved central bow with fluted Ionic columns that again rise to the parapet line. The wings on the front side have deep colonnades with Doric columns and the end pavilions are in the Doric manner, incorporating pairs of columns. On the garden front the wings and the pavilions do not repeat the Doric features of the front but make an accent of the Venetian windows; these, like the other windows, are set slightly low, which allows for a pleasing area of stonework above them before the parapet is reached.

In 1797 a Frenchman, Le Chevalier de la Tochayne, who visited Castle Coole and was shown round by the proud owner Lord Belmore, described it as 'a superb palace' – and then added, somewhat cryptically, that it might be better to 'leave the Temples to the Gods'. Perhaps what he was implying was that to have created such a paragon might be a statement of such heavenly quality that mere mortals might not be able truly to appreciate what they saw.

(above) The library, like
almost every part of Castle
Coole, is in the hands of the
conservators. They face a task
of a magnitude which would
daunt the less dedicated. The
fabric is quite literally being
skinned. When the house was
built the blocks and slabs of
Portland stone were fixed in
position with iron clamps, but
two hundred years of Irish
damp have made the clamps
rust and cause spalling,
chipping and cracking.

(left) Detail through a
doorway at Castle Coole.

Enter from the driveway into the hall, which has a screen of Doric
columns in porphyry scagliola at the far end, and on opposing sides two
small Doric chimneypieces by Westmacott. A Doric frieze of delicate
modelling is the sole decorative feature. The hall connects to the library
which is to the left just inside the main door while the breakfast room is to
the right. Through the screen of columns doors give on to the main
staircase and the subsidiary stairs. And, above all, on to one of those rooms
which may quite rightly be described as great: the saloon, its oval shape
fitted behind the garden front bow, has that atmosphere of reticent
splendour which marks great rooms. The walls are lined with grey scagliola
Corinthian pilasters and matched with a frieze of refined swags, while the
ceiling carries a gentle, sensitive ornament which expresses the approach of
the stuccodores working at Castle Coole: it seems that Wyatt's vision held
complete control over every feature, including the techniques of his
craftsmen, to ensure that none should overshadow the others but rather that
the whole should be orchestrated into chords of perfect harmony and
quality.

The main staircase leads upward from the almost stark simplicity of plain
walls and a wide doorway with a delicate fanlight – what richness there is

comes from the scagliola columns. It has been suggested that this area may have been worked on by Sir Richard Morrison, who was employed quite considerably at Castle Coole during the first two decades of the nineteenth century; it was he who designed the stables, which have quality and taste. Apparently Morrison must to some degree have failed the expectations of the 2nd Earl as he is said to have referred to the architect's work as being 'Gate houses in the Grecian Cottage Style' – which does seem a rather harsh judgment on the man who was responsible for the excellent classic treatments at Fota and other places.

One feature of particularly high quality in the interior of Castle Coole is the woodwork. Whoever the joiners, cabinet-makers and carpenters were, they certainly understood to the full the working qualities of the different woods. Examine the double doors that divide the hall from the saloon. They are hung on pivots with no visible sign of hinges; more than this, they are gently curved to follow the oval shape of the saloon. When the architectural woodwork was finished, so inspired was this talented band of craftsmen that they turned to making furniture for the house, some of which can still be seen.

On the first floor the most impressive room is the so-termed State Bedroom, the centrepiece of which is a magnificent canopied bed supplied by John Preston of Dublin, who was responsible for much of the fine furniture in the main rooms. The drapes of the half romantic, half theatrical bed were suspended from an earl's coronet fixed to the ceiling. The walls are covered with a richly textured crimson flock paper. Here indeed was a place for majesty.

Across from the State Bedroom is one of those rooms one sometimes finds in these great houses that give one instantly a sense of intimacy, of glancing into the lives of those who lived here. Strictly speaking it is called the Bow Room or Museum. As far back as 1816 it served as a sitting-room and was described as a needlework room. Here can be found personal objects and memorabilia: a wheelbarrow and silver spade used by the 4th Countess for ceremonial tree planting when her husband was Governor of New South Wales, two fine Etruscan vases, a somewhat Rococo carved rent table, and other pieces. But the most interesting are the architectural drawings connected with the house – in particular the elevations by Wyatt and Johnston.

Castle Coole has so much to offer, so much for the exploring eye, so much to give to the student of architecture. It is a great place of such style and quality it would be impossible to repeat today – not least because of the cost that would be involved.

But slowly something was happening to the building. When the house was built the blocks and slabs of Portland stone were fixed together and into position with iron clamps. Just about 200 years of that 'soft rainfall' which some think one of the delights of the west have badly rusted these

iron clamps and the result is that round each one the stone has spalled, chipped and cracked. The destructive force of water and iron has done its work – leaving the National Trust of Northern Ireland with one of the greatest conservation and restoration problems of its history. In simple words it means that the whole bulk of Castle Coole must be dismantled, every single iron clamp must be replaced with a stainless steel tie, and then the whole building must be reassembled. Fresh supplies of Portland stone have been brought from Dorset and a team of highly skilled stonemasons are working away on a task that it is estimated will take ten years. Their task is aided by the fact that they can use modern stone saws, jackhammers and mechanical transport and hoists. But it remains the most impressive signal that there are still some who have that urge for perfection that the original builders must have felt.

The grounds echo the economy of detail that makes the house so fine. The spread of gently undulating grassland is soothing to the eye, studded here and there with some truly great trees. Look down from a window of the garden front across the park, beyond the drive to the lake on which lives a colony of rather special birds, the oldest non-migratory flock of greylag geese in the British Isles. Tradition has it that if ever these birds seriously take wing to leave Castle Coole so will the Belmores.

Castle Leslie *Glaslough, Co. Monaghan*

The site is an ancient one and stands just to the north of the small town of Glaslough, which itself is a few miles north of Monaghan. Things were astir in this area long before Glaslough came into being. O'Nial of Ulster granted it to O'Bear McKenna on condition that he and his descendants should pay 'bonaghty', or tribute, and furnish white meat and oats to the Gallowglasses of O'Nial on the particular days on which they visited the Holy Well of Tubber Phadrick, near Glennan, and that they should never wage war against the O'Nials. Nearby is the hill and rath (or earthen ring-fort) of Drumbanagher where on 13 March 1688 a fierce battle was fought between a detachment of the Irish army which was on its way to join in the siege of Londonderry and Protestant forces drawn from the district; the latter had a convincing victory, although they lost their much admired leader, Colonel Matthew Anketell.

The district was a part of the MacMahon country until the Flight of the Earls at the beginning of the seventeenth century. Then it was confiscated and made over by grant to Sir Thomas Ridgeway, and in 1664 it was bought by John Leslie, the Bishop of Clogher – a man of some spirit and courage, nicknamed the 'Fighting Bishop'. His father was George Leslie of Crichie. John, a devotee of the House of Stuart, had defied Oliver Cromwell and refused to give up his episcopal duties. Such was his passion for royalty that at the age of ninety he rode from Chester to London in twenty-four hours so that he could celebrate the Restoration of Charles II. Charles sadly deemed him too old for an archbishopric, and so the gallant old gentleman came back to Castle Leslie and managed to build a church overlooking the lough where the Leslies of his persuasion have been buried ever since. John Leslie was 100 when he passed away in 1671 leaving a wife fifty-two years younger than himself and a fine cluster of children, many of whom were to become personalities themselves and beget more children who carried on the tradition. John's eldest son, Charles, was elevated to Dean and, though an Anglican, refused to take the oath to William whom he regarded as a usurper; in this he was joined by other bishops, only to find that their opponent was too powerful. But Dean Charles Leslie kept up his vendetta against William. He also went into combat against Dr Johnson, who had the grace to admit that 'Leslie is a reasoner against who it is difficult to reason'; Oliver Goldsmith, in some ways his rival, said of him that he was 'a reasoner of some wit'. So far as the establishment was concerned, the last straw was when Leslie went full-blooded into the attack against the Penal Laws and made a spirited defence of the Catholics; he was arrested for high treason but managed to escape while his captors discussed some obscure point of the law that Leslie had put forward.

Charles's eldest son, Robert, came next; he and his younger brother were close friends of Dean Swift, who when on a visit wrote a poem to 'Robin and Harry'. Of Robert's children, the first became by his marriage an uncle to the Duke of Wellington.

The atmosphere of Co. Monaghan has drawn many writers and artists, including George Moore, Yeats and Thackeray, Millais, Lavery and Lady Gregory. Sir Shane Leslie, the father of the present incumbent, wrote more than twenty of his books here. The tangles of the family tree stretch across the Atlantic: Leonard Jerome's youngest daughter, Leonie, married Sir John Leslie, father of Shane; her elder sister, Jennie, was the mother of Sir Winston Churchill. The present owner's mother, Lady Marjorie Leslie, was the daughter of Henry Clay Ide of Vermont, one time Governor-General of the Philippines and later American Ambassador to Spain.

The original castle was a medieval stronghold, a redoubtable fortress flanked with circular towers, with a keep, a donjon (or inner defensive tower) and a moat and drawbridge. Since then it has been rebuilt several times.

The present Castle Leslie may seem to be somewhat strangely named as there is nothing warlike about it, but in Ireland there has always been quite a fashion for calling mansions castles. It was built by Sir John Leslie, 1st Baronet, Member of Parliament and famous traveller and painter, who spent years in Italy studying and collecting the precious and the rare. He employed Sir Charles Lanyon and William Henry Lynn as architects and the somewhat sombre grey stone house was built around 1870. Undoubtedly Sir John must have incorporated into the project many ideas culled while in Italy, not least in the very fine colonnaded loggia or cloister which was said to have been copied from Michelangelo's cloister at Santa Maria degli Angeli in Rome. It matters not, for it is a distinguished feature in its own right, set beside a rose garden with pool and fountain where a strange figure lurks and where it is not unknown for a fine grey horse to stray, adding a touch of surrealism as it wanders along the cloister and then steps regally down into the garden.

A stone Cupid readies his bow while a stained stone Venus stares upwards from the fountain at Castle Leslie.

The house is superb, sited alongside the lough whose waters, placid and mirrorlike on a fine day, are thought by some to hide a monstrous relative of the Kraken, that legendary Norwegian sea-monster. Probably Lynn was mostly responsible for the exterior of the house, while the interior – which is more exciting – came from Lanyon and Sir John. The great hall has Ionic columns and a shallow barrel-vaulted ceiling and various details, such as the cornice, inspire something of the feel of the Italian Renaissance and this carries through the main rooms of the house. The drawing-room, which has

Castle Leslie, the fastness of the Leslie family, stands beside the placid spread of Glaslough lake. Or is it, in imagination, on a private island surrounded by the waters of a fantasy sea? A place that has inspired not only the family but others such as Thackeray, Keats, Millais and Lavery who came to the area.

a ceiling with modillion cornices and a frieze carrying pleasantly decorative festoons, houses the jewel of Castle Leslie – a piece not quite unique but of great rarity: a superb example of the ceramic art of Andrea Della Robbia – not just a plaque or minor object but no less than a complete chimneypiece. Winged angel heads with sprays of leaves, floating ribbons and bunches of fruits, the top frieze finished at each end with bravura scrolls. Maybe it is just a little chipped and scratched, but not enough to spoil the pleasure of gazing at this object of eternal beauty.

Elsewhere there is a long top-lit gallery which contains some rather exciting frescoes in a manner probably inspired by the Pre-Raphaelite Brethren; they were executed by Sir John, who also hung here portraits of himself and other members of the family. The dining-room, a room of some architectural elegance, displays a number of quite striking family portraits. On the north side of the hall is a small drawing-room and from this a door leads into a large and somewhat unexpected Winter Garden which houses among other objects a fine terra-cotta head by Carpeaux. A second door on the north side of the hall leads to the stair well and billiard-room and the library, which is well stocked with many rare reference and other books.

It is said that it never gets really cold or really hot up here. Thus many shrubs such as rhododendrons and azaleas flourish with bright colours as their season comes. At the summer solstice it seems that some magic hand holds back the darkening shades until there hardly appears to be any night at all. The harvest season brings a change of many colours, leaves that have been so green turning to golden-reds and warm sienna browns. Cast the eye across the lough to the Old Wood, as it is half-affectionately called, and see how the waters pick up the copper tints, producing a richness reminiscent of a Titian glaze.

The Old Wood has a presence that seems to reach out long beckoning fingers across the water towards the gentle lawns of Castle Leslie. Some say that on a very quiet night bumbling, rustling, bumping sounds are heard coming from among the dense tree-trunks of the place. Yet these are not feared by those who know, but rather are regarded as the presence of good, benign beings that are possibly part of the guardian host that keeps an eye on the Castle and cares for the Leslies.

The year wears away and with the gentle winter come other friends of Castle Leslie, great birds from far places, and the lake surface ripples with the landing of whooper swans and wild geese. In fact birds like the place, for they are never absent throughout the year – rooks come in their thousands for a winter's food and peace, often broken only by their staccato babbling.

Castle Leslie remains a fascinating place, a place out of time, a place that is a kingdom, small maybe, but entirely of its own.

Castletown *Celbridge, Co. Kildare*

This is the 'big one', the largest of the Irish Palladian houses, and it was also the first: a statement of substance put up by a man who probably needed such a demonstration to realize his own position. Castletown is a vast, grey cliff of a place, separated from the slow, sliding waters of the Liffey by a stretch of flat, green parkland, a fence and a row of trimmed yews lined up as a frontal guard. The approach is from the small town of Celbridge, the entrance guarded by two sphinxes that stare for ever into each other's eyes from lofty perches on the stone gate-columns. Then, straight as a dart, the drive passes through an avenue of tall limes, perhaps a little ragged, but still fragrant in the warm evenings. On taking this entrance, keep the eyes straight to the front, for in this way the invasion by a latter-day housing estate will not be seen. Slow down as the avenue ends, so that the first sighting of the house is not spoiled by the need to take snap decisions.

To live here must have filled the builder with the spirit of a great landowner, a prince above the rest, a person of property. At the end of his duties in Dublin, he could transport himself to a private world of self-sufficient splendour. The demesne wall and an army of retainers kept out the herd. Here was a rich man's state within a state – a pivotal place for entertainment that might at times go on almost round the clock: food, wine, spirits made into lethal punch, hunting, shooting, dancing, play-acting and amours played out in the smaller chambers.

The man who brought this Castletown into being was one William Conolly, who was born in 1662, the son of a provincial publican in Ballyshannon in Co. Donegal; apart from this one fact, his origins remain hidden. From early on, it would have been evident to those alongside him that Mr Conolly was set to be one of those self-driven dynamos who would make his way fast and to a degree regardless: a man who was to lay the foundations of his great fortune, so hearsay has it, by dealing in forfeited estates after the Battle of the Boyne in 1690. The scheme worked well, for Mr Conolly ended up with property in at least ten Irish counties, as well as estates in north and south Wales. Money brought influence and in 1715 he was unanimously elected Speaker of the Irish House of Commons, a position which he held until his death in 1729. In 1716 he was appointed a Lord Justice, the status of which enabled him, with other Justices, to exercise viceregal authority if the Viceroy himself was out of the country.

Work on Castletown started in 1722. The architect employed was the Italian Alessandro Galilei, who is also known for his façade for St John-in-Lateran in Rome, which ranks high even beside the great St Peter's. Speaker Conolly's house had to be something special, the showpiece of everything that was finest in the land, as we may gather by this extract from a letter written to Bishop Berkeley, who was acting as an adviser to the Speaker on

the finer points of building and possibly aesthetics as well. It was penned by Sir John Perceval, a rich landowner from Cork who was later to become the Earl of Egmont:

You will do well to recommend to him the making use of all the marbles he can get of the production of Ireland for his chimneys, for since this house will be the finest Ireland ever saw, and by your description fit for a prince, I would have it as it were the epitome of the Kingdom, and all the natural rarities she can afford should have a place there. I would examine the several woods there for inlaying my floors, and wainscot with our own oak, and walnut. My stone stairs should be of black palmer's stone, and my buffet adorned with the choicest shells our strands afford. I would even carry my zeal to things of art: my hangings, bed, cabinets and other furniture should be Irish, and the very silver that ornamented my locks and grates should be the produce of our mines. But I forget that I write to a gentleman of the country who knows better what is proper and what the Kingdom affords.

So the big house started to rise under the direction of Galilei, and later of Sir Edward Lovett Pearce. The growth of this great place must have been followed with interest by a large part of the Ascendancy, the ruling or overseeing class that was a fusion of the descendants of Norman lords, Tudor officials, freebooting Cromwellian adventurers, as well as some Gaelic families – those of the stamp of Buck Whaley and the notorious, almost impossible, character, George Robert FitzGerald. There was little that FitzGerald would not do to stimulate his lust for pleasure – as example, he chained his father to a bear for entertainment and ended his days at the end of a rope in Castlebar after one too many killings.

Sadly for Speaker Conolly, time ran out before his dream palace could be completed. He died the richest man in Ireland and one who had endeared himself to the people because of his patriotic ideas. At his funeral a large crowd followed the magnificent procession to Celbridge where he was buried: it was noted that many wore linen scarves on this occasion for the first time, the intention being to promote the linen industry. In 1694, the Speaker had married Catherine, daughter of Sir Albert Conyngham, a Donegal estate owner who was connected with the Conynghams of Slane. There had been no children and thus Speaker Conolly was succeeded by his nephew, William, though his widow lived on in the growing house until her death in 1752.

Among other matters that took Catherine's attention was the provision of relief work during the famine of 1739 and afterwards, and one such project was the construction of an immense obelisk designed by Richard Castle. To the north of the house there were radiating avenues: the site she chose was at the end of one of these, about two miles from the house and apparently

(top) Rusticated column surmounted by a reclining sphinx, one of two that mark the main entrance drive to Castletown.

(above) The peerless quality of the so-called Conolly folly. This piece of magnificence rears up some 140 feet and stands on an axis two miles from the house.

on land then owned by the Earl of Kildare; Castle was at this time working on Carton for the Earl. The base of the obelisk consists of counter-poised arches and semi-domes, rising to the great central viewing-chamber, with well-balanced pediments and arched openings to a north-south axis – the final obelisk rears up to a height of 140 feet. It is said that the lonely lady would sit by one of the windows in the long gallery and dream as she looked at this rather wonderful object, which sadly today stands with its base defiled in what is little more than a confused and messy rubbish dump, the construction itself the helpless victim of mindless scribblers with aerosol paint cans. Another work Catherine put in hand was the so-called 'Wonderful Barn', intended as a large granary. The construction is conical, with four brick domes of diminishing size; at the top there was a winch and the exterior was faced with stone and hung with slates. There is also a corkscrew external staircase that leads right to the top. A stone bears the inscription: '1743 Execut'd by JOHN GLINn' – a builder who, apart from this, seems to be unknown.

With Catherine's passing, William, his wife and seven children moved from the Conolly house in Capel Street, Dublin, into Castletown. Two years later, in 1754, William died, whereupon his widow moved to England and Stretton Hall in Staffordshire. In 1758 Thomas Conolly married Lady Louisa Lennox, a daughter of the Duke of Richmond; the couple moved into Castletown the following year and straight away took up the immense task of finishing the interior in particular. During the Speaker's time, only the hall, the long gallery on the first floor and some other rooms of simple design and finish had been completed. Tom Conolly, a noted and popular patriot, became fired with his wife's enthusiasm. The famous Italian stuccodores, the Francini brothers, were sent for, and they applied their art to the walls of the great stairwell, creating a pleasing ornament of putti, swirling, plant-inspired forms and modelled portraits of the two owners. The fine, cantilevered, stone staircase itself was installed in 1760 with an unusual use of brass columns for the balustrade – an idea probably of Louisa's; these bear the signature of 'A. King, Dublin 1760', the work being under the supervision of Simon Vierpyl, a student of Sir William Chambers. The ground-floor reception-rooms are supposedly decorated and handled by Chambers.

It is said that in the dining-room a strange happening once took place. Tom Conolly had been hunting and on his way back had encountered a dark stranger; being of a generous nature, Tom asked the man in for some hospitality. The story has it that during dinner Tom may have dropped something, a napkin or suchlike; as he bent down to retrieve it, he saw that his guest had removed his boots and now displayed some very hairy feet with an appearance of cloven hooves. Tom was more than a little shocked, for he realized that he was giving dinner in his beloved Castletown to no less than the Devil. He at once asked his now unwelcome guest to leave and

(opposite) Castletown – a stately statement of substance put up by a man who must have felt the need to demonstrate his position. Within the demesne and the house in the 18th and 19th centuries might have been witnessed a standard of entertaining and behaviour never to be seen again.

The Batty Langley Lodge on the secondary drive to Castletown. An architect and romantic in the van of the Gothic Revival, Batty Langley published his 'Gothic Architecture Restored and Improved' in 1741; it provided much leaven for the growth of the movement which swept across the land, gaining influence also from writers who found an inspiration back in the centuries.

was greeted with an offensive response. He bade a footman fetch his priest, who then received the same rude and crude treatment; the holy man, infuriated by this, hurled his breviary at the Devil, missed and cracked a large mirror on the wall behind. The Devil was so shaken by this action that he leaped over the table, stamped on the hearth stone, split it and then vanished up the chimney, presumably followed by sulphurous fumes. The cracked mirror and the split hearthstone remain today, to be seen – and considered!

The preparation of the rooms and much of the major decorations were watched over by Louisa, who was certainly responsible for the Print Room, which is now possibly the sole surviving example of the fashion in Ireland. The walls were prepared with a fine linen, which would then have been given a coat of good distemper, and onto this Louisa and her sister, Lady Sarah Napier, pasted cut-out prints, rather in the manner of a large collage.

Louisa also turned her attention to a full decoration of the Long Gallery, where she commissioned Thomas Riley in 1776 to paint some involved decorations in the Pompeiian style. This he did to good effect, though it cannot be discerned if he used the *stucco lustro* employed by the ancients. She ordered costly glass chandeliers from Venice, which took a long time to arrive and disappointed the lady when they did, having too much blue glass in them. The Long Gallery has a fine form to it, the proportions complementing the doorways and windows. It would have been for much of the time a meeting place for a number of possible entertainments. At one end there could have been a chamber-orchestra playing, somewhere else a card school, in another part some amateur dramatics, and at the other end a general discussion group, perhaps with ladies working at their embroidery.

Castletown must have seen a level of entertaining that could not even be approached today. Guests were in the care of their own servants, whose task it was to see that the guest lacked nothing: at whatever hour he called for food or drink, his requests would be answered immediately. There would be inside and outside pursuits: games would be organized; mounts to follow the hunt would be ready in the stables.

Although many of the rooms at Castletown are now somewhat sparsely furnished through the vicissitudes of changing ownership, more than enough remains to feel the pulse of this great wonder beside the Liffey. The impression created by the front elevation, with its three storeys – the top two with a line of thirteen window openings, the ground with twelve and the entrance door – the roof-line balustrade, the massive chimney blocks, is one of skilful handling of large architectural forms. The two-storey pavilions on each side are joined to the central mass by colonnades of columns with Ionic capitals, and these are surmounted again with balustrades and an ample supply of those favourite ornaments – slightly flamboyant urns. How many rooms are there? A casual reply might be approximately one hundred, with well over two hundred windows. Search round the items to be seen, study notices in the rooms and pleasant, intimate details are found – a Mr Nicholls was engaged to polish the brass balusters of the main staircase at a fee of £3 a year; there are particulars of the effect of diets on Louisa's health; a small lacquered cabinet, decorated with copies of Dutch and other pictures thought to have been painted by her; and a letter to her sister, Sarah Napier, dated 29 February 1768 (the latter part of

The print-room, one of the pet projects carried out by Lady Louisa Conolly with the assistance of her sister Lady Sarah Napier. Onto the linen-covered walls these two ladies stuck large and small prints, many of which, if they could be salved, would be collectors' items today. In their time such a practice was a fashion.

it referring to the painter Robert Healy): 'Lord and Lady Gore are here and many more gentlemen. There is a man in the house who draws very good likenesses in black and white chalk – we have made him draw some of the Company which is good entertainment . . .'

The true era of Castletown and its like must surely have ended with the departure of Louisa and her husband. As the nineteenth century brought new modes, industrial revolution, different transport, so did it erode the great demesne walls and the social life that went on behind them. Faster travel meant faster communication; factories drew in workers from the countryside, and on their return they told of many things that opened up the thoughts of the simple souls who for so many years humbly – and most of the time willingly – served at the rich men's tables.

Castletown now seems a little withdrawn, a little uncertain of just how to handle the late twentieth century, perhaps wondering if the well-masoned stones will carry through into the twenty-first. But surely they must, for if ever there was a monument to a period in all its facets, the upstairs and downstairs of Castletown stand as an irreplaceable example. There is something unique about the way this perfect expression of the thoughts of Andrea Palladio, the master architect of sixteenth-century Italy, stands here on a spread of Irish turf beside the waters of the Liffey. Palladio worked to revive the ancient Roman ideas of symmetrical planning and harmonious proportions. Castletown reflects these characteristics and is much more than a statement by a man about his wealth; it is a model of telling strength for good taste and fine workmanship, as well as a marker in the story of design and an accomplishment by all those connected with it.

After you leave the lime-lined avenue-drive, the thoughts stay with the two ladies of Castletown – sitting up there in the long gallery, gazing across to the great finger of the obelisk, lost in their own world for ever.

Celebrated bracket clock with painted face and superbly modelled ormolu figures. (opposite) Part of the great gallery on the first floor, showing the entrance doors with a large painting of Aurora over them and some parts of the painting in the Pompeiian manner by Thomas Riley in 1776.

Castle Ward

Strangford, Co. Down

Strangford Lough, Loch Cuan, is a large expanse of water some twelve miles long by up to three miles wide. It is almost entirely landlocked, being separated from the sea by a narrow channel. The Norsemen gave it the name of Strang Fiord – literally the 'violent inlet' – no doubt after encountering the fearsome ebb and flow of the tides that bear down on this channel. Numerous islands which have been formed by submerged drumlins, streamlined mounds of glacial drift, are scattered down the west side of the lough. Today the whole area has a quiet beauty individual to itself, and this has encouraged the setting-up of nature reserves: the Strangford Lough Wildlife Scheme is run by the National Trust.

The gently hilled landscape exhibits neatly kept farmsteads, the houses mostly brightly whitewashed. But centuries back, this haven from the wildness of the seas must have been witness to strife and the comings and goings of wild characters not only from Ireland but also from over the waters: from Scotland and the north of England, and earlier still the Vikings, probably reinforced with unwilling or willing recruits from the Isle of Man. In an attempt to control matters, castles were built liberally around the landscape in positions that could survey and guard approaches by sea and land. The Normans erected the once imposing but now much-restored Quintin Castle that looks out across Knockinelder Bay on the Ards Peninsular; on the west side of the narrow strait that connects the lough with the sea is Kilclief Castle, built about 1440 probably by John Cely, Bishop of Down. On the lough itself, between Downpatrick and Strangford, stands Walshestown Castle, a good example of a sixteenth-century four-storeyed tower house and bawn, and one mile north of Castle Ward is the remains of Audley Castle. All these have some features of interest and years ago could, in their own way, have been imposing – but nothing like as startling or puzzling for the uninformed traveller as the mid-eighteenth-century house that was built by Bernard Ward, later to become the 1st Viscount Bangor, and his wife Lady Anne, daughter of the 1st Earl of Darnley.

The husband and wife just could not agree on the style and design. From this disagreement grew surely one of the strangest of architectural fantasies to be found anywhere. His lordship – for his side of the noble dwelling – chose the manner of Palladio, with all the required though dignified classical trimmings; her ladyship was impelled to have her side in the form of Strawberry Hill Gothic, set with ogee arched windows on the two bays at each end and three bays of more formal pointed arched windows in the centre. It is her ladyship's façade that looks down on the waters of Strangford Lough. One can imagine that some seaborne visitor might sail for an anchorage and on landing set his steps towards the Gothic elevation,

The Coat of Arms of the Wards in the pediment of the Classical side to this unique house. When it was built husband and wife could not agree over the design, so one side is Classical and the other in the Gothic manner.

but as the drive swings around and trees hide the house he would emerge close to the building to find himself confronted with the Palladian elevation – which could cause considerable consternation.

The Castle Ward estate was originally called Carrick na Sheannagh, and has been with the Ward family since the second half of the sixteenth century, at which time it was purchased from the Earls of Kildare by Bernard Ward, the father of Sir Robert Ward, the Surveyor-General of Ireland. Bernard himself had come over from Capesthorne in Cheshire. One of his more notable successors was another Bernard, a great-great-grandson who rose to be High Sheriff of County Down and was apparently very much a man not to be trifled with. During a hearing in 1690 in the grand jury room at Downpatrick a fierce argument arose between the High Sheriff and a certain Mr Hamilton – so strong indeed did feelings run that the two gentlemen went outside and fighting beside the ruins of the Abbey, managed within minutes to dispatch each other in a rather oddly conducted duel: the High Sheriff put his bullet in a lethal place, whereon Hamilton made a mighty lunge and ran his blade nearly to the hilt in his opponent's breast.

Michael, the next in line, was elected Member of Parliament for County Down and, ignoring his father's behaviour, rather bravely took up the law and became Justice of the Court of the King's Bench in Ireland. But he did not neglect the estate and among other projects furthered the production from lead mines on his lands, procuring vessels to transport it and even providing an adequate quay for the loading. Michael had one son, christened yet again Bernard, and two daughters. Bernard succeeded in 1759; he also sat as Member for County Down and was appointed Deputy Governor for the County.

He already had a fine house, but following the fashion for bigger and better houses he decided to build – and then came the contretemps with his wife Anne. Just which architect was prevailed on to sort out this marriage of styles is not known, but it is thought he was probably brought over from England, as was the considerable quantity of Bath stone that was used for the facing. The façade on the classical side has seven bays, with the windows of the first storey carrying simple pediments; the ground floor is rusticated. The three central bays are contained in a breakfront and from the first-storey level carry four elegant columns with Ionic capitals supporting a pediment with coat of arms on the tympanum and surmounted by three urns. Lower the eyes and move round to the garden side for her ladyship's Gothic: seven bays and three storeys – certainly no rustication, no classical columns, but the parapet does carry an urn at each end of a run of rather mild flattened battlements and standing atop the breakfront three central

The interior can provoke strange sensations as the visitor enters the classically treated hall
and then passes through a classical door suddenly to find himself in a completely different
period – ceilings hang down with variations of Gothic vaulting, the drapes are heavy,
window shapes are pointed or in the ogee form. How a harmony of living was reached is
difficult to imagine. But some were greatly impressed, one Sir James Caldwell remarking
that it was the 'finest place in this kingdom'. (opposite) Castle Ward today, with the woods
full grown, sits well into the landscape.

bays are three small spires with some lightly carved stones in the manner of crockets.

The two end elevations are quietly neutral in this collision of tastes. But enter through the main door, set in a semi-octagonal bay on the eastern side, and very soon the division of taste becomes apparent again. Broadly speaking, the rooms on the classical side show the same preference and those on the Gothic side, such as the saloon, have the trappings of quatrefoils, fretting, pointed doors of carved mahogany; the ogival windows have seventeenth-century glass panels probably of Flemish origin, set in later coloured glazing. The hall on the classical front reflects the eighteenth-century need for space for assembly, combined with a sense of richness. There is a screen of Doric columns of light-toned scagliola surmounted with a Doric frieze. The walls above the dado rail are panelled and the main door, classic in proportions, is surmounted with a strong broken pediment; interspersed between panels and doorways are light-hearted vertical trails of ribbons carrying musical instruments, arms and objects associated with farming and sport.

Castle Ward may have started out as a changeling when it was built between 1760 and 1773, but it has become a place of sheer delight. The journey through the house titillates the imagination and the thoughts of those who lived here seem to gather substance. Hundreds of miles away from the influence of London, Paris or Brussels, the Wards cultivated here an atmosphere brimming with intellectual satisfaction and taste. To find one room of pure escapist whimsy, open the door of the Gothic Boudoir: here, the blossoming forms of Gothic fan vaulting hang downward, to give the ceiling almost a sense of motion – the source of this fantasy is undoubtedly to be found in Henry VII's Chapel in Westminster Abbey, and this is confirmed in a letter to Bernard Ward from Lord William Gordon dated May 1764. The romantic unreality of the room is enhanced by a richly patterned carpet, eighteenth-century furniture, many paintings and other pictures, and a fireplace with columns and a bold round opening for the grate.

Paintings of a house and its grounds are worth seeking out because the artist's eye can fix a period, a season, often more surely than the camera – the painter with his sensitivity locked into his subject can put down nuances of tint and tone beyond catching with a lens. In the library, a room of fine carved and figured mahogany bookshelves, there is a work by that master of the wide view and tall skies, William Ashford. He has taken as his viewpoint the steps of Lady Anne's Temple looking towards Old Castle Ward, with the new house away almost on the skyline in the distance; the scene was worked in 1785. Other views of the house and estate that hang above the bookcases have been attributed to another Irish painter, Jonathan Fisher.

Sir James Caldwell of Castle Caldwell, Co. Fermanagh, visited Castle Ward in October 1772 and declared that he found it to be the 'finest place in this kingdom'. His account of how he was received and dined shows he may have been grateful on one hand but was not going to admit that all was perfect:

Monday, 12th October 1772. – A little before dinner I got to Castle Ward. Lord Bangor received me with great cordiality . . . he also asked me to dine and stay all night. This was a great compliment, as his house was full of company, and not quite finished. . . There was an excellent dinner, stewed trout at the head, chine of beef at the foot, soup in the middle, a little pie at each side and four trifling things at the corners. . . . The second course of nine dishes [was] made out much in the same way. The cloth was taken away, and then the fruit – a pine apple, not good; a small plate of peaches, grapes, and figs (but a few), and the rest, pears and apples. No plates or knives given about; we were served in queen ware. . . During dinner two French horns of Lady Clanwilliam's played very fairly in the hall next to the parlour which had a good effect. . . .

Of the musical part of the evening Sir James would have been an instructed critic, as so fond was he of this branch of the arts that he even had provision for his musicians to take to the water. Arthur Young, that competent traveller through Ireland, noted after staying with Sir James: 'Take my leave of Castle Caldwell, and with colours flying and [Sir James's] band playing go on board his six-oared barge for Enniskillen. That evening reached Castle Coole.' In that rather special period of history, at the end of the

Delicately carved scroll on the classic side connecting balustrades that separate the lawns from the ground floor.

eighteenth century, the noble dwellings of Ireland seem to have offered a quality of life that was often a dimension larger than similar places elsewhere. Their demesnes, often set far out in the country away from the watchful strictures of city eyes, could provide an environment for indulgence and frivolity, and also a setting seemingly unreal in the contrasts it afforded between the way of life of those who had and those who just did not have.

Away from the main house there is not only the Temple of Lady Anne, with its massive portico with Doric columns and pediment, and the Temple Water, an artificial lake made around 1724, but also something much more mundane but much more useful: the laundry. It is likely that such a building would have been built at the same time as the main house and, as was normal with many of the domestic offices, it is situated away from the residence. It is a place of fascination – so much do we take for granted today when more and more of the time-consuming and tiring chores are being done by machine. Although many of the objects on show date from the nineteenth century they would not be all that different from their predecessors. Possibly it is the sheer magnitude of the operation that is so impressive. It needs to be remembered that not only would the ladies and gentlemen of the great house have their personal servants but also – when friends came to stay – they would bring with them their maids and menservants, coachman and all. The quantity of fine linen used for daily living was immense: damask tablecloths up to fourteen feet long, countless napkins thirty inches square, sheets, bolster and pillow cases – a daunting prospect for the poor laundry maids when they rose around five o'clock in the morning and set to. First everything had to be listed in the Laundry Book and then it would have to be sorted, with some items being put to soak in warm water with a little soda. The handkerchiefs used by snuff-taking gentlemen could cause particular trouble. Spend time here and you can learn much about the sartorial manners of our ancestors.

Sadly the patina of graceful living in this strange great house cracked when the schism of taste went deeper and Lady Anne took herself away from the beauty of the Temple, the lime avenue, and all the household affairs over which she must have wrestled with Bernard; travelling eastwards she crossed the Irish Sea, never to return again – to Bath, where she died in 1798.

Clonalis House Castlerea, Co. Roscommon

Clonalis House – overhanging foliage and trees give a sense of presence and dignity to this place that holds within its archives so much of the history of Ireland. (left) Bracket clock mounted in a delightful porcelain case, late 18th century, surmounted by a small putto and the whole supported by twisting scrolls.

Travel out of Dublin almost due west as far as Athlone, cross the Shannon – still a great river even this far from the sea – and then follow the road for Roscommon. On a clear day, as the town comes close, the bluff, sturdy round forms of the once great Norman castle appear. The massive stoneworks seem cut off, things apart, almost as though the long running memories of what those invaders could do and did do have given them eternal isolation. Sweep past the town and tackle the fiercely undulating bog-roads to Castlerea and one is nearly there – this almost mystical place, the heart-hearth of the O'Conor sept. A bare mile out of the small town, a hard right turn, and the searcher seems to draw clear of the twentieth century as the entrance gates to Clonalis are passed. This demesne may be of material woods, rich grass fields, but the overpowering sensation is one of timelessness.

Tread gently on the turf which has felt and carried the steps of mighty heroes – the High Kings of Ireland, the Kings of Connacht who by tradition came from the O'Conor sept. It is a family that far outstrips all others for sheer length of lineage. None in Ireland or elsewhere in Europe can match the total of ninety-six generations which takes their earliest ancestors back to Milesian times around 300 BC. Genealogical tables record in detail that the O'Conor family are in direct descent from Feredach surnamed the Just, Rex Hiberniae c.75. This royal line ran through until the coming of the Normans during the reign of Roderick, or Cathal Crovedearg of the Wine Red Hand, when the High Kingship was terminated, although the O'Conors remained kings of Connacht until the end of the fourteenth century.

The selection of the Kings of Connacht was carried out strictly in accordance with the Brehon Laws, more correctly named the *Feineachus*, meaning the laws of the *feine* or *feini*, who were the free Gaelic farmers. These laws, which were of universal application and could be administered only by duly qualified judges, were termed *Cáin* laws, while minor ones which could be administered by nobles and magistrates were called *Urradhus*. Regular courts and judges existed in Ireland from prehistoric times. The Anglo-Irish word *brehon* is derived from the Gaelic *brethem* – literally judge.

The particular law for the selection of the Kings of Connacht was the *Derb Finor*, a uniquely Irish law of succession. When the time came a list of candidates was made; these had to be no more distantly related than third cousin to the previous king and it was of great importance that they were in possession of all their faculties: it was not unknown for a jealous rival to arrange that a favoured candidate should have his eyes gouged out and thus render him ineligible. After the election the chieftains, bishops and abbots would present the successful candidate with tributes, often in the form of cattle. They would then gather round the Inauguration stone. This large, weatherbeaten block still exists today and rests on a strip of turf just to the left of the front door of Clonalis. It has no determinate shape and the one unusual feature is a sunken footprint on the top side. Its supposed date is about 90 BC and a pendulum dating confirms this: the results from two separate swingings came out at 70 BC and 100 BC.

The new king would approach the stone and lay down his sword; he would then place his right foot into the footprint on the stone and would then probably have proclaimed an oath of dedication to his people. Next he removed his foot from the stone and took up his sceptre – a simple wand of hazel with the bark stripped from it. Now he walked three times anti-clockwise round the stone to signify a survey of the cardinal points of his kingdom; this was followed by three circuits clockwise. The meaning of these latter circuits in pre-Christian times is uncertain, but after the coming of Christianity they pointed to a recognition of the Trinity. At the completion of the circuits each chieftain advanced and threw a slipper over the head of his new king, thereby implying an act of submission and a token for good fortune. The act of the king in placing his foot in the footprint on the stone symbolized a marriage with the earth – he was establishing a relationship with Maev, mother earth or mother of the earth.

The historical associations of the stone have made Clonalis much more than just a material house of stone and mortar, more even than the spiritual home of the O'Conor Dons ('Don' signifying king or leader). It has become a place of pilgrimage with a unique aura of its own, heavy with the ingredients of Ireland's history – courage and oppression, deeds of valour and of brutality. But lift the head and focus the eyes towards the distance and let the imagination take in those myth-charged days of the legendary champions of the land.

The family's early homes have long since withdrawn themselves behind the curtains of time, weather and dereliction. But there is a ruin not far from today's house giving evidence of a comfortable mansion that must have been erected in the early part of the eighteenth century. It would have been double gable-ended, with two storeys over a basement and five bays, the windows being grouped together slightly away from the corners. There were two large chimney stacks and in later years a form of Gothic glazed porch was added. This house had been sited alongside the turgid waters of the river Suck, and later generations decided that the place was unhealthy – one reason for this may have been the attentions of myriad swarms of a particularly powerful black midge with an unsatiable appetite for blood.

Between 1878 and 1880 the Right Honorable Charles Owen O'Conor Don took action to remedy matters by commissioning F. Pepys Cockerell to design the present house, but although deserted, the older house stood more or less firm until a fearsome storm in 1961 produced the ruined pile that can be seen today.

The Cockerell house has been variously described by critics as having vestiges of the Italianate, the Victorian Italian style and a form of Queen Anne. Looked at with a gentle eye it gives the impression that it was conceived as an unpretentious three-storey house to which have been applied various classical elements – pilasters with Doric and Ionic capitals, and nautilus twirls over some of the windows. Balustrades enrich part of the roofline and horizontal mouldings and other architectural refinements have been used to hold the whole together and impart a satisfactory substance.

Lawns and flowerbeds with clumps of long-planted evergreens and shrubs lap the main front of the house, while the entrance is approached through an arch of intertwined branches of dense green. In through the double white doors and the visitor finds an unexpectedly lofty and ornate hall with graceful arches held up by Ionic capped, richly coloured, marble columns. Over the staircase hangs a rather special banner. In 1911 Denis O'Conor attended the coronation of George V. This was the first time that the head of an Irish Gaelic family had been invited to represent his country on such an occasion and he must have borne this very banner.

From the hall into the drawing-room, which is larger than might have been expected and which holds some fine examples of Boulle furniture and also a number of beautifully modelled figures and groups from continental manufactories. The library has been sought out by scholars since the house was completed. Here on shelves that reach to the ceiling are some five thousand books and manuscripts. In fact the collection at Clonalis lays claim to at least 100,000 letters and documents recording the pains and joys of Irish history. Among them are the diaries of Charles O'Conor of Belanagare, the eighteenth-century historian and antiquary. These are in Irish and provide an almost unique record of the lives of the native Irish in Connacht. Among the larger volumes and folios can be picked out fine facsimiles of the *Book of Armagh*, the *Book of the Dun Cow* and the *Book of Fenagh*; there is also a fine copy of Queen Anne's *Book of Hours*, with exquisite illuminations. For those seeking information on the details of the O'Conor lineage there is generally on display an illuminated genealogy of the House of O'Conor hand-scripted and illuminated on parchment.

The billiard room has surrendered its original purpose and become a small specialized museum. The focal exhibit is certainly the Irish harp that was once played by that most celebrated of Irish bards, the blind Turlough O'Carolan. Like many others, he used to ride the countryside calling on friends far and wide, generally following a warm invitation. The leading bards were often men of some substance and culture. Carolan found a favoured place on his visits to Clonalis and is credited with saying, 'when I am among the O'Conors, the harp has the old sound in it'.

Glass cases hold a changing display of some of the letters and paper ephemera that light up the story of the house and point to just how important the family was and remains in the history of the land. There are intimate notes from Douglas Hyde, Daniel O'Connell, Charles Stewart Parnell, Gladstone, Samuel Johnson, Napper Tandy, Anthony Trollope and numerous others – and often beside them can be found faded household accounts and orders from local tradesmen. There is a clear facsimile of the death warrant for Charles I with the signatures and seals of the regicides. On one wall hangs a slightly buckling parchment carrying the details of the Composition of Connacht in 1585 – an outline for a title to land in Connacht that never existed and a rather illuminating comment on the craftiness of some courtiers.

Turn from the main reception rooms, pass through a simple doorway at the back of the hall and step down a narrow passage to find the most precious, indeed most sacred, centre of Clonalis: the Private Chapel, which has the unrestricted right to celebrate Mass and reserve the Blessed Sacrament. It is a small place yet has a feeling of unlimited dimensions. The altar came from an earlier, secret chapel built between the older house and the stables during the Penal Times when devotions were strictly forbidden. (The Jus Patronatus was upheld and confirmed by the Council of Trent.) On the altar is the simple chalice used by Bishop O'Rourke to celebrate Mass in a cave at Belanagare at that time. Examined closely it gives mute but telling evidence of those cruel strictures: the priest, generally disguised, had to be careful that his chalice was not discovered, and this one can be unscrewed into separate pieces to make concealment easier. Beside the

The entrance hall is surprisingly lofty; tall, richly coloured marble columns topped with Ionic capitals and graceful arches hold up the ceiling. Over the staircase hangs a unique banner; it was carried by Denis O'Conor when he attended the coronation of George V in 1911 – the first time that the head of an Irish Gaelic family had been invited to represent his country at such a ceremony.

One of the principal bedrooms on the first floor. Furniture, drapes and decorative treatment have been retained and fix the atmosphere at the turn of the century. The house and that before it must have welcomed many of the famous, not least the blind Turlough O'Carolan, most celebrated of Irish bards. His harp can be seen in the billiard room below, which now displays letters and documents precious to Clonalis.

chalice is the Bishop's pectoral cross and ring given to him by the Austrian general, Prince Eugene of Savoy.

The atmosphere that pervades Clonalis today seems to have carried right through the history of the family, from Turlough Mor O'Conor, the High King of Ireland, who reigned from 1119 to 1156. A wondrous man, he built stone bridges over the Shannon and the first stone castles in Ireland at Dunloe, Galway and Collooney, and commissioned the magnificent Cross of Cong, a masterpiece of the metalsmith's art originally intended as a reliquary to hold a fragment of the True Cross. When he died he was buried under the altar of St Kieran at Clonmacnoise. The deeds of the latter-day O'Conors may have been carried out in a more muted manner, but none the less they show the vital spirit of those far-off kings who planted much of the soul of Ireland that flourishes today.

A last note, a simple one: outside, towards the far side of the house, is an outdoor museum of farm machines and implements from a century or more ago, and sheltering under a roof stands one of those fine coaches that ruled the roads and tracks of the past. The present owner is doing his best to keep together something which he and his wife – and fortunately some others – know is a keystone of the past and a foundation for the future.

Dublin Castle   Dublin

By their purpose and nature castles usually dominate their sites. Coming towards them one may be guided by a towering keep or other high parts of their construction. But if a castle has its site chosen, later, as the core of a city it may, along with other valued buildings from the past, find itself obscured, even submerged, by the creeping needs of trading and living. Glass cubes on cubes, concrete elevations and medium-rise flat-blocks may change the view within days. Start from Trinity College, face the Bank of Ireland opposite, and then take Dame Street which passes the Bank on the right and walk on. Keep the eye sharp or you may miss the sign pointing towards the castle entrance on the left.

Informed voices will state that it is almost certain that in those long lost days the ridge on which the castle stands would have been crowned by a Celtic rath, or those with a more romantic thought might whisper that it was one of those fairy places in which the country abounds. The Vikings would also have thought of fortifying it, for it was then a commanding position, with a water barrier on two sides if the little stream of the Poddle is counted – although the defence value of this was increased later when it was made part of the castle ditch.

In 1169 the Anglo-Normans landed in Wexford and linked up with Dermot MacMurrough, who insinuated that an attack on Dublin should be made. Word has it that Dermot was fired by vengeance rather than cupidity, because the people of Dublin had murdered his father and apparently as an added insult had then buried the body in a dunghill with a dog. The combined forces came north and cut their way into the capital. The Danish king escaped by sea with some of his men. Later the Danes returned with some sixty ships and a powerful force of ten thousand men levied from the Isle of Man, the Orkneys and Norway. The attack was repulsed and the king was taken prisoner, subsequently to be put to death.

Battle at that time must have been a gore-drenched exercise. One of the Danish king's henchmen was a Scandinavian giant named John le Dene, who was of such enormous strength that he could with one blow of his battle-axe cut the thigh-bones of horsemen like cheese, their legs falling off like so many cabbage stalks to the ground.

King John set about planning for a castle in Dublin and directed a mandate, written in Latin, to Meiler FitzHenry ('the Tameless Tamer of the Irish Nation all'):

The King to his trusty and well-beloved Meiler, son of Henry, Justiciar of Ireland, greetings. You have given us to understand that you have no safe place for the custody of our treasure and, because for this reason and for many others we are in need of a strong fortress in Dublin, we command you to erect a castle there in such

a place as you may consider to be suitable for the administration of Justice and if need be for the defence of the city, making it as strong as you can with good ditches and strong walls. But you are first to build a tower, to which a castle and bailey and other requirements may be conveniently added: for all of these you have our authority. At present you may take and make use of 300 marks from G. FitzRobert, in which he stands indebted to us.

The castle was built – four great towers with walls many feet thick and with curtain walls. Just how long it took to complete cannot be certain as records are few, but it must have been functioning by the second decade of the thirteenth century and continued to do so with minor fracas until the reign of Elizabeth I, when the castle became the residence of the Lord Deputy, or Viceroy. It continued in this role, and as the headquarters of the British administration, until the establishment of the Irish Free State in 1922.

Of the Norman fortification only two of the towers remain and a part of the curtain wall, and the towers have been considerably altered. The main entrance at Cork Hill occupies the site of the original main gate, where all too often the macabre remains of Irish chieftains were displayed when the English had them beheaded and then rammed the dripping exhibits on spikes above the entrance.

This gateway leads into the Upper Castle Yard, which gives access to the State Apartments. The entrance is marked by a massive arch with a heavy broken pediment surmounted by the figure of Justice; there is a second similar gateway to the west which carries the figure of Fortitude, but this is not used; both figures are by Van Nost. Between these two gates stands a stately and dignified building – the Genealogical Office that was erected about the middle of the eighteenth century. It is surmounted by the clock tower called the Bedford Tower after the Lord Lieutenant John Russell. It was from here that the regalia known as the Crown Jewels were stolen in 1907 – a strange, and still unsolved, mystery, for this was surely one of the best guarded places in the country, with security officers on the alert round the clock. Yet somehow the jewels were spirited away from a safe in the library which was used as a public waiting room. Never has there been a sign of them since – were they broken up for ease of 'fencing', or are they still somewhere snug as objects to be gloated over? The theft was discovered just four days before the state visit of Edward VII and Queen Alexandra.

The entrance to the State Apartments is across the Upper Yard and through a colonnade into a reception hall, then mount the stairs to Battleaxe Landing, which takes its name from the chosen weapons of the Viceroy's ceremonial bodyguard. The fanlight over the central door shows the arms of Ireland and flanking these on either side of the doorway are the personal

(opposite) St Patrick's Hall, built after 1746 to replace the earlier viceregal hall, became from 1783 the ceremonial meeting place for the Order of the Knights of St Patrick. The ceiling was painted by Vincenzo Valdré in 1778.

(right) Scene in the main courtyard with the clock tower known as the Bedford Tower after the Lord Lieutenant John Russell.

arms of the Presidents of Ireland. The atmosphere of Battleaxe Landing will have raised the expectations of what may come but will hardly have prepared the eyes for the sheer controlled magnificence of St Patrick's Hall. This is indeed a place for heroes, wide and spacious, its lofty ceiling coffered to receive elaborate paintings by Vincenzo Valdré: the subjects, partly factual and partly allegorical, include George III, Hibernia, Justice and Liberty, Henry II and the chieftains, St Patrick, and the Paschal Fire on the Hill of Slane.

Built after 1746 to replace the earlier viceregal hall, this magnificent room became from 1783 the ceremonial meeting place for the Order of the Knights of St Patrick. Around the walls are the stallplates, marking the places of the knights, in chronological order; higher up are crests and helmets and just under the cornice the standards of those who have aspired to this Order and contributed to the full story of the land – Earls of Dunraven, Mayo, Granard, Iveagh, the Duke of Abercorn, and Viscount French of Ypres. The splendour of the Hall is overwhelming: no wonder the ear strains to catch the flourish of silver trumpets and the sound of the full trappings of a state occasion of the age of chivalry.

After St Patrick's Hall the Bermingham Tower room presents a marked contrast – a room of peace and quite splendid decorative taste: tall pointed windows in the lancet style and an ornamented ceiling the intricacies of which are repeated in the carpet; the focal point is a nineteenth-century chandelier in brass incorporating the motifs of the shamrock, the rose and the thistle. From the Bermingham Tower into another wholly delightful colour experience: the Wedgwood room, with walls and ceiling in blues associated with the Jasper ware of the Wedgwood manufactory and carrying white motifs. Through an ante-room and there is the George's Hall, which was built as a supper room for the visit of George V and Queen Mary – who were, incidentally, the last British royalty to stay in the castle. One of its most interesting features is a set of grisaille paintings by the Flemish artist Pieter Jan Balthasar de Gree which were carried out late in the eighteenth century. Basically works of this nature are made by painters to explore the possibilities of a composition before they commit themselves to full colour, but often – as here – the use of chiaroscuro can give a highly realistic effect. Sadly, few such works survive today: because of the nature of the materials used and the fragility of the supports, without careful conservation and consolidation they are likely to deteriorate, particularly where the atmosphere inclines towards damp.

The Picture Gallery is a long, dignified room that was originally three smaller apartments, the divisions being indicated today by graceful Ionic columns. The paintings include a number of portraits of Knights of St Patrick wearing the emblem of the Order. But on to another of the glories of the castle: the Throne Room, glowing and glistening – the gilt fluted Corinthian columns with their ornate capitals; the massive chandelier, its many branches gleaming with still more gold; ornate festoons with ribbon bows and still more gold; the substantial canopy on heavily scrolled corbels, and beneath it the Throne itself – a seat that must surely bring comfort to the most substantially made noble figure. The room, first known as the Battleaxe Hall, dates from the time of William of Orange. The atmosphere seems to shimmer with a million flecks of golden light that are picked up by the splendid carpet and absorbed into its already rich colouring – if design and the controlled use of colour and gilding can give an effect of sheer glory and pageant, they certainly do so here.

There is one more pleasure for the eyes in the seemingly humble State corridor which serves the Apollo Room, the former bedrooms and the State Drawing-room. In this long narrow space the art of the interior decorator has triumphed. Through careful use of soft pastel shades, and with no outside windows to lean on for effect, the architect has created a sense of space and at the same time intimacy, an area of perfect taste and enchantment.

To return to the outside once more is to step down from the Elysian to the other world which we call today. What of the other parts of this stone-girt demesne? The Lower Castle Yard which adjoins the Upper has on its south side the Record Tower, with sixteen feet of good solid wall around it; the upper storey was rebuilt in 1813 and at the same time a parapet was added. On the same side is the Church of the Holy Trinity, which dates

The Throne Room or Presence Chamber, originally called the Battleaxe Hall. Now glowing with full restoration – gilt throne, canopy, fluted Corinthian columns and capitals, a fine coffered ceiling and a magnificent carpet.

from 1814 and was designed by Francis Johnston, replacing an earlier garrison chapel. On the outside of the building more than one hundred carved heads adorn the walls: they include sovereigns of England, bishops and many notable persons from the past – the north door is watched over by St Peter and Dean Swift, while the east door is under the safe eyes of St Patrick and Brian Boru.

No one could list the catalogue of the great, the brave, the heroes, the romantic souls who have marched in and out of this place. Can one hear the voice of Henry de Loundres, Archbishop of Dublin from 1212 to 1228, or the anger of Thomas Fitzgerald working itself to the climax of renouncing his allegiance to King Henry? The old cobblestones by the main gateway would have borne the footsteps of them all. Close the eyes and dream a little that history can live again. Sir Henry Sydney rides out on his sturdy charger preceded by lines of mounted pikemen and a single herald who blasts his brazen notes from a trumpet held high. The years which are the pages of history flick over and are gone. Here in the castle's secret being must always have been nurtured the precious seed of Eire.

(opposite) Dunsany Castle – an impressive pile of ancient and more recent stonework, the earliest parts possibly dating from around 1200. It has stood a positive bastion of defence through the centuries, later generations of the family gradually converting it into a place of comfort as the need for warlike reception faded.

(below) A simple wayside Cross carrying the Crucifixion that stands just across the road opposite the main gateway of the castle.

The demesne of Dunsany lies nearly due north-west from Dublin; drive out across Phoenix Park and leave by the Castleknock Gate and head up the road to Navan. Watch for signposts, not always very clear, and a slight minor road will lead to the entrance. Again it might mislead, for what appear to be the ruins of some old church, abbey or castle come up on the right-hand side. But this is the gateway to one of the great monuments of the past: actually the building that guards the driveway was put up about 1760, a time for the building of follies. It is well done and deceives even close and careful examination. Directly opposite, on the other side of the road stands a thin column of ancient stone which widens at the top into a cross: just visible is the Body of Our Lord. How old? Lord Dunsany mentioned one thousand years; it has that appearance – the base of the column wrapped in layers of dark green moss, further up grey, silver-green lichen spreads in patches, and in between the old stone carries the stains of weather and drips from overhanging trees.

This is one of those areas of the land that carries an aura that the twentieth century cannot explain away. There is a scent to the air of something primordial, a beginning of special things – maybe the notes of ancient music are coming down from the north. Invisible messengers scurry down to the castle bearing a rolled vellum, a call to one of the most sacred and proudly revered spots. The great Hill of Tara lies a bare three miles to the north, and from time immemorial Tara has been the setting for High Kings, heroic figures of real and legendary life. The hill stands a little over five hundred feet high but do not expect stone ruins – in those early days forts were built of timber – but there are signs of quite large earthworks.

Tradition has it that St Patrick came here at the beginning of his mission in an effort to convert the High King Laoghaire. King Laoghaire is said to have looked out from the earthen ramparts and seen away to the north-east the Paschal fire of St Patrick flaming upward from the hill of Slane. Druids friendly to the king warned of the saint's intentions, so the king laid an ambush for the holy man and his followers. But Patrick with his friends passed by the waiting soldiers in the guise of a herd of deer – the druids were defeated in a struggle of magic and the king, although not converted, did give his consent for Patrick's mission.

With tales such as these in mind pass under the seemingly old arch of the folly gateway and bump over the cattle-grid. Old weather-battled trunks stand on each side; some, over-tired, lean on younger ones for support. The ground is rich in inches-deep leaf compost and pheasants peck and squabble in their dozens. Before passing the enormous pile that is Dunsany Castle, turn off to the left and bundle through an overgrown walk to where a genuine ruin stands – the fifteenth-century church of St Nicholas. The roof is open to the sky and the east window has been renewed. But step inside, for there is a fine old font, its basin and shaft covered with sculptured figures of angels, apostles and saints, though the carvings are too weather worn for any of the figures to be identified. A little way from the font in a large alcove stands a large altar tomb that carries on its top the recumbent figures of Sir Thomas Plunkett and his wife, early ancestors of those across at the castle.

The effect of this massive stone pile – pecked at, reconstructed, added to as it has been throughout its history – is of sheer strength. The façade, with its great towers largely built of random rubble, stands defiant to the assaults of time and weather, a solid monument to dignity and chivalry.

A castle seems to have been first built on the site around 1200 by Hugh de Lacy; this, with another nearby castle, Killeen, came by way of marriage to Sir Christopher Plunkett. On his death Killeen went to his eldest son, who was an ancestor of the Earls of Fingall, and his second son, the 1st Baron Dunsany, received Dunsany Castle.

The building that evolved consisted of two tall and sturdy blocks, each of which had square corner towers; these were joined together by a hall range so as to enclose a small court. Much of what happened in the intervening centuries can only be guessed at. But in the latter part of the eighteenth century, probably around 1780, the 13th Lord Dunsany put in train extensive reconstructions aimed at greater comfort for those living there. The court was filled in to form a staircase hall from which could spring the fine curving staircase which rises through three storeys in a series of gentle curves. From the first-floor landing a doorway leads to the library, a room decorated (probably by James Shiel) in the manner of the early part of the Gothic Revival and lit by tall mullioned windows at each end. From here pass through to the elegant drawing-room, with its delicate plaster ceiling worked in fine detail by Michael Stapleton. A door at the far end gives access to a small wooden spiral staircase.

The stairwell that was put in where the court once was is well lit by large windows; when the conversion was first made these were of Gothic tracery, but Shiel – working at the castle for the 14th Lord Dunsany – replaced them with mullioned windows. At the base of the staircase, fitting into the serpentine curves of the rising steps, is a delightful Venus which was probably copied from one in the collection of the Medici in Florence.

Just beside the base of the stairs is the entrance to the ground-floor dining-room; on the table in the centre rides the Duke of Wellington, splendidly modelled and cast in auriferous bronze, seemingly indifferent to a sadly bowed head in darkened bronze of his mortal foe, Napoleon. On a table of rare craftsmanship between the windows stands an amazing piece of nineteenth-century metal-working – a large cup about fifteen inches high with cover, on its top a masterly depiction of the savage combat between St George and the dragon.

The bottom of the main stairwell guarded by a delightful Venus, probably copied from one in the collection of the Medici in Florence. The glass-fronted cupboard on the half-landing contains a superb service of Meissen.

In the present century a large, panelled billiard room was added as a single-storey wing at the back of the main block; the work of George Jack, it suits well, with stepped gable and simple mullioned windows. At the right-hand side of the main range is an imposing stable block which is likely to have been the work of Sir Gilbert Scott, who worked on and off at Dunsany from 1875 to 1878: following the vogue for 'Revival', he battlemented the entrance and in his treatment of the window shapes maintained the feeling for romanticism. Although the castle may have been liberally spattered with excessive battlements, corbelled details and other pieces of imaginative 'medieval' builders' work, none of this disguises its underlying structure.

The texture of old stonework can be a lovely thing; each random block has a personality of its own. The textures vary, the myriad tints call for a special palette to portray them. Look closely at the work of long-past masons, touch the surface with the fingertips, and you will almost feel the current of history passed across.

Dunsany stands on its gravelled patch surrounded on three sides by lawns and woods that seem to show a certain deference and courteous respect for the ancient building.

Emo Court Coolbanagher, Co. Laois

Emo Court – framed by the avenue of huge Wellingtonias that may have been rudely torn about by winter gales but still stand regally dwarfing other timbers nearby.

A few miles to the north of Port Laoise stands the small village of Emo, at one time a post-town in the parish of Coolbanagher. About 150 years ago it consisted of 14 houses and 102 inhabitants; there was a public school and a constabulary police station and in the centre of this tiny place stood – and still stand – the gates to Emo Park or, as it is now, Emo Court. Limestone abounded and it was quarried for building, road-making and for burning into lime for fertilizer. The Dublin Grand Canal passes close by and there were a number of large estates that included Woodbrook, the home of Major Chetwood; Lauragh, owned by the Reverend Sir Erasmus Dixon Borrowes, Baronet; Knightstown, belonging to Joseph Kemmis; and Shane Castle, the seat of Thomas Kemmis, which gentleman – to ease unemployment in the area – had established an iron-foundry in his grounds. But the pride of place must inevitably be given to the distinctive mansion within the demesne of Emo Court.

The creation of this refined and noble building was an act of inspiration between two men: James Gandon, the English architect, a man of considerable taste and architectural knowledge; and John Dawson, later Viscount Carlow and from 1785 the 1st Earl of Portarlington. The highlight of James Gandon's work in Ireland before Emo is the magnificent Custom House beside the Liffey in Dublin, which illustrates his faultless sense of proportion and his use of carefully culled classic elements and motifs. Other important public buildings confirm these skills, and his only early ventures into domestic architecture – villas at Rosslyn Park, Sandymount and Emsworth – were carried out with the same fastidious touch. He was also very much involved with town planning in Dublin, working to ideas associated with the Dublin Wide Streets Commissioners during the 1780s and 1790s.

Gandon had not, however, previously entered the arena of the big house. Then he found himself faced with the desire of the 1st Earl of Portarlington for a great house, to be set some fifty miles out of Dublin away from the sophistication of that teeming and erudite city. The challenge must have been a fascinating one for Gandon. Should he follow the well-trodden paths, or choose to erect something quite original – perhaps take a leaf from the sculptor's method and create a form related to the space in which it stands and to the landscape surrounding it. What James Gandon eventually evolved for Emo was a deed of architectural genius: his house is not put into the landscape so that it obtrudes, rather it is of the landscape and has a harmony with it which is remarkable. Emo Court must have had then and certainly has today that timeless quality associated with true design, unmarred by vanities or needless additional decorative features.

Emo Court (the name Emo is derived from the Italianized version of the original Irish name for the estate, which was Imoe) replaced an earlier house on a site some distance away, called Dawson's Court. The Dawson family had settled in Ireland during the reign of Charles II, one William Dawson being the tax collector for Antrim and Down, and also for the port of Carrickfergus. His son bought the Portarlington demesne in the early eighteenth century – at that time he was known as Ephraim Dawson of Imoe in the Queen's County. Ephraim had a son William, who married a Mary Damer from Dorset, and in 1744 was born John, destined to be the 1st Earl of Portarlington. The father was raised to the rank of Baron in 1771 and Viscount in 1776. John married Caroline Stuart, daughter of the 3rd Earl of Bute, a young woman talented both in music and in portrait-painting. But her letters hint that she did find the Irish scene to her taste: in one written to her sister, Lady Louisa Stuart, she writes: 'perhaps you will be shocked at our Irish Manners when I tell you I am writing over a jug of whiskey punch, which I enjoy very comfortably.' But nobly born as she was, she carried on and undoubtedly gave much to the union and to her husband's standing socially. When the Coolbanagher church was built by Gandon – probably to a degree under the influence of the Earl's own dilettante ideas – Caroline busied herself with a copy of a Raphael for the building. This small church stands today – a dignified design shorn, like Emo itself, of unrequired detail. Adjoining it is Gandon's mausoleum for Lord Portarlington – which his lordship was to come to earlier than he would have hoped, for sadly he never saw Emo complete: during the 1798 Rebellion he was taken sick, as a result, no doubt, of the rigours of campaigning in the field, which would have been a harsh contrast to the comforts he had been used to.

Against this background Emo rose into being. It was basically two storeys over a basement. The entrance front has a seven-bay centre with a portico of four columns surmounted with particularly fine Ionic capitals and an almost severely plain pediment; the portico reaches to the line of the first floor windows. The flight of steps up to the entrance is guarded by two fantasy lions proud in their trust. To the left and right are single-storey pavilions with pedimented windows and quoin stones at the angles, laid with deep joints and lending just that right show of strength to hold the façade together. The central front is balustraded at parapet level, while the two pavilions have blind attics on which are placed two notably fine Coade stone reliefs, the one on the right being a delightful scene with amorini engaged in a light-hearted study of the arts, music and drawing – one may even be holding up a plan that could symbolize the work on the house, and to the left are more of these gentle cherubs set in a pastoral landscape.

The 2nd Earl, lacking money, discontinued serious work on the building until 1834, when he brought in another English architect, Lewis Vulliamy. He finished the garden front with another portico with tall columns topped

One of the Coade stone plaques mounted on the blind attics of the end pavilions of the entrance front. The scene shows 'amorini' engaged in a lighthearted study of the arts – the two on the right possibly examining Gandon's plan of the building.

Detail of the façade, illustrating the classic purity achieved by James Gandon: the portico is a thing of proportion, dignity and taste, with its tall columns surmounted by Ionic capitals.

with Ionic capitals; the entablature was balustraded and the whole complemented Gandon's front elevation. Assisted by a firm of Dublin architects named Williamson, Vulliamy also did some work on the interior. But in general it was a time of suffering for Emo and the estate must have slipped badly, for around 1860 rumour had it that the Encumbered Estates Court was close to ordering a compulsory selling-up. Somehow, though, the 3rd Earl found the courage and the funds to carry on. Another Dublin architect, William Caldbeck, was summoned and he it was who designed one of the most notable features of the house – the rotunda with the copper clad dome rising above it. He also erected a detached wing at the back and to the left of the house, connected to the main building by a curved corridor.

In the latter part of the nineteenth century much of the interior became obfuscated under the weight of Victorian taste, including some heavy panelling which had little relation to the design of the rooms involved. In 1930 Emo was sold to the Society of Jesus for use as a seminary, and thus it remained until 1969 when it was purchased by C. D. Cholmeley-Harrison who, working with the advice of Sir Albert Richardson and Partners and his own well-developed aesthetic taste, has carried out a most commendable restoration. Like Kylemore Abbey, it seems clear that Emo was waiting for just that right combination of understanding and foresight to bring it truly to life.

The court of the rotunda under the dome is a splendid place; the rich glow of the gilding of the Corinthian pilasters, the capitals full of detail and other decorations of plant and fruit forms, the overall colour scheme of carefully muted and matched tones – the total impression is of one of the most beautiful interiors to be discovered anywhere. The great salon is a surprise: here are more Ionic columns and capitals, the drums being of multi-tinted green marble, and the walls have most courageously been distempered a powerful apple green. On them hang some notable paintings: *Figures beneath Roman ruins* by Jean Lemaire (called Lemaire Poussin); over the marble fireplace a large canvas of *Christ and the woman of Samaria at the well* attributed to Francesco Trevisani; close by, *Ornamental fowl in a landscape* by Abraham Bisschop; also a fine work by the Irish James Arthur O'Connor, *Travellers in the Hartz Mountains*.

Outstanding among the furniture are two excellent Louis XV style kingwood or Brazilian wood commodes with *verde antico* modelled marble tops and rich ormolu decorations to the legs and supporting fronts. At the far end there is a rare Irish mahogany settee, dating from about 1750, with acanthus leaf motifs; the back is lattice-work with spandrels; and the front legs are cabriole with acanthus knees and lion's-paw feet. Around the salon are shown many examples from the best of the European ceramic manufactories. From Lowestoft a blue and white coffee pot, soft-paste ware *c*.1775; from Germany a wondrous Meissen two-handled little tray decorated with quite extraordinary delicacy and powder gilt; from Delft what might be termed a fun-jug, showing a bewhiskered farmer in a linen bag; and nearby a Renaissance ewer and dish in majolica with voluptuous snake handles, the decoration showing satyrs in ochre tones on a blue ground – place of origin almost certainly Stafford. (During the late eighteenth century and well into the nineteenth Wedgwood and most of the other great manufactories were hard at it imitating each other's best work and wares from the past – the whole scene could become really confusing, especially when they started imitating each other's imitations.) Survey the whole salon as a unity, with the colour scheme, and it is indeed a notable room.

The dining-room, with plasterwork ceiling designed by Vulliamy, has dark, cool, green walls that set off perfectly portraits of the family from the past. The library also has a plasterwork ceiling with sinuous Rococo modelling, but the eye-catching centrepiece here is a superb white marble fireplace of considerable size, with carvings of putti and vines heavily in fruit. The sheer detail and depth of the carving are amazing, as is also the skill of the maker in disguising just where the joins of the marble come.

There are two ways to approach Emo Court after the main drive has threaded its way through a somewhat tousled area of forestry. One is to come through a gateway which was probably the work of Gandon, and follow the drive round; all the while the house is hidden by a mass of trees, until – as they clear away – the façade appears and gives a rather lovely impression, as though it had suddenly been slipped into position at the last moment. The second and more impressive approach is to work round through the woods and so come on to what was intended to be the main drive. Straight as an arrow it directs the eyes to the great portico and behind it the blue-green copper dome. But what makes it the more memorable is the avenue, not just of any old trees but magnificent Wellingtonias. Pole-straight Douglas firs at the far end – trees which can put up a fair challenge in any wood – are here outclassed as the immense Wellingtonias, their trunks cased in rough flaking bark and wrapped in their

The library has an eye-catching centrepiece in the superb white marble fireplace of some considerable size. The sculptor has worked in putti, grapes and vines with much skill and delicacy, and very deep relief.

shaggy foliage, appear to regard their neighbours with a form of almost gentlemanly disdain and then turn their eyes heavenwards and go on up. Walk towards the house framed by these great trees and appreciate something of what good tree-planting is all about. For the final approach the last of the Wellingtonias stand back. They give it all to Gandon – Gandon, that is, plus that dome by Caldbeck. Yes, Emo Court is unique, erected from true inspiration and not in competition (as some have suggested) with that master of the stately greats, James Wyatt, who at the same time Emo was being built was bringing into being that vast presence of Castle Coole in Co. Fermanagh.

Florence Court
Enniskillen, Co. Fermanagh

Approach this graceful house from which direction you will. Come out from Enniskillen crossing over the little Arney river, or come up from the south by way of Swanlinbar with its sulphur well, whose waters were much sought after during the eighteenth and nineteenth centuries and earned the little town the nickname of the 'Harrogate of Ireland' – threading the way through the peaks of Cuilcagh, Benaughlin, the 'Peak of the Speaking Horse', and Benbrack, with the high ground running along on the left and over yonder to the right the waters of Upper Lough Erne set with turf-green islets. But perhaps best of all come through that truly lovely genuine wild country that the road from Sligo will take you. Keep straight on at the cross in Manorhamilton and bear right in Blacklion and the road will pass through the magic Cladagh Glen. Here the Cladagh river runs underground for about a mile, with many natural caverns hollowed out by the action of water and decorated with stalactites and stalagmites. Perhaps the best known of the natural formations round here is the span of the Marble Arch, which is an outstanding feature of the Glen. But move on towards the landscape that inspired a patron to build, a landscape that took to its heart the great house of Mullach na Seangain, the Hilltop of the Ants – Florence Court.

There are without doubt parts of Ireland that seem to the listening ear to hold the 'song of the little people'; round Florence Court is one. An old wise head might say that they have so many places to hide – all those tunnels under foot, the caverns up the mountains, the dark green depths of the valleys. Stuff of the fairies – maybe it is, but also the background for the stuff of romance.

Despite the Gaelic inference about the place being the Hilltop of the Ants, it is pretty certain that the Court took its name from Florence, the wife of John Cole, who died in 1718. But most of the facts about dates of building and just who did what in those early years are missing or obscured in documents that can be confusing. The fair lady who gave her name was from a west-country family in England, the Boucher Wreys, who came either from Cornwall or near Barnstaple in north Devon. The earliest house on this idyllic site was probably quite small and may have just served as a hunting-lodge, but all traces of this have now disappeared.

It was John the son of the aforementioned John Cole who seriously set about erecting the magnificent façade to be enjoyed today. He was to be ennobled as Baron Mount Florence in 1760. Under his eye arose the centre block of three storeys with seven bays, but there is no reliable information about who the architect could have been. This façade is plentifully decorated with deep-set quoins, rustication, pediments, balustrades and other artifices to proclaim its presence as a thing of beauty and substance out here in the lonely country. Later, probably around 1770, arcades and end pavilions were

*The plasterwork in Florence
Court has a character almost
entirely of its own. It takes
the form of a refined Rococo.
Motifs used include horns of
plenty, plant-inspired corbels
under a frieze, fruit and
extravagant curved shapes, all
put in with a masterly light
touch so that at times they
hardly seem connected to the
walls and ceilings. In the
dining-room birds are to be
found feeding among
acanthus-like growths; the
span of decorative features
moves from intricate
splendours to simple swags of
draped cloth.*

added, almost certainly by William Cole, 1st Earl of Enniskillen, and they may have been designed by Davis Ducart or at any rate inspired by him. It is the colonnades that transform the appearance of the house, with their arches joining the columns and necklets of balustrades running along above. This is not just another house: it is a building that embodies the full spirit of the Baroque – that imaginative bravura spirit drawn from places like Würzburg and Pommersfelden that jumped the Channel, touched down at Blenheim, to light out here. There have been many guesses about just who would have had the skill to design such a place. The Rev. G. N. Wright, who is normally reliable with dates and facts, states in his *Scenes of Ireland*, published in 1834, that 'the mansion, after a noble and classical design by Cassels, was raised about the year 1771 by the Lord Mount Florence'. The trouble with this is that Richard Castle (Cassels), who built so many fine places in Ireland, died at Carton in 1751. But what matter? Someone conceived and erected this incomparable façade, reaching across the hillside for all of 350 feet. It seems as though all the inspiration and love went into this front elevation, as the side and rear elevations are by comparison quite simple – rumours have said that the reason for this is that the money ran out. The element of fire visited Florence Court in 1955 and struck to the heart, gutting much of the interior. But skill and care under the supervision of Sir Albert Richardson brought back the spirit and the look of the house – the only real loss being the nursery on the top floor, which had an unusual ceiling with plasterwork incorporating rocking horses, drums and other toys, recalled today from early photographs.

The entrance hall is almost square, with a bold entablature with a frieze of triglyphs supported by rusticated Doric pilasters. Pass through an arch and mount the stairs, which have a handrail of superlative craftsmanship in exquisitely used tulip wood. The walls carry some of the finest Rococo plasterwork in the country, almost certainly executed by Robert West, one of the top stuccodores from Dublin. The motifs include horns of plenty, fanciful curvaceous plant-like corbels under the frieze, fruit and extravagant curved shapes that seem so light in form that they might just have floated in and landed feather-light into their place in the scheme of decoration.

The dining-room has more of this frothy beauty – the frieze spills over with cornucopias of fruit, birds happily ensconsed in acanthus growths feed from corn cobs. Mercifully this treasure was saved by builders who, as the fire subsided, drilled small holes through from the room above to allow the great weight of water to drain away – if this had not been done the enormous weight would almost certainly have brought the whole ceiling down. This room was more fortunate than the drawing-room, where the original ceiling with a demi-dragon emerging from clouds and the family

Florence Court – despite its impressive physical size it has more than a touch of mystery. The surrounding area is one of the special places – here many would state they can hear the 'song of the little people'. Certainly as the afternoon light softens with the approaching dusk the stone yields up its hardness and for a few escapist minutes the whole range of Florence Court sits across the brow of the slope as something ethereal; hard lines soften, dark tones blend into the surroundings and the great house takes on a delicacy of substance that can leave in the mind a picture that lingers.

crest was destroyed by the fire, although the plasterwork which fills the coved cornice did escape. This repeats the exuberance of the work in the dining-room, with foliage, flying birds and baskets of fruit. These motifs are very much the hallmark of Robert West and versions of them can be seen in houses in Dublin such as 86 St Stephen's Green and Grove House, Milltown. The dignified fireplace is a later addition and was brought from Innishmore Hall, Co. Fermanagh in 1946. The style is neo-classical, with flanking Ionic columns supporting a frieze with winged horses and chariot.

It is interesting to compare a photograph of the hall as it was in 1910, cluttered with the trophies of chase and war, and the charming finish that can be seen today. The clean lines of good design give a restful sense of space where before there was almost a feeling of claustrophobia.

The house and fourteen acres of land were acquired by the National Trust in 1955 and twenty years later most of the rest of the estate was purchased by the Department of Agriculture. The park of some ninety acres in front of the house is being restored to its eighteenth-century appearance by the Forest Service, who are using aerial photography to position trees that have gone over the years.

Florence Court is a name known worldwide because of one tree: the celebrated Florence Court Yew, *taxus buccata 'Fastigiata'*. Tradition has it that it was discovered on Aghatirourke mountain as a seedling between 1740 and 1760 by George Willis, who was a tenant of Lord Enniskillen. The strange little tree was brought down and transplanted in its present site alongside one of the walking trails used today. The yew is a freak which can only be reproduced from cuttings, any seedlings reverting to the common type of yew. Widely known as the Irish Yew, it is regarded as the patriarch of all such in the country. Cuttings have been taken from it since 1830 and propagated by the nursery trade, and have been available for sale to the public since that year.

To draw the most from Florence Court you should view it from well back in the parkland that swells up gently to meet the house. Then go up to the Court and stand on the entrance steps and look out across the green sweep of turf that guides the eye down to where the distant waters of Upper Lough Erne sparkle mildly in the declining sun of an afternoon. These two views tell really all there is to tell about putting a house into a landscape.

Go back once more to the first viewpoint as the afternoon moves softly into the evening and watch a transformation scene. If the sunset is a rich one the palette of colours will brush in the heights behind – a scumbling finger will erase any hard lines; just for a moment the architectural fantasy of the façade stands clean cut, almost as detailed as an engraving; then down come the curtains of the night, at first diaphanous, then more and more opaque until the last sight of Florence Court is little more than a cut-out of blue and grey.

Fota
Carrigtohill, Co. Cork

The name has a vague Norse ring to it; literally translated, it comes out as 'warm turf', 'warm sod'. The site of this hidden place is on an island of the same name in the outer reaches of Cork Harbour. A very well-preserved tall stone wall surrounds the demesne, which is approached from the mainland along a causeway that just about keeps dry when the spring tides are pushed into the harbour by the equinoctial gales.

The whole area, including large tracts and properties on the mainland, has been 'Barryland' since the time when Henry II came with a mighty cluster of knights bent on conquest, fairly polite and chivalrous if possible, but prepared to be as rough as necessary. The family that lived in Fota until 1975, the Smith-Barrys, were the direct descendants of Philip de Barry, who was mightily involved with Henry's invasion; he was the founder of the great Irish Anglo-Norman family of De Barry.

In the early period the Normans had made a vast land grab and the De Barrys seized huge estates from the MacCarthys. The battle cry of the De Barrys resulted from a particularly fierce tussle between the two families near the small town of Killnemullagh – to rally his forces the De Barry leader shouted 'Boutez en avant' (very literally translated by someone as : 'Kick your way through'). The day was won and the little town changed its name to Buttevant, while the stirring cry was adopted by the Barrys as their motto. Various fortified places watched over the plunder of this fearsome family, but slowly a quieter and more civilized life settled on the descendants. A barony had already been bestowed as early as the thirteenth century. In the sixteenth century Castle Lyons was built near Fermoy and became the seat for the Earls of Barrymore, whose creation dated from 1627. Another and earlier foothold for the family was at Barry's Court, Carrigtohill; this ancient medieval castle had been remodelled in 1585 and the Earls of Barrymore used it through to the seventeenth century.

Eventually the attraction of great stone walls and bleak surroundings began to pall, as it did for so many warlike families. In 1714 some of the Barrymore estates, including Fota Island, were given to the Hon. John Smith-Barry, a younger son of the 4th Earl, who set about erecting a hunting lodge which must have inspired the family to abandon finally the rigours of medieval life. They moved into John's Lodge, and – assisted by the celebrated architect Sir Richard Morrison – turned the somewhat humble lodge into an impressive Regency mansion.

During the latter part of the eighteenth century certain prominent members of the Barry family were absentee landlords of the most wanton type; they had estates in some 30 parishes with an overall total of 79,000 acres. Three brothers, orphaned as small boys and as they grew up grossly spoilt by their guardians, quickly displayed the family contempt for money.

Richard, the eldest, who became Lord Barrymore on the death of his father, got the bulk of the fortune and is reported to have been given £1,000 for pocket money while still at school. With his brothers Henry and Augustus, Richard became a close associate of the Prince of Wales, later King George IV. Legend has it that the Prince dubbed these three wild, almost lunatic, characters with suitable nicknames. Richard was Hellgate; Henry – the clubfooted one – Cripplegate; and Augustus, Newgate. There was also sister Caroline, who got the title of Billingsgate because of her raucous tongue and pithy oaths. Gillray took full advantage of their behaviour and labelled one drawing of them 'Les Trois Magots'. Together, and often in the company of the Prince, they went the full round of the social bravado scene: horsemanship in all its forms, cockfighting, boxing, gambling. By day the threesome would charge around the countryside, ripping down signs, misdirecting travellers, breaking windows. One of their more spectacular feats was achieved by Augustus; on one spree, he rode his horse upstairs into the attic of Mrs Herbert's house in Brighton, probably in search of buxom chamber-maids; whether he found them or not, it required the services of two blacksmiths to get the unfortunate horse down again. The monies of the three, substantial as they were from all their rents, poured away. Richard died after nearly blowing his head off in a stupid gun accident on a journey in his gig – shortly after his twenty-fourth birthday.

Around 1820 the transformation of the hunting lodge gathered speed. Morrison was noted for the classical purity he brought to his designs; here at Fota, certainly with the interior, he excelled himself, and left behind a building with a heart of great beauty. Additions were made to each end of the old lodge and a fine single-storey Doric portico was added to the front door in the centre. This has sturdy fluted columns, with plain Doric capitals, and is surmounted by acroteria. Pass through into the long entrance hall and one senses an amazing change of atmosphere from the cool, simple treatment of the exterior; the few steps forward take the viewer into the grandeur of a palace, albeit on a reduced scale. The ceiling is supported by carefully proportioned ochre-orange scagliola columns with Ionic capitals, and on the lintels are representations of the Barry crest. Between the windows are plaster casts made under the direction of Canova from antiquities in the Vatican Museum. These had been ordered by the Pope to give, with others, to the Prince Regent, who gave them to the Cork School of Art in 1818. Some then passed, in 1840, to the new Queen's College, which is today University College, Cork, and the College kindly loaned these two to Fota.

In 1975 a joyous thing happened to Fota. University College, Cork, purchased the island from the last of the Smith-Barrys; this act brought

Fota – another of those private places that hide themselves away in Ireland. Its vaguely Norse-sounding name translates roughly as 'warm turf' or 'warm sod'. The house, which started out as a shooting lodge, stands as a pivot to the whole complex of the demesne. Within it are gathered not only the graceful interiors of Sir Richard Morrison, but fine furniture and paintings that bring credit to the Irish School. Outside, a magnificent arboretum encircles the house on two sides; a bee farm provides the pollenators and a home farm supplies the cattle for the wide parkland in front. Further back strange animal calls give evidence of a lively and promising habitat where endangered species can survive: cheetahs, rare antelopes, flamingos and others browse and breathe without fear. (opposite) A painting of the Flemish school close to the Breughels that suggests aptly what those directing Fota strive for; it hangs in a room next to the drawing-room.

with it a sturdy flow of lifeblood for the house, the demesne with its agricultural projects, the gardens and the splendid arboretum, and the bee farm – and not least a hope for the future for some endangered species of animals, since in 1983 the Royal Zoological Society opened a large wildlife park in the grounds. For the house also this was a happy year. Mr Richard Wood opened it to the public after an effective and dedicated conservation and restoration in conjunction with University College, a special feature being one of the finest collections of Irish paintings outside the National Gallery in Dublin.

From the select and refined delight of the hall pass into the drawing-room, which is one of the most successful rooms that was added to the lodge in the 1820s. In the 1870s there was a catastrophic crash when the ceiling fell down. Looking up at it today one can only wonder at the power the restorer can wield; the exquisite tonal passages of Mr Sibthorpe's decoration and the gilding of the mouldings have been done with just the right degree of reticence for pure success. Gold is a lovely metal, but when used for decoration its power needs to be carefully bridled or the result may be overpowering. In this room have also been gathered landscapes by such as Robert Carver, Thomas Sautell Roberts and George Mullins, who seem to have absorbed the mastery of golden light achieved by the Frenchman Claude Lorraine and the Dutchman Aelbert Cuyp.

Through into the library, and note that the ceiling here carries a moulded decoration almost identical to that in the drawing-room, but left uncoloured and ungilded – a most fascinating comparison. The lovely, rich, draped curtains are exact copies of a set made in the 1830s for the library of a house called Ballinagall in Co. Westmeath.

On the walls are more paintings of the Irish School and notably three by William Ashford (*c.*1746–1824), who many would claim is the master of his time. There is his amazing composition *Cloughoughter Castle, Lough Erne, county Cavan*, in which a massive chunk of rock, half muffled in creeper, threatens to roll over and engulf the small party of the gentry who have come by boat for a picnic. A servant unloads the hamper, one venturesome soul clambers up on a high rock; but first and last here is a great experiment in the handling of a landscape, significant for the quality of landscape itself rather than for the narrative that is being told in an undertone.

Back into the hall and walk through to the dining-room where Morrison produces yet more of his classic skill. This time the pillars are of sombre-toned scagliola and are surmounted by good Corinthian capitals, thus completing the placing of the three great orders in Fota. The heavy sideboard is a good illustration of what a watchful eye can find: not all that long ago it was found in the hands of the 'travelling people', and a close examination of the left-hand side of the top reveals ugly score marks where the 'people' were using it as a workbench.

Before the stairs are ascended, it is worth spending a while in the watercolour room. A fine study of Blarney Castle by the Cork artist Nathaniel Grogan senior is brimming with life and fun, and has many historically interesting features: the bridge, the mock battlements, the player of the uileann pipes. There is a perspective for the proposed railway station for Cork by the mid-nineteenth-century architect Benson, while another that should certainly hold the eye is an evocative and moving study of Clonmacnoise by Petrie.

The staircase itself is of interest, for here again brass balusters have been used – perhaps the influence of Lady Louisa Conolly from Castletown came down as far south as this, although it would have been a coach drive of around 170 miles from the gates of her great house.

The Shamrock Room still preserves its mid-nineteenth-century wallpaper and between the windows hangs a study for the very large canvas in the Royal Dublin Society of a scene from Shakespeare's *Cymbeline* by James Barry, the Cork artist who left his native country to attempt to storm the London scene. A strange, irritable man, he fell out with his fellow painters at the Royal Academy. Today his work has been reassessed and a higher judgment passed upon it – at his best he was capable of showing great power and control of light and shade, with subjects that portrayed heroic scenes often with a mythological content. Life did not cosset him and his last years were spent in considerable poverty, alone and avoided, but he did find a resting place in St Paul's Cathedral.

Close by the Shamrock Room, in another bedroom, is a remarkable marine painting by Edwin Hayes; it depicts the scene when an officer fell overboard from H.M.S. *Shannon* while rounding the Cape of Good Hope. The painting of the vessel is meticulous, with details of the rigging put in with great care, and the facial expressions of the whaler's crew as they approach the waterlogged figure stand out; but perhaps best of all is the way Hayes has captured the massive quality of the huge seas of the southern hemisphere.

Fota is a place with a number of faces: the interior of the house, the exterior, the gardens and the wilder places for the animals. It was J. H. Smith-Barry in the mid-nineteenth century who first seriously set about laying out the gardens. He supervised construction of a temple and an orangery, as well as a formal area guarded by tall yew hedges and delightful iron gates with rusticated piers. He also started the planting of the arboretum, which work was continued for more than a century by his descendants – the soft gentle climate of the area has fostered many rare specimens and made the arboretum world-famous.

The demesne of Fota actually takes in the whole island and is skirted by the rail and road connections between Cork and Cobh. The fine classical entrance-gateway and surrounds were a final touch by Morrison. They carry on each side not only the Barry crest, but also the motto 'Boutez en Avant'; and for some reason which is not clear they are surmounted by the figures of two seated wolves.

To wander in through these gates when the foliage is at full splendour is to become immersed in a great harmony of myriad greens, studded here and there with the flowers of rare plants and common ones. The paths wind through this careful planting, leading past great conifers that soar up over the more lowly specimens and the bright sparkling foliage of evergreens. Those who persist will reach a secret fern garden. Here exotic tree ferns sprout from contorted moss-wrapped trunks; finally, when they find air space, they open out as multi-ribbed, green-feathered umbrellas, swaying gently to fret the lancing sunbeams that find their way through the serried branches of the surrounding woods.

Perhaps it is only in areas such as this that our need for green is recognized. Radiating out from the fern garden is an atmosphere that carries within itself an irresistible peace and harmony, in the end embracing the whole of Fota: the subdued, satisfying joy of the house, its contents and those who care for it. It is picked up by the animals that may have come from very far-away places, yet have found here a haven that has become an acceptable home.

As the day gives place to the pastel, soft-lined forms of the evening, and as the evening gives place to the night, the sounds of Fota are different – the harsh crowing of the peacocks, the muted mewing of a cheetah, the calls of native wildlife. But it is all part of that special Kingdom of which Fota has found a portion.

Fota surely is a magic place.

Glin Castle
Glin, Co. Limerick

Glin Castle – a bow-shot from the south bank of the Shannon. A pleasant, peaceful place that shows little of the battle-torn history of the FitzGeralds.

The FitzGeralds, who have had such an impact on the history of Ireland, were intermingled in the early centuries with the neighbouring Lords of Kerry, the FitzMaurices. Both these families originally came from the same, somewhat unexpected source. Way back in the twelfth century their mother was that generous lady, Princess Nesta of Wales; she was the daughter of Rhys ap Griffyd ap Tudor Mawr, Prince of South Wales. Princess Nesta married Gerald FitzWalter, Constable of Pembroke Castle and President of that county. Those early members of the family would have come to Ireland with Strongbow or soon afterwards.

There was, and is, strong blood in the FitzGeralds – in the branches of the family tree can be seen the Earls of Desmond, the Earls of Kildare, the White Knights, the Knights of Kerry and the Knights of Glin. Search out individuals among these and the list will include brave men and women, indomitable tribal chiefs, aspiring monarchs, eccentrics, villains, kindly generous souls, priests, yeoman farmers, sportsmen and, more especially, an impressive array of lords and ladies of fashion, wit and sheer style.

Members of the family were noted for building castles from which they could assert their authority. Probably the earliest of these stone fastnesses was the castle of Shanid, set high on a motte that by its size must indicate immense labour from a workforce armed with little more than primitive shovels and baskets. Originally Shanid had a fine polygonal tower which would have given to those holding the castle an unobstructed view over a large part of Co. Limerick. Today only part of the tower remains, and this has been eaten away by the elements and in all probability by damage from early sieges, as well as by those hungry for a ready supply of cut stone for building projects of their own. From here was taken the war-cry of 'Shanid a boo' (literally, 'Up Shanid'), a rallying call for the knights and their men.

Later signs of the family's domination appear in many places, particularly in the southern half of Ireland. At Maynooth massive walls are the remains of a stronghold of the 8th Earl of Kildare, uncrowned King of Ireland for forty years until his death in 1512. The large late-fifteenth-century Castle Mattress in Co. Limerick was first under the command of the FitzGeralds; Kilbolane Castle in Co. Cork was built in the thirteenth century by the Cogans and later 'acquired' by the Earls of Desmond; Kilkea Castle in Co. Kildare was long associated with Gerald, the famous Wizard and 11th Earl of Kildare – today it continues life as a hotel. In Co. Offaly there is Lea Castle, dating from the thirteenth century, with a massive towered keep standing in a roughly oval ward and commanding a large walled courtyard with a gatehouse; and at Minard in Co. Kerry once stood a FitzGerald stronghold, which was blown up by the Cromwellians.

Nearer to the site of the present FitzGerald Glin Castle is Desmond Castle, which was one of the chief fortresses of the Earls of Desmond. Of mostly fifteenth-century construction, it stands on an island in the river Dee that flows through the pleasant little town of Askeaton. The most interesting feature that can still be glimpsed here is a fine fifteenth-century great hall, raised on a basement of vaulted chambers, with windows indicating a florid decorated style. Within the bailey are some strange remains of a house of rubble stone with red brick dressings, which at one time – according to the evidence of old pictures – had a high pitched roof and tall chimneys. It was in this building that the Limerick Hell Fire Club made their headquarters in the 1730s, though the main features of the castle had been sadly disfigured by the gunpowder of the Cromwellians.

In those distant times, there would often be little showing of chivalry; informers made good money with their whispering tongues, and massacres would flare up. One such incident illustrates the unbridled savagery that could be expected. A particularly fierce marauder, Sir George Carew, had set himself to savage the Knight of Glin and his forces, who were occupying Old Glin Castle, as it is now known. Carew brought up a great cannon and some lesser ordnances – then by chance the six-year-old son of the Knight of Glin fell into Carew's hands. A message was sent to the Knight that he must surrender or the child would die; to back up the threat Carew ordered that the young child should be bound and tied across the mouth of the great cannon. A letter from Carew to Sir Robert Cecil, dated 27 June 1600, has these lines which show clearly the temper of the commander: 'I am unwilling to be cruel to infants, but where fathers be unnatural, I know no reason why other men should use pity towards them. I will bring the boy before the castle, on whom if the parents will not take compassion, I am afraid that I shall be enforced, for terror's sake to use severity.'

The Knight was in no way daunted and the Constable of the Castle replied for him in a rich and earthy manner: 'Gread leat. Tá an ridire go meidhreach fós agus a bhean go briomhar. Tá an phit oscailte fós agus an bod briomhar. Is fuiriste leanbh eile do gheiniúint.' The gist of this shocking reply was that the Knight was virile and his wife was strong, and that it would be easy for them to produce another child.

The surprise of this bold and seemingly callous reply caused Carew to have the child removed. He then commanded the cannonade to begin, resulting in a crushing and bloody victory for him.

After the capture of Glin Castle, the Knights no longer sought to live there. About 1675 Gerald fitz John erected a large house with a thatched roof close to the site of today's Glin Castle: this was called Glin Hall. It was here that one of the most celebrated ladies of the family lived: the 'bean tighearna' (the female chieftain), Mary, who was married to Thomas FitzGerald. During the famine of 1739–40 Mary turned herself in the nicest possible way into a lady highwaywoman; with her staff and others around

The remaining stump of an earlier Glin Castle in the village.

A few miles away on an earthwork stands the ruin of Shanid Castle, which was one of the earliest FitzGerald fortified posts. Originally, Shanid had a fine polygonal tower from the top of which the defenders would have had an unobstructed view over a large part of County Limerick. In early years many must have been the times when the battle-cry of the FitzGeralds – 'Shanid a boo' (literally 'Up Shanid') – was heard as the knights and bowmen marched forth.

her she rustled and raided for cattle in west Limerick and north Kerry, drove the herds back to her district and then had them killed and the meat sent out to the starving.

Mary FitzGerald had children aplenty and of assorted characters. There were five boys, who passed away in what might have been thought a convenient order in that four of them were able to take the title of Knight of Glin. Gerald went in childhood. John married Isabel Butler of the House of Ormonde and died on 10 August 1737, the day after the ball to celebrate his marriage. Edmond went in 1763. And then came the colourful and somewhat lethal Richard, the duellist, who was wont to go out of his way for a chance to engage in personal combat. He kept alive the feud between the FitzGeralds and the Moriartys, which had started when the latter family murdered the 14th Earl of Desmond in 1582 – on entering some public place, Richard would issue a challenge to any Moriarty present. He was a tall, strong man with a great eye for a target – his opponents were nearly always offered the choice between pistols at twenty paces, or the frightening prospect of that unpleasant weapon, a short sword, wielded at close quarters within a ten-foot ring. In the castle today there hangs a portrait of him by the Dutch painter Herman van der Mijn; this shows Richard's servant offering him a challenge to a duel with a Spaniard. The latter gentleman must have known of the danger from the sword of the Knight and had taken precautions. Repeatedly Richard lunged at his adversary, but each time his blade failed to penetrate; then, to save his master, the servant called: 'Sáidh é mar a sáidhtear na muca' ('Stick him where they stick the pigs').

The dining-room, like other rooms at Glin, is noted for its fine Irish furniture – the work of the native craftsmen has been well cared for. On the walls hang portraits of famous earlier occupants: a lady who practised a gentle form of highway robbery, the 24th Knight of Glin who recruited his own cavalry and artillery, and the 25th Knight who acquired locally the sobriquet of The Knight of the Women. (opposite) A bedroom that reflects the sense of home and comfort, with gentle furnishings and a wall covered in pictures to study.

The Knight complied with the instruction, inserting his blade into the neck of the Spaniard. When the body was examined, it was seen that the crafty fellow was wearing chain mail under his clothes.

The fourth Knight that came from Mary was Thomas, who survived Richard by six years, dying in 1781. One other lady connection of the family finds a niche in the story and that is Celinda Blennerhassett – she distinguished herself as the only female member of the notorious Limerick Hell Fire Club.

The thatched Glin Hall was accidentally burned down in 1740 and appears to have been quite speedily replaced by another Glin Hall of unremarkable construction. The year 1740 is remembered by traditional legend as 'bliadhain an air' – the year of destruction. The power of the Knights of Glin as they came into the latter part of the eighteenth century remained as strong as ever, but it changed character, for the leading members of the family sought comfort rather than the rigours of living behind yards-thick, icy-cold walls, and a new site was chosen for a more gentle home. The area selected was one that looked out over green parkland towards the flowing waters of the Shannon, not far from Tarbert, where the fresh-run floods joined with the cool waters of the Atlantic. The Shannon, the greatest of the Irish rivers, rises way up in the midlands, flows roughly south until it comes to Limerick and then turns to the west. A way out for the emigrant and a way in for the invader, this is a part of the country which has had more than a fair share of cold steel, blood and conquest: as mute proof, both the north and south banks at intervals carry jagged, wrecked and blasted ruins of castles and lesser fortifications that sit slumped on bluffs or artificial high ground, seeming still to eye the traveller on the waters or land with a watchful and threatening suspicion.

On these lands Colonel John FitzGerald, the 24th Knight of Glin, built between 1780 and 1789 an almost fairy-like castle, an apparently frail construction after the early defensive fortresses, a place of pale whiteness and decoration rather than warlike castellations. In the silver haze of the morning or dusty shadows of evening it still has an ethereal quality reminiscent of the French Château Ussé, which is also set beside a river – the long Loire that flows across the waist of France and also out into the Atlantic.

Basically it was a three-storey, double bow-fronted house, with a long service wing on the western side which may have contained some parts of the earlier house. The house was never completed, for John Bateman FitzGerald, the 24th Knight, succumbed to the family trouble that shadowed the Knights of Glin through the eighteenth century and into the nineteenth: the common fate of those who lived too freely, gambling, wenching, banqueting and indulging in expensive entertainments. The 24th Knight designed his own uniform, with liberal amounts of gold lace; he recruited the Glin cavalry and artillery, and marched them around the countryside to martial music to impress, though not to frighten, the locals. The year 1801 brought rumours of his impending bankruptcy. Still today one may pass through the ground and first floors admiring their quality and condition, and then climb to the second floor and enter a place of desolation. The rafters are exposed, no ceilings in sight, and the walls are scored for the top coat of plaster. The Knight could no longer pay his craftsmen, and so they downed tools and left. Here it is still 1801.

The 25th Knight must have found some more money because, between 1820 and 1836, this gentleman – known by the locals as 'The Knight of the Women' – added two turrets and enough plain battlements for the name of Glin Hall to be dropped. From then on, this confection on the bank of the Shannon became Glin Castle. It may be a little on the plain side, almost severe on the north front, but behind the sturdy front door there is a dignity and quality unsuspected. The front door has just a single large central handle – no knocker, for there was a superstition in the family that some invisible hand might give three blows on a door knocker, which would signify impending calamity.

The hall has generous dimensions, with a fine decorated plaster ceiling, and features two convex fluted columns surmounted with carved wood Corinthian capitals. The plasterer who worked the ceiling shows the influence of Michael Stapleton, the most skilful stuccodore of his time. Into the drawing-room, and again a decorated ceiling, but this time not quite the

A detail from the plasterwork in the entrance hall. The delicately handled decoration certainly shows the influence of the Irish stuccodore Michael Stapleton if it is not actually by him. The Irish harp is commemorated in lines by Thomas Moore:

'Tis believed that this harp, which I wake now for thee, Was a Siren of old, who sung under the sea: And who often, at eve, through the bright waters roved, To meet on the green shore a youth whom she loved

One of the 'pepper-pot' lodges that stand close to the south bank of the Shannon. In the background the great river and the folded hills of County Clare.

refinement of the hall, suggesting that it was carried out by local workmen from Limerick. The delightful fireplace is the work of the Italian Pietro Bossi, that supreme master of the art of inlaying fragments of coloured marbles; he worked in Ireland between 1782 and 1798.

The far door of the drawing-room leads through into the library, which is pointed up with a fine gilt-wood, pedimented mirror bearing the trade label of the great craftsmen, Francis and John Booker of Dublin. There are also two outstanding pieces of what might be termed manipulative furniture. The first of these is a delicately worked reading or drawing table with a double action. Lift one side and a variety of slopes can be provided. Lift the opposite side and a clever ratchet system allows the whole height of the working surface to be raised, so enabling the little table to be used from a standing position; it can then be lowered by turning a small brass handle which lifts a pawl and allows the notched curved arm to fall. The table was originally made for Francis Thomas FitzMaurice, 3rd Earl of Kerry, and carries his crest and coronet on the escutcheon.

The other piece of cabinet-maker's skill is a pull-out desk with an adjustable reading top and a swan-pedimented bookcase. This also has a sliding, baize-covered inner top to the pull-out section, as well as numerous compartments, including a swing-out, quarter-circle tray to hold pens and inks.

On one wall there is a tall bookcase which runs for the whole length in four sections. Three are what could be expected, but the fourth holds a surprise. Turn the handle and it comes forward in the manner of a conventional door: the way is clear to the staircase hall and one of the private wonders of Glin Castle. Here is something almost unique in Ireland, a masterpiece of the joiner's craft: the so-called 'flying staircase' which rises first on two ramps, one on either side, and then – in the final ascent – by a central tongue. Walking up this tongue one has the feeling of literally moving upward into space. It is likely that the staircase was modelled on the one in Mellerstain in Scotland, brought into being under the hand of Robert Adam. Rare indeed for Ireland and Britain, such a design is apparently quite common in the villas around the Bosphorus.

The second half of the twentieth century has witnessed careful and generous restoration and conservation to this Shannon-side castle, so ensuring that it will survive as a fit palace for the Knights, their heirs and whatever problems may come their way. Problems may not now be solved as Richard would have done, with dripping blade and smoking pistol, but the courage which has been the staff of the FitzGeralds will hold steady. Today, in the spring, a mighty carpet of rich, glowing, yellow daffodils sweeps down to within fifty yards of the house; flowering shrubs and conifers and other trees jostle with each other to complement this personal and private castle.

Kilkenny Castle Co. Kilkenny

Kilkenny Castle – one-time cold stone fortress of oppression, today it has yielded its strength to more peaceful purposes. Late sunlight caught through two aligned windows blazes out from the grey wall across the rose garden.

Today the castle stands proud and splendid, restored and dominating the pleasant city of Kilkenny which bustles with divers interests – it is still one of the most important centres of the country. The name according to some writers was derived from *Coil* or *Kyle-Ken-Ni*, 'the wooded head, or hill, near the river'. Of the early history little has been reliably recorded and it is not until the latter part of the twelfth century that facts become firm. Across the seas from Wales came the longboats bringing the Normans, who attempted to follow out to the letter Pope Adrian's Bull 'Laudabiliter' which authorized King Henry II to carry out the conquest of Ireland.

The greater part of what is now Co. Kilkenny fell to Strongbow who, having married Aoife the daughter of Diarmait Mac Murchadha, laid claim to the territory when her father died. The Normans found their way up the Nore and the Blackwater to areas of Ireland from which they could spread out to further the royal wish for conquest. In Kilkenny, in a commanding position above the river Nore, Strongbow set up the first fortress in 1172. This was probably a wooden tower on an earthen motte, possibly with a defensive palisade, the idea being to defend the crossing of the river; the exact position is not certain and there are no visible traces left today.

Strongbow had no male heir and was succeeded on his death in 1176 by his daughter Isabella, who in 1189 married William, the Earl Marshal, thereby conferring on him the Lordship of Leinster. It was he who started to build the first stone castle around 1192. From him the castle passed via his daughter to Gilbert de Clare, Earl of Gloucester and Hereford, whom she married. The de Clares held on until 1314 when – by marriage – the fortress came to Hugh le Despenser. The Norman settlers were jealous of their birthright and the purity of their family lines, and their efforts to preserve them resulted in 1366 in the Statute of Kilkenny – an Act put together in London, presumably as a sop to supporters of the Irish enterprise, which was a sad mixture of smugness, oppression and deliberate divisiveness. It set out clearly the rules of conduct and social behaviour for settlers in Ireland; for example: marriage with the Irish and nurture of Irish infants should be deemed high treason, and any man of English race taking an Irish name, using the Irish language, or adopting Irish customs was to forfeit goods and chattels, unless he gave security that he would conform to English manners; further it was declared illegal to entertain an Irish bard, minstrel, or story-teller – or even to admit an Irish horse to graze on the pasture of an Englishman. In 1391 the castle changed hands yet again; the Despensers sold out to James Butler, 3rd Earl of Ormonde, and this family were in almost continuous occupation until 1935.

The great building seems to have attained in 1307 the basic plan and shape that it still has today: four sturdy round towers, of which three remain, with curtain walls and ranges of buildings on three sides sheltering a large courtyard. Various owners in their time carried out alterations but these were mostly to the interior. One such was the 10th Earl of Ormonde, nicknamed Black Thomas. In the last half of the seventeenth century, after the Restoration, the Great Duke of Ormonde set out to transform the interior, which still had its somewhat oppressive medieval atmosphere, into a place pleasant to live in on the lines of some of the French châteaux and German castles. External vanities were also added in the form of high-pitched roofs with cupolas and weathervanes with gilded coronets surmounting them, thus changing the look of the old towers. The Duke had constructed elegant terraced gardens and an ornate fountain, the figure of which was probably carved by William de Keyser; and two statues copied from those in Charles II's Privy Garden added a feel of changed circumstances to the lawns in front of the castle.

The Duchess was as enthusiastic as her husband for the transformation. It is probable that Sir William Robinson was brought in for some of the finer points. He was the Surveyor-General and architect of that masterpiece, the Royal Hospital, Kilmainham, Dublin. The dignified quality of the main entrance gateway points very much to Robinson. Constructed from Caen and Portland stone, it is an outstanding feature – the pilasters capped by well-carved Corinthian capitals, the main arch balanced by the niches each side, the decorative festoons giving an air of lightness under the great pediment. In 1791 the 17th Earl built the extensive stabling across the road in front of the main gate; today this houses the Kilkenny Design Centre, which does much to exhibit the best of Irish design and allied craftwork.

The story persists that some forty years later the Kilkenny architect William Robertson was walking with the current Lady Ormonde around the courtyard when suddenly he paused and pointed out to her ladyship that a main wall was apparently out of true and in his opinion was unsafe. This turned out for him to have been a well-rewarded act of observation because he very soon found himself with a commission to carry out rebuilding on a massive scale. The basic intention seems to have been to undo some of the work that the Great Duke had carried through: in effect to restore the earlier medieval look. Fortunately, from the aesthetic point of view, the exterior walls were left, as were three great towers and – mercifully – the fine entrance gateway.

One of the better features carried out by Robertson was the construction of the Great Hall or Picture Gallery to replace the original one on the top floor of the main range, which was then converted into extra bedrooms. Robertson's gallery was 150 feet long, 27 feet wide and 30 feet high to the apex of the hammer-beamed roof. Between 1859 and 1862 this great gallery was remodelled by Benjamin Woodward, who introduced a partly glazed roof which enables the huge space to be amply illuminated with daylight. Crane the neck upwards and examine the paintings on the members of roof

Two details from the white Carrara marble double fireplace in the Great Hall or Picture Gallery. It was designed by Pollen, one-time Professor of Fine Arts at the Catholic University, Dublin, who also carried out the carving.

trusses and a strange collection of birds, beasts, waterfalls and languorous ladies are revealed; these are the work of John Hungerford Pollen. Here and there are vestiges of Celtic motifs – strap patterns and the sinuous forms inspired by the La Tène. Taken with the brightly gilded, sharp-beaked fantasy birds carved on the ends of timbers the overall effect is strangely unreal – there are whispers of the Viking, the Scythian, blended with the romance of the Arthurian legends, the Pre-Raphaelite world of Dante Gabriel Rossetti, and a whisper of Wagnerian extravagances. On one of the long walls is a large double fireplace which carries on the sloping top an intricate low relief carving of imaginative plant forms and on the front over the openings for the firegrids a number of bas-reliefs illustrating incidents in the history of the Butlers. The whole is constructed of pure white Carrara marble and this also was the work of Pollen, who not only designed the fireplace but carried out the carving himself. He was at one time Professor of Fine Arts at the Catholic University, Dublin, and another example of his work may be seen in the University Church there.

Sir Thomas Newenham Deane, a senior partner with Woodward, added internally some rather curious but impressive stonework. In one of the staircases the carved stone arches and the placing of the columns has a slight feeling of the Moorish. He also inserted a number of Gothic windows. Two of these in the east wing are in line through from one side of the building to the other, thus creating a strange effect towards evening as the sun sinks: for a few short minutes there is a stab of brilliant gold light that stares out across the fountain and rose garden like some stone-bound latter-day Cyclops.

The huge kitchen has an unusual plan, for it was fitted into the original site of the south-east tower: it is slightly below ground level with walls all of four feet thick supporting a high domed ceiling with pendentives. Today the kitchen has been converted into a tea and coffee shop, but it still retains much for the curious to examine. There are the old iron cooking ranges with great double-doored ovens, dampers and hotplates. Hanging above these and around the walls is a superb display of copper saucepans, frying pans, boilers and other kitchen utensils from the past. Over the entrance door was the necessary bell signal box with tallies that would swing when a lady or gentleman called for attention, meaning someone had to heft a large copper can of hot water or a scuttle of coal down draughty passages and up many stone steps. On the subject of fires, the nineteenth-century travellers Mr and Mrs Hall – in their account of journeying round Ireland – note:

From the turrets of the castle, there is a striking view of Kilkenny, and a magnificent prospect of the winding Nore, and the fertile valley through which it passes. One is instantly startled by the singular effect, to be witnessed nowhere else in the world, of a large assemblage of houses, with the usual chimneys, from which

Kilshannig

Rathcormack, Co. Cork

The Fermoy road out of Cork pulls itself along the valley before starting to ascend a series of switchback inclines and declines leading up into clearer air after Watergrasshill; then one enters the beautiful landscape watered by the river Bride that has come down from the small village of Rathcormack. The uplands that encircle this blessed spot lead the eye away to the mauve and grey forms of the Nagle mountains; a little way north of Rathcormack these offer up to the skies a large pile of stones known as 'the Lord's cairn or pile'. Legend has it that it was here that the Tierna (or chieftain) called his followers together to choose their leaders. Others have suggested that it could have been a place of pagan worship to the sun. In 1933 a cross was erected during the Holy Year. Search the lower slopes and a Holy Well will be found.

Looking for Kilshannig while driving north from Cork on this road may be a fruitless effort, so well is it hidden by trees and tall undergrowth. But come south from Rathcormack and it can be made out towards the top of a hill on the left-hand side. What was once a main drive wends its way across parkland to an impressive gateway with stone pillars surmounted by modified heraldic horses; the fine iron gates are now closed, for entrance is by a side drive from a small road at the top of the hill on the left.

The meadows here even in late October were thick with luscious moist green grass, which was obviously being greatly enjoyed by some spirited hunters and their young. Although the whole scene breathes a sense of peace and gentle living it was not always so – earlier this century, during the times of the Troubles, many was the skirmish that crackled into life and left behind bloodied reminders of man-against-man duels.

The side drive leads through a positive jungle of laurels grown beyond their ordained size, twists once or twice and then debouches on to an open space of turf with a solitary hardwood in the centre – and there is Kilshannig, one of the lovelier of the smaller noble houses.

This delightful building was the work of the Italian architect Davis Ducart and was erected in 1765. One of its most attractive features is the red brick of the walls: it has surrendered with subtlety to the passing of just over two hundred years, the tone has lightened and the warm red has faded to exquisite tints of pink-grey-ash green; the stonework dressing has also mellowed and its surface is flecked with small stains of lichen.

Designed in the Palladian manner, Kilshannig was built to the order of Abraham Devonsher, a Member of Parliament and a leading Cork banker. The general ground plan is symmetrical – in the centre the main house from which arcaded walls stretching out on both sides connect with a series of offices and stables, each of which comes round with a right-angle range stopping wide of the house and then connects back to it with a form of

curtain wall with gates to the two yards. The front entrance to the house is approached up a shallow flight of steps and a slabbed forecourt. There is some similarity to Vanbrugh's huge conception at Castle Howard in Yorkshire, only here the scale is greatly reduced; yet this in its own way seems to give an atmosphere of substance to the house – it sits there so obviously happy with its surroundings.

The façade has seven bays with three storeys, the centre feature being a three-bay Doric frontispiece in stone; this contains circular spaces with corbelled frames and is surmounted by a niche, all of which would originally have contained statues or urns. The back has something of the look of the Custom House, Limerick, which was also designed by Ducart: it has the same five bays and arcades of blind arches as the Custom House, but not its central feature with Corinthian pilasters. The two-bayed pavilions on the extremities of the office and stable blocks were originally adorned with copper domes – an impecunious incumbent in the last century apparently had them stripped to relieve his debts.

One could be content with the outside of Kilshannig, but make an entrance and there is more to delight – above all the supreme plasterwork, which surely cannot be bettered by any other house in Ireland. Some state it is by the great Francini brothers during their later period and at full strength, others more timorously suggest that it was carried out by Patrick Osborne. Let them argue – look up and wonder at the sheer consummate skill of those forgotten hands.

The hall has Corinthian columns supporting an entablature which curves inwards at the corners. The decoration has many free-moving forms including birds, one sadly flying forever on outstretched wings but with no head – tradition reports that in the early 1920s it suffered at the whim of a Black and Tan who could not find anything more dangerous or harmless to shoot at. Pass out of the hall into what is today the drawing-room but in earlier times was the ballroom. On the inside the doorway is framed by wooden pilasters with Ionic capitals and surmounted by a richly scrolled broken pediment – the same being repeated on the other two doorways of the room. On one wall hangs a giltwood mirror which is of considerable delicacy, telling some fable of animals or other fairy fantasy. To increase the sense of unreality here the architect – by clever use of a mezzanine floor – has made the drawing-room half as high again as the entrance hall, thus opening the way for highly imaginative treatment by the stuccodores. Here the central group has a quite fantastic plastic quality which, combined with the high relief, gives one the sense that the figures are actually emerging through the plaster. The three leading figures are Pan, Bacchus and a delightfully seductive Ariadne, caught at some moment after

Kylemore Abbey *Letterfrack, Co. Galway*

The search for the great buildings of Ireland brings a seemingly endless number of surprises and few are more dramatic or unexpected than the position of Kylemore Abbey. Connemara is a hidden kingdom; whichever way the approach is made, it is well protected from the casual traveller by miles and miles of wandering narrow bog roads. Come in from the city of Galway and it is more than fifty miles, from Westport nearly as far. The wild and lovely country has nothing quite to match it anywhere. To the north the pinnacle of Croagh Patrick stands guard, behaving at times almost like a chameleon, so rapidly can it change colour – harsh grey green on a late winter's day, yet the last beams of the falling sun can soften the edges and instil a warm mauve with, perhaps, torn shreds of cloud worn with all the abandon of some rakish scarf. Or come the other way and skirt round the slopes of the Maamturks that bulge upwards, sparkling with reflected light from embedded fragments of quartz and possibly mica. Either way the journey is almost certain to end up at Kylemore pass – a place of such extraordinary beauty that it rivals and many think surpasses the Gap of Dunloe in Kerry, or Barnesmore in Donegal.

This gap in the mountains runs for about three miles, deep set almost as though some colossal giant had slashed it out with a couple of strokes from his mammoth sword. The sides of the hills are in some places raggedly clothed with stunted, twisted shrubs and trees, although on the narrow floor of the valley, sheltered from the gales, some tall conifers stand interspersed with vast clumps of rhododendron. Waterfalls toss themselves from the heights falling as long lengths of part-spun white wool until they reach the swiftly running river. This is the heart of Connemara – a place apart, lonely yet comforting, savage heights and rock faces scoured by the elements, but holding within itself a warmth, a welcome. Some celestial brush has already painted this scene with a palette of colours that challenges the eye to believe what it sees.

Press on until the mountains move back and the waters of Kylemore Lough appear on the right-hand side and there across those waters stands the Abbey – an amazing statement that seems at first glance to be a marriage of some fairy-tale castle with elements of a Gothic cathedral. The name is quite simply derived from Coill Mór, 'a big wood'.

How did this place come into being so many miles away from anywhere? In 1852 Mitchell Henry, later to be elected Member of Parliament for Co. Galway, a surgeon and financier of Manchester and Stratheden House in London, had just married a sweet young girl, Margaret Vaughan from Co. Down. They had chosen to come out here for their honeymoon. By report, as they entered the Pass of Kylemore they stopped the carriage to picnic. For miles they would have seen practically no houses and very little sign of

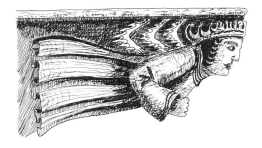

(above) A carved water-spout on the Gothic church that lies about two hundred yards along the lough from the Abbey.

(above, right) Details of three of the carved stone capitals by the front door of Kylemore – they present rather charming little fantasies with their presentation of strange lizards and birds.

habitation at all. Suddenly Margaret Vaughan looked up and saw one single little building set into the opposite hillside, possibly a shooting-box. She exclaimed to her bridegroom, 'How I should love to live there!'

Back in England Mitchell Henry found out who owned the property. But much larger ideas were working away in the minds of the two of them. He learned that a huge estate of some 9,000 acres went with the shooting-box, expanses of moorland, mountain, water and woods. He bought the lot and together they created in their minds a picture of an ideal, a fantasy that would come true – Kylemore Castle, as it was to be called at first.

The joyous couple employed two architects, Ussher Roberts (brother of the Field Marshal) and John F. Fuller. The list of what had to be incorporated must have daunted the architects, bearing in mind that the site was so many miles from any centre, any builder's yard. It included the following: drawing-room, dining-room, morning room, breakfast room, library, study, billiard room, ballroom with sprung floor, thirty-three bedrooms, sundry bathrooms and quarters for the staff. The list continued with a model farm with all necessary buildings, laundry, Turkish bath, saw-mill, an ornate chapel. Then there were to be all kinds of gardens, walled for rare fruits, and glasshouses; acres of bog would have to be reclaimed for the planting of specimen trees and shrubs; and finally there would be a Gothic church set about two hundred yards along the lough from the Castle. This was in part to be a replica of Norwich Cathedral, which was originally built by the English Benedictines – a scheme that proved later to be a happy foresight.

The building of this place took about seven years and came to completion in 1868. It served a useful purpose as famine relief work for the area, which was among the worst hit.

The style was definitely to be Gothic Revival. This fashion, that was basically inspired by the literature of the day, was popular beyond all other with the moneyed gentlemen of the late nineteenth century. The writings of

Kylemore Abbey – originally built as Kylemore Castle, it lies back against the tree-girt mountain that rises heather- and boulder-strewn to a mist-covered peak.

Sir Walter Scott, Goethe and Victor Hugo evoked a nostalgia for the dreamed Romanticism of earlier centuries. The Pugins, father and son, were among the leading protagonists; the father wrote *Specimens of Gothic Architecture*, the son *The True Principles of Gothic Architecture*; both books were valued as reliable guides.

Advance and inspect the building from close to and marvel at the task the builders faced – how many masons, craftsmen of all types must have been needed. The stonework is not just any old job; the blocks are carefully dressed and bear the marks of skilled cutting – not least the ornamental capitals at the entrance door where strange little birds and lizards creep in and out of cunningly arranged flowers and leaves. The labour was supplied almost entirely from local sources, just a few specialists coming in from Dublin and a few Italian experts who were needed for ceiling details and other intricate work. Perfection was what the Mitchell Henrys sought, even if it meant that drinking water had to be piped and pumped from natural springs on the Mweelin mountain a mile away – an echo here of Neuschwanstein and Ludwig, who had his water brought through a lengthy pipeline down from the mountains.

The final bill came out at around one and a quarter million pounds sterling.

The happy couple – by now with a family of no less than nine children – had lived in the Castle for seven years when Margaret decided she would join a lady friend on a visit to the wonders of Egypt. Tragically, while there she was taken with 'Nile fever' and after a few days she died in Cairo. Mitchell must have felt that all this great dream had suddenly shattered and become little more than wind-blown dust. He had Margaret's body brought back and placed in the mausoleum which had been part of the original plan. He could hardly bear to stay in Kylemore, and spent most of his time in London feebly attending to his business interests. The reaper struck again: his daughter Geraldine was driving a pony-trap out at Derryinver, the pony shied and she was thrown out while crossing a bridge; she was hurled helpless against the cruel rocks below and killed. Shortly after, Mitchell's businesses started to fail and he was forced to seek a buyer for Kylemore.

Mr Zimmerman, a Chicago businessman, bought it as a present for his daughter when she married the Duke of Manchester, the price a twentieth of the value. The new owners had no true love for the place and made changes which would have saddened the Mitchell Henrys.

In 1903 there was a rumour that Edward VII was looking for an estate in Ireland and among the properties being considered by his advisers was Kylemore. Perhaps encouraged by these stories, the chef in charge advised that the lovely ballroom should be converted into an enormous kitchen, and this was done. Excitement grew as the British Fleet arrived in Killary Bay for manoeuvres and the Duke and Duchess imagined that the King and Queen Alexandra would be pleased to stay at Kylemore; but no – they preferred the royal yacht. However, the royal couple did eventually tour the district and much to the chagrin of the chef and no doubt his Grace as well, their Majesties merely took a cup of tea at the Castle.

In 1913 the Duke, who was always short of cash, mortgaged the estate to a moneylender in Liverpool.

Many of these great buildings seem to pass through the same phases in their history – neglect, disaster, desertion – as though the spirits of these places are wandering through some desert of hopes. At times it seems that the rightful possessor just fails to come along. But for nearly all eventually the proper owner does appear who will applaud everything about the building. Then that house will have attained its true purpose. As the summer months of 1914 went by, a chain of events was about to be forged that would bring that fulfilment to Kylemore.

As the armies began to tear great chunks out of Europe it was not long before the fighting reached Ypres in Belgium. In that town was the Irish Abbey of the Nuns of St Benedict, founded originally in 1572 in Brussels by Lady Mary Percy and moved to Ghent in 1598. In 1665 the Abbess, Dame Lucy Knatchbull, established the abbey for the Irish Nuns in Ypres.

Just before the shells and explosives started to wreck their abbey the ladies set their brave steps for the west, taking with them some of their precious treasures. The road must have been hard, with military traffic taking priority. One sister died from exhaustion at Poperinghe; snow fell; but at length they reached the coast and found a passage to Dover. From there they went first to Oulton Abbey in Staffordshire. The Benedictine Abbot Columba Marmion set about the task of helping the sisters. Over the Irish sea they found another temporary haven at Macmine Castle, Co. Wexford. The Archbishop of Tuam lent his support, and eventually in 1920 the brave band of holy ladies came across the flatlands, the hills, the peat-lands to the Pass of Kylemore: the castle quite suddenly stopped being a castle and became an Abbey, with all the rights and privileges of Ypres Abbey transferred to it by the Holy See. Somehow the purchase money was raised by a public appeal.

Here now the nuns have brought into being a famous girls' school, which is attended not only by pupils from Ireland but also from countries far afield.

The ballroom turned into kitchen has now been transformed once more, this time into a chapel which has become a special place in the Abbey; not only has the conversion been done with great care and love but also here can be seen at divine service some of the precious objects that were brought from Ypres: a most splendid monstrance in silver and gilt silver embedded with rare stones, donated by the faithful; an exquisite chalice and also a fine censer. In a private room at the back is something out of the ordinary: an ebony tabernacle of superb workmanship, with small columns encased in tortoiseshell, bronze gilt angels and small painted panels by an early Flemish

Details from a fine white Carrara fireplace in the reception room. The quality of the carving is noteworthy and was probably carried out by an imported Italian hand.

painter, possibly around the time and place of Rubens – an unknown hand but most beautifully worked.

Down in the hall are other things brought by the nuns; vestments embroidered in gold and silver thread on rich velvet, a chasuble dating from the time of James II – reputedly the foundation velvet came from the drape of the royal charger. Close by is a poignant reminder of the careless brutality of war: a delicately modelled figure of Our Lord in silver torn from the cross and with one arm broken off. This was found in the rubble and returned to the nuns after the war. Another valued object, dating back to 1706, is the flag of Ramillies, which was captured from Marlborough's army by the Irish Brigade under the command of Lord Clare, who was a kinsman of a nun at Ypres Abbey. It was his prowess with arms that saved the French from total disaster. A verse from a popular marching song expresses the spirit of that victory:

> *The flags we conquered in the fray*
> *Look lone in Ypres Choir, they say*
> *We'll win them company today –*
> *Or bravely die like Clare's Dragoons!*

In 1956, on 25 January, the Abbey was threatened when a fierce fire broke out during the hours of darkness, but mercifully the alarm was quickly raised and no nun or pupil was hurt. Temporary accommodation was found for all while the restoration took place and at the same time a new wing was added in the same Gothic Revival style and improvements made to the decoration of the chapel.

Behind Kylemore a steep mountain gives protection from the cold north winds; the lower slopes are well wooded while the top reaches are a massive natural rock garden, with immense outcrop boulders and coverings of deep mauve heather studded at intervals with tiny jewels of wild flowers. Climb up the path to the Statue of the Sacred Heart. Glistening white against the rocks and turf the figure mounts guard over the Abbey and those who serve and are served there – the castle that metaphorically laid down a material sword and was transformed to find true fulfilment as the Abbey of Kylemore. The pure sweetness of the scene is watched over by 'De Iersche Damen' from Ypres and those Reverend Ladies who have followed.

PAX BENEDICTINA

Lismore Castle Lismore, Co. Waterford

Lismore Castle – it looks as though it might have stood on the bluff above the river for many centuries, but in fact dates from the early 19th century. Battlements and turrets were faced with cut-stone brought all the way from quarries at Chatsworth, Derbyshire.

The valley of the Blackwater river is a pleasant place today, edged as it is by dense woodlands alternating with luscious green alluvial meadows. The road on the north bank follows closely the windings of the water, each sweeping turn bringing up fresh views. Not long after leaving the little town of Cappoquin the road narrows for a moment as a sharp right-hand comes up; rounding this, there it is: a fairy-tale scene, with the great castle of Lismore seeming virtually to hang from the top of a lofty cliff beside the town. If it is mid-morning and the sun is shining, the illusion can be more complete as the battlements split the sunbeams into slivers of gold and the details of the landscape are just for a while robed in gently swirling mists.

Lismore Castle today presents the romantic picture of towers, turrets and battlements beloved by those nineteenth-century lords and ladies who were content, it seems, to pour nearly all they had into huge Gothic Revival piles. But at Lismore, underneath those cladding stones and mock threatening fortifications, there is evidence of a widely varying past. In a way the castle, with its precincts, is a splendid example of an architectural layer-cake.

The name Lismore literally translated means 'great place or enclosure'. None can be certain exactly when the first settlement was made here, or the first building erected. The site became famous during the period between the seventh and ninth centuries when the celebrated teacher St Carthach (also named Mochuda) founded a monastery here and also, according to ancient records, a university and at least twenty churches round about. Students seeking the wisdom of the saint came often from great distances – it is likely that one was the English King Alfred – and those trained by St Carthach journeyed far, one St Kathaldus even venturing down to the heel of Italy in the eighth century.

Unfortunately the waterway from the sea was an open invitation to the Vikings, who came at least five or six times to burn and loot. But with a resilience bred from a spiritual fire the inhabitants went again and again into the forests to seek sturdy timbers to rebuild and carry on their work. By the end of the twelfth century Lismore had become one of the leading Christian centres in Ireland – others included Armagh, Bangor, Clonmacnoise and Durrow. The calibre of these early inhabitants must have been considerable because – apart from the Vikings – in 978 the town and abbey were burned by the Ossorians – Ossory was an ancient kingdom in the south-west of Leinster; in 1095 there was much destruction following an accidental fire, and in 1116, 1138 and 1157 the monastery was again and again ravaged by flames.

In 1171 King Henry II made his historic journey to Cashel to claim his sovereignty; he spent two days with the Bishop of Lismore and probably with secret thoughts of future conquest made a note of the ford through the

Blackwater at Lismore which would allow for the speedy crossing of a large army.

In 1173 Raymond le Gros, one of Strongbow's chief assistants, who later married Strongbow's sister Basilia, marched down the valley, preceded, it is said, by a huge herd of cattle to conceal his coming. During this time the Irish chiefs were confused about the exact intentions of these Normans, who were rapidly spreading out over their country. In 1185 Prince John, son of Henry II, was sent over, initially for an eight-month assignment. At Lismore he ordered the sacking of the episcopal palace and the building of a castle on the site. Irish chiefs, encouraged possibly by false rumours, crowded to see the Prince and to pay their respects. But the stupid youth and his ignorant and brash followers insulted the Irish nobles, making mock of their dress and long hair and beards – the fashion with John and his Normans was for short hair. They plucked the hairs from the Irish, who speedily retired to plan unpleasant things. Only four years later, in 1189, they returned in force and sacked the castle thoroughly, the commander Robert de Barry and all his men being savagely put to the sword.

A few more years passed and an episcopal palace was built on the ruins and for many years was lived in by bishops of the see. Later it was the residence of the celebrated – or notorious – Pluralist Bishop Myler Magrath. This astute gentleman was consecrated Bishop of Down in 1567 by the Pope; by 1569 he was Protestant Bishop of Clogher, and a year and a bit later he became Archbishop of Cashel, to which position he calmly added the bishoprics of Lismore and Waterford and for good measure seventy-seven benefices. In 1589 the bishop's palace and demesne were leased to Sir Walter Raleigh for a peppercorn rent, but Raleigh preferred to live in his house in Youghal, which is today called Myrtle Grove. Tiring possibly of the chores of upkeep of Lismore and his other considerable properties in Ireland, he sold the whole package to Richard Boyle, the 1st Earl of Cork, in 1602 for £1,500.

Richard Boyle had a remarkable life. He arrived in Ireland in 1588, the year of the Spanish Armada; he was just twenty-two and the records state that he had no more than £28 in his pocket, a diamond ring, a bracelet and the clothes he was wearing. When he died in 1644 he was close to being the richest man in all Ireland. He had seven daughters and seven sons, the most famous of the latter being the justly described father of modern chemistry, Robert Boyle, who was born at Lismore in 1626.

The 1st Earl carried out considerable rebuilding of the castle; he surrounded the courtyard with three-storeyed gable ranges that joined the old corner towers, one of which survives today as a reminder of the ill-fated castle of Prince John. He also built the rather fine gatehouse tower with a Romanesque arch purloined from a nearby twelfth-century church. Three outlying forts were erected, one in the park, another at Ballygarran and the third at Ballyinn. Under his hand a charter of incorporation for the town

Detail of doorway in the gatehouse which guards the drive in from the town of Lismore: evidence of the mixture of architectural styles and manners, traces of which can be found around the castle.

Detail on marble fireplace surround in the Banqueting Hall. It was first seen as part of Pugin's Medieval Court in the Great Exhibition of 1851.

was obtained, as well as licences to hold a market and fairs. The Earl did much to develop the district – roads were made and improved, bridges constructed and schools established. There are account books among the Lismore manuscripts in the National Library, Dublin, and the Earl's diaries are at Chatsworth; from them can be gleaned a fair idea of his construction work and also details of costs and other matters that illuminate the early seventeenth-century scene.

The walls of the gardens were built up to a considerable strength, being so wide at the top that it was possible to walk along them; in fact they were to act as outer fortifications during the war of 1641. At the start the castle, which was under the command of Lord Broghill, the Earl's third son, was besieged by a strong force of some 5,000 Catholic Confederates under Sir Richard Belling. Lord Broghill reported matters to his father and an extract from his letter shows the spirit of the writer:

I have sent out my quarter-master to know the posture of the enemy; they were, as I am informed by those who were in the action, 5,000 strong, and well armed, and that they intend to attack Lismore. When I have received certain intelligence; if I am a third part of their number I will meet them tomorrow morning, and give them a blow before they besiege us; if their number be such that it will be more folly than valour, I will make good this place which I am in.

I tried one of the ordnances at the forge, and it held with a pound charge; so that I will plant it upon the terrace over the river. My Lord, fear nothing for Lismore; for if it be lost, it shall be with the life of him who begs your Lordship's blessing, and styles himself your Lordship's most humble, most obliged, and most dutiful son and servant. BROGHILL.

The attack failed and the enemy retreated, but the insurgents unfortunately were not done yet, and in 1643 a band of about 200 struck at the city as a gesture of revenge for the destruction of nearby Clogheen by a party from the castle; thatched houses and cabins were burnt, sixty of the inhabitants were killed and several prisoners were carried off. In July of the same year Lieutenant General Purcell, commander-in-chief of the insurgent forces, attacked at the head of 7,000 foot and 900 horse and with three pieces of artillery. First he roughed up Cappoquin for four days and then, joined by Lord Muskerry, went on to Lismore. After a siege that lasted only a week but during which much damage was done to the castle, both sides agreed on a truce and the insurgents retired. Two years later there came another Confederate army, under Lord Castlehaven, and this time the strife-battered building was mortally wounded and reduced almost to a ruin.

It was made habitable once more by the Earl of Cork; but subsequent Earls of Cork, who were now also Earls of Burlington, tired of the affrays and commotions of Ireland, greatly preferred the peace and quiet of their other estates in England.

Lissadell House *Drumcliff, Co. Sligo*

The far west is a land of many moods, a land that will not always invite exploration, but rather chooses those who will be allowed into the private recesses of its kingdom. Such a location is the peninsular in Co. Sligo that reaches out towards the Atlantic with Sligo Bay on one side and Donegal Bay on the other. The land itself is low lying and gives a footing to small hamlets and fishing villages. The backcloth is of mountains: the Dartry range to the north-north-east, with the bold escarpments of King's Mountain (1527 feet) and the proud head of the mighty Benbulben (1722 feet); to the south Lugnafaughery (1472 feet), the one with the great cliffs. To the east and sheltering under the slopes of the Dartry is the beautiful Glencar Lough, in part fed with waterfalls that have gathered their force from the heights above. Traditionally Drumcliff is the site of a monastery founded by St Columba about 574; possible relics of this include the stump of a round tower and a tenth-century High Cross showing scenes from the Old and New Testaments, including Adam and Eve with the serpent, the Tree of Knowledge, Cain killing Abel, Daniel in the lion's den, the Virgin and Child and the Crucifixion. One person perhaps above all others who saw, felt and embraced this wild, entrancing area was the Irish poet William Butler Yeats, who died in France in 1939 but lies buried in his soul-land in the churchyard of Drumcliff.

Out here have lived for generations one of the ancient families of Ireland: the Gore-Booths can take their records back to the Elizabethan Sir Paul Gore who was the direct ancestor of the family – including the Gores, Earls of Arran. A branch of the family have lived around Drumcliff for centuries, their habitations having included a castle and a house that must have been overdamp owing to its proximity to the shore.

It was probably this fact that persuaded the 3rd Baronet, Sir Robert Gore-Booth, to build a new house farther inland. Sir Robert at this time (1830) was twenty-five and carried in his line of descent not only the strength of the Elizabethan Sir Paul but more romantically the blood of Brian Boru 'of the Tributes', High King of Ireland, who with Malachy broke the cruel yoke of the Norsemen. Sir Robert commissioned the London architect Francis Goodwin to design Lissadell. What rose into being was a two-storeyed house over a basement; the entrance front has a pedimented and pilastered three-bay projection. The lower storey of this has open sides and thus forms a porte-cochère – wide enough to allow a coach and horses to draw up underneath. The opposite front has three bays on either side of a curved central bow with a parapet standing above that on each side. The façades are almost clear of any decoration apart from some Doric pilasters. The stones are set close jointed and smooth cut – in the

sunshine the surface has a warm silver-grey tint, after the soaking of months of rain the tone deepens almost to a light lamp-black.

To find Lissadell, take the road north out of Sligo which is signed to Rosses Point as you leave the city, but take the right fork for Drumcliff; then on to Carney and on again weaving through the stunted trees, over the petrified swell of the peat-bog roads. The gateway is on the left; enter and follow the twists deeper and deeper into a green tunnel that on an October day drenched the passer-by with heavy drops of rain that pierced the close-packed leaves. The sound of the dripping waters seemed to build to a climactic chord that was silenced only as the timbers thinned and the house broke into view a bare thirty yards away.

It seems that almost every member of the Gore-Booth family has contributed to the story out here, far from the cities and clamour of the crowds.

Sir Robert, like his successors, loved to travel and record what he saw – his sketchbook is a treasured possession in the house, as is his travelling library of forty-eight leather-bound miniature books. During the Famine he freely mortgaged the estate so that the hungry of the district could be fed. At the little cove of Raghley he shared with the government the expense of building a harbour. His son Sir Henry found his expression at sea. He had his own yacht called *Kara*, which must have been very well found because

Lissadell House – six miles to the north-west of Sligo town a narrow drive branches off to the left, feeling its way through dark pines, at times close to the water's edge until quite abruptly it debouches into a small clearing where stands the dark stone mass of Lissadell – another place that breathes out history. Here the great central hall, tall columns and pilasters give an impression of some long-forgotten Egyptian temple.

The main staircase, its finely cast balusters decorated with winged birds; an Irish elk looks down on the scene. On the walls drawings by members of the family – on the half landing an unusual feature of a fireplace. (opposite) The great bow on the western side of the house stares out westwards, the glistening afternoon sun lighting the sombre building. A window here which Yeats might have glanced through and found inspiration.

on one occasion he took her far north into Arctic waters. It was a voyage of rescue, for Sir Henry's friend, the explorer Leigh Smith, in his ship the *Eira* had got caught by the ice – the crew of the *Kara* arrived in time.

Sir Josslyn, the son of Henry, had a passion for horticulture and was largely responsible for the valued planting in the grounds – a secondary interest was founding local creameries.

His sister Constance, with others of her spirit, joined the Irish Citizen Army on the same footing as the men. She was given the rank of staff lieutenant and worked as a 'ghost', the name given to those who stood secretly behind the leaders of the Rising; these 'ghosts' would have known enough about plans to have enabled them to carry on if the leader was incapacitated. Constance must have cared little for herself – driving through the thick of the struggle, put in charge of trench digging in St Stephen's Green by Commandant Mallin – who also told her to be ready if need be to take up a sniper's rifle. Constance survived the horror days of 1916 and became a member of the first Dáil and a person who will stay long in the memories of her countryfolk. She also painted, and married an artist, Count Casimir Markievicz, who himself left behind a unique series of portraits at Lissadell. These over-life-size figures, painted straight on to the plaster of the walls, portray members of the family, and also Thomas Kilgallon, the butler who loyally followed his master on the voyage of the *Kara*, and the forester and the gamekeeper.

Cross the loose shingle to the shadows of the porte-cochère and enter the dimly lit hall. It is a place of height with square Doric columns and Ionic

163

The dining-room – over the black marble Egyptian-influenced fireplace hangs a double portrait of the sisters Constance and Eva Gore-Booth by Sarah Purser; around the walls over-life-size figures, painted straight on to the plaster by Constance's husband Count Casimir Markievicz, include likenesses of the family, Thomas Kilgallon, the butler and the gamekeeper. (opposite) The drawing-room, with a white marble fireplace which also shows Egyptian influence; treasures here include Sir Robert Gore-Booth's travelling library of forty-eight leather-bound miniature books.

columns above. Kilkenny marble is used for the floor, and for the double staircase, which has one rather unusual feature: on the half-landing there is a fireplace. The billiard room has been sacrificed to become a display room for the family memorabilia – sporting trophies, banners given to Sir Robert in gratitude for his help during the Famine, certificates, photographs, the little things that even big people like to harbour.

The core of Lissadell is the great gallery. It is a surprise chamber – entered from the hall it towers up with smooth columns surmounted by Ionic capitals and light coming in through a clerestory and skylights. It is one of those places that command a respectful silence; on these boards have stepped not only the family but also how many of their famous contemporaries – not least the man, William Butler Yeats, whose words brought immortality to Lissadell and to those two sisters, Constance and Eva, whose double portrait by Sarah Purser hangs in the dining-room.

Withdraw slowly from this place – here may have been glimpsed one of the arteries that has given of its life to the weave of Ireland. In winter the late gales of November lash themselves to fury far out on the Atlantic, then bear down on the wild coastline of Sligo to blast the rising waves against the rocks and send the salt spume flying over the land, to regenerate that salt of the earth that has made this solemn house of Lissadell a point for pilgrimage.

Lucan House   Lucan, Co. Dublin

*Lucan House – the form was the thought-child of Agmondisham Vesey, probably assisted by
Sir William Chambers and James Wyatt, plus Michael Stapleton the stuccodore.*

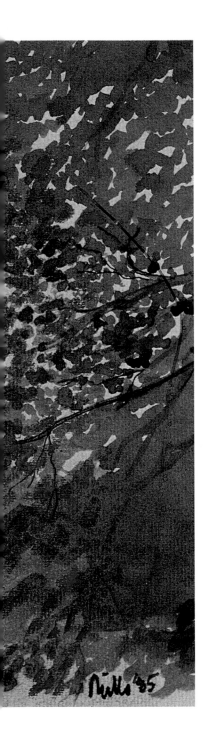

The little town of Lucan has a happy setting on the banks of the Liffey over which in 1794 a handsome bridge was built; it had a single arch ornamented with balustrades of cast iron from the Phoenix ironworks near Dublin and its design is credited to Isambard Brunel. The road passing through is one of the main thoroughfares to the west for Galway and Sligo. During the eighteenth century it was fashionable to come to Lucan to take the waters of the so-called 'Boiling Spring'; this gave up heated draughts of mineral water strong with carbonic acid and sulphurated hydrogen, which was supposed to have healing qualities for those brave enough to swallow it down. There was a fine spa-house of generous dimensions where the folk who came from far and wide could attend concerts and balls.

The demesne of Lucan House is tucked into the back of the west side of the town, slightly to the north of the main road, close by the brown waters of the Liffey. The early history of the estate is a little indeterminate; with the coming of the Anglo-Normans it appears that a grant was made to a Richard de Peche, an adventurer with the invaders, and in 1220 the property was owned by Waryn de Peche, who founded the monastery of St Catherine near Leixslip. In the reign of Richard II it was in the possession of the Rokeby family and then it came to the Sarsfields in the sixteenth century. In the grounds are the ruins of their old castle.

Patrick Sarsfield, Earl of Lucan, hero of the siege of Limerick, was succeeded by his daughter, who married the elder Agmondisham Vesey. They had a daughter and she was the ancestress of the Binghams, the Earls of Lucan. The same elder Vesey married again and had a son, also christened Agmondisham, and it was to this son that he left the estate.

Agmondisham Vesey the younger was one of a number of young men who fancied themselves as amateur architects – in fact his prowess came to the notice of James Boswell, who is reputed to have said of him: 'He understood architecture very well and left a good specimen of his knowledge in that art by an elegant house built on a plan of his own at Lucan.' Just how much of this plan and the elevations was his own is not clear; it is almost certain that he consulted with Sir William Chambers and very likely also with James Wyatt and the skilled stuccodore Michael Stapleton regarding the interior.

In any event the result was successful. The house has about it a quiet dignity with no over-pretentious features. It is of middle size: two storeys over a basement with seven bays and a well-proportioned central feature. This consists of a light pediment raised over a three-bay attic and carried by four engaged Ionic columns. The ground floor is rusticated – alternate long and short quoins go right up to the parapet at the corners. The two side elevations reflect the simplicity of treatment round the windows of the front. The whole sits harmoniously in its garden setting, set on an area of slightly rising ground with well-raked gravel drive and well-kept lawns bordered to one side with flowering shrubs behind which a somewhat frail span crosses the river.

It was built circa 1776 and a graceful compliment was paid to Agmondisham when in 1797 the 1st Viscount Monck built Charleville at Eniskerry, Co. Wicklow: his architect Whitmore Davis made an almost perfect copy of the Lucan House façade, except that it had nine bays instead of seven and a pediment was added above the front entrance.

The front hall at Lucan has a screen of Doric columns marbled to give the appearance of yellow Siena – there are also pilasters treated in the same way. The walls and cornice carry some refined and delicate plasterwork with roundels of groups of figures and the cornice has a continuous flow of festoons. The most impressive of the rooms is the so-called Wedgwood room, the ceiling of which is unusual in that at the corners it curves down, to give the impression that the whole ceiling is actually a very shallow dome. The roundels contain paintings by Pieter Jan Balthasar de Gree – a Flemish artist born in Antwerp in 1751 who studied with Geeraerts, from whom he acquired the skill of painting bas-reliefs. About 1786 he came to Ireland and settled in Dublin where he died in 1789.

The house has some notable fireplaces, particularly the one in the dining-room which has outspread Ionic curls and delicate marble inlays with wavy festoons of coloured fragments underneath the mantelpiece.

The ceilings of the Wedgwood room and the dining-room both carry similar plasterwork to the entrance hall. The ideas of James Wyatt are clearly visible in the general arrangement, and the plasterwork has similarities to that by Wyatt in the dining-room of Westport House – the authenticity of which is proved by Wyatt's working designs for the room. How much of the design at Lucan can be traced to Stapleton would be impossible to state, or how much of the actual decorative work he did.

The first floor is reached by a staircase of some lightness and elegance; from the landing there is access to a circular drawing-room that lies above the oval dining-room. A small classic touch on the landing is an iron stove in the likeness of an urn which today has had its blackness blanched with white paint.

As in a number of the larger houses in the country, a tunnel connects the house to most of the domestic offices, stables and estate buildings. The stable yard is approached at ground level through a strange little archway in a wall. This arch is made up of just a few rather large, very rough-dressed stones that were apparently dredged up from the bed of the Liffey.

Range round the demesne and there are a number of points of interest. There is a monument to the great Sarsfield, which consists of a graceful classic urn made from Coade stone and designed by James Wyatt; it stands on a short column carrying various architectural motifs, raised on a bank

The small doorway that leads to the stables and other domestic offices – as in a number of Irish houses, there is a connecting tunnel between these places and the main house. The massive rough stones forming the arch are said to have been dredged up from the turgid depths of the Liffey.

(right) The Sarsfield monument designed by James Wyatt, the urn made from Coade stone; the main mass is supported on the backs of four tortoises. The monument today is somewhat obscured by full-grown shrubs and long grasses.

approached by a small flight of stone steps. In another part is a rustic Gothic hermitage which is somewhere between a summerhouse and a folly. In earlier times the demesne supported a fine walled garden which was entered via a tunnel running underneath the Galway road, but this was disposed of in the 1930s.

In this century the ownership has changed several times. Captain Richard Colthurst, later 8th Baronet, inherited the demesne from the Colthurst-Vesey family. He sold it in 1932 to Hugh O'Conor, President of the Irish Association of the Order of Malta, of the O'Conor family whose seat is Clonalis House. Hugh O'Conor's son-in-law, Sir William Teeling, Member of Parliament after the 1939–45 war, sold it to the Italian Government for use as their embassy. How grateful His Excellency must be to drive those short miles from the hustle of Dublin, to enter the iron gates and come into this private place. The Liffey may not be the Arno or the Tiber, but what it lacks in breadth and majesty it can more than compensate for with its own inimitable sylvan banks and gentle ways.

Malahide Castle Malahide, Co. Dublin

Malahide Castle – sited on flat ground near a waterway and the coast, this venerable stone mass in earlier times saw much bloodshed and swordplay, heard intrigues and at times waited silent to see who might be the next to throw themselves into battle.

The site for this grey stone pile lies some ten miles to the north-east of Dublin; the land is low-lying and flat, and is deeply steeped in the history of Ireland both from the earliest periods and later. The little town of Malahide lies on the north side of the Broad Meadow Water Estuary, a sheltered spot that must have been a welcome sight for invaders from afar. It is likely that the first of those who came in force were the Firbolgs, who made a three-pronged descent on Ireland. One of their parties pitched into this estuary – the *Leabhar Gabhala*, the book of invasions, contains traditional mention of a race known as 'the Children of the Goddess Danu'; others now refer to them as the Firdomhnainn or 'the men of the deep pits', a name that they came by from their habit, when cultivating, of digging deeply into the soil. They also have associations with supernatural and magical rites that might be traced, through the early migrations, to India, where the earliest mythological pantheon shows a goddess Danu. The place where these people landed was for a lengthy period afterwards called Inver-Domnainn, the river mouth of the Danannans, and it has been positively identified with the little bay of Malahide.

The tenuous threads of deep history inevitably become woven into a partly obscuring curtain that lifts here and there as fertile imagination, stimulated by legend and distant fact, becomes a foundation from which heroes and goblins can grow.

The overall name for the district holding the great castle is Fingal – the place of the 'Fair Foreigners'. The name Malahide itself comes from the Gaelic 'Baile Atha Trid', pronounced 'Ballahid', the town of the 'Ford of Trid'. Until the late eighth century it was almost certainly a centre for one of the leading Celtic chieftains. Then, in 793, the fiercest of all sea warriors arrived – the men of the longboats, with their threatening carved figureheads. The Vikings, who already had settlements in the Orkneys and Hebrides, made a base at Malahide, from where they could continue their depredations and in particular the cruel sacking of the monasteries of Meath. To the simple folk, the sight of these men from far over the seas must have stilled their hearts: nothing, it seemed, could stop the marauders, who at times even dragged and carried their slim craft over the land to launch into new lakes and rivers in furtherance of their looting.

The Vikings, however, were not the last of the invaders. In 1170 the Normans seized Hamund MacTurkill, the last Danish King of Dublin, and accepted a surrender of his forces. The King was allowed to retire to his estate at Malahide, but this Viking could not live under the thrall of others and rebelled, an action which brought his execution. His lands were confiscated and were granted in 1185 by Prince John, Lord of Ireland, to Richard Talbot, a knight who had arrived in 1174 with Henry II. This marked the beginning of one of the longest tenures by the same family of a property in Ireland. The Talbots remained masters of Malahide Castle until 1973, some eight hundred years, punctuated only by a short period during the Commonwealth in the seventeenth century, when they were dispossessed for being Royalists.

Like so many ancient buildings, Malahide Castle has been subjected to much alteration and addition, but part of a massive fifteenth-century tower remains as the core. Battlements of varying design vie with window shapes that represent different periods; worn stone steps lead upwards in one part, a well-constructed timber staircase fulfils the same function in another. But, despite the amalgamation of styles, the lighting, the heating, and other amenities more associated with comfort than the active life of a stronghold, the place retains in good measure the feel of a true castle. The modern additions appear wafer-thin and cannot dispel an atmosphere rooted far back in time – in part surely pre-Norman and springing from the mists of something primordial and totally basic.

The demesne today is a leisure area, with large expanses of well-kept turf and tidy paths. The driveway, some half a mile in length, provides the first glimpse as soon as one enters it – two large oak trees frame the castle, which remains in sight as one sweeps forward. The front door, if that is the right term, opens from a carefully raked gravel patch and at once the twentieth century seems to be lost; the walls, substantial and thick, embrace a slight chill which is left behind as one climbs the broad, winding, stone steps, helped by a thin rail held to the wall by bronze hands. Malahide, like many other places, has many minutiae that are worth seeking, little fantasies of the craftsmen's imagination, or perhaps a display of supreme skill, a small gesture of vanity. In the rooms ahead can be glimpsed small, bronze sash-holders which feature the Talbot lion; intricate decorative motifs engraved in metal, carved in wood, worked on leather; and on to the incredible marble inlays in the side-table by Pietro Bossi, where the fragments are so tiny that they really call for magnification to be properly appreciated.

From the top of the stone steps one passes into the Oak Room. The entrance way and the front part were added during a reconstruction in 1820, but the inner and larger part of the room is considerably older and is a fine example of a sixteenth-century panelled room. The timbers have now darkened and hardened until they present the appearance of ebony, and there is much fine carving and decoration. On the wall facing the window there is a set of Flemish seventeenth-century work, added perhaps to replace earlier damaged areas, or brought back by some returning collector member of the family: it shows incidents from the Scriptures – the Garden of Eden, the Expulsion and others for which the carver has taken his inspiration from frescoes by the School of Raphael in the Vatican.

Furniture here includes one of the oldest so-called 'Guild chairs' in Ireland – sturdily made in hard oak, it carries symbols and signs cut out in a naïve

(opposite, top) One of a number of late 17th-century Restoration chairs, richly carved and with cane seat and back. (centre) A lively bronze head mounted on a sash holder – no doubt inspired by the Talbot lion. (bottom) A 'Sheela-na-gig', an 8th-century red sandstone carving built into the south edge of the east gable of Malahide abbey. Such figures might be carriers of good fortune or the reverse.

manner, the meaning of which is obscure. In contrast, there is a set of Restoration chairs, cane-seated and backed with rich foliate decoration.

The fireplace could cause confusion unless it is explained that it was a nineteenth-century idea to celebrate Nelson's victory at the Battle of the Nile; thus there appear sphinx-like figures and other such images from Ancient Egypt. But let the eye now wander upwards to the area over the fireplace, where there is a work of considerable beauty and quality. It is a sixteenth-century Flemish carving of the Coronation of the Virgin, the four angels making a symbolic pattern of protection round the simple figure of Mary, who stands humbly with praying hands as the crown is raised over her head. It is round this group that one of the legends of Malahide is woven. As the Talbots were Royalists, they were turned out of their castle after the defeat of the King's forces. One of the regicides who had signed the royal death warrant was made Chief Baron of Ireland and came to live in the castle. This unsavoury character was Miles Corbet, a Norfolk barrister. It is said that as soon as he took up residence the carving of the Coronation of the Virgin disappeared. Corbet, according to local tales, had some regret for what he had done; some said he spent many a sleepless night riding a great white horse called the Pooka round the estate. With the Restoration, Corbet and the other regicides were high on the wanted list. Corbet was arrested on his way from church, but managed to escape to the Continent. With two other signatories, Okey and Barkestead, he was betrayed by Sir George Downing, a Dubliner, who had once served as a chaplain in Okey's regiment. The three fugitives were taking a glass in an ale-house in Delft when they were seized and taken back to London to meet their end at Tyburn, where they were hanged, drawn and quartered. On 19 April 1662 Samuel Pepys made an entry in his diary: 'This morning, before we sat, I went to Aldgate and at the corner shop, a draper's, I stood, and did see Barkestead, Okey and Corbet drawn towards the gallows at Tiburne.' Local legend in Ireland completes the tale by recording that soon afterwards the figure of the Virgin made a miraculous reappearance on the wall above the fireplace.

Another writer has made a mark at Malahide. In the 1920s American scholars instigated a hunt for the literary papers of James Boswell. The upshot of what became a major pursuit was that some of this precious material was found not only in a Flemish ebony cabinet that stood in the Oak Room but also in other unlikely places, such as a box that was supposed to contain croquet equipment in an outhouse. Negotiations were finally closed and this unique material followed much of like matter across the Atlantic, where it now resides in a new fastness in the library at Yale University.

The Oak Room would have been the centre of living in the early centuries; a fire probably burned round the clock, a watch could be kept on approaching strangers, and who knows what gossip and planning went on?

Group portrait of the Talbot family; it shows the late Lord Milo Talbot with his mother and surviving sister Rose.

16th-century Flemish carving of the Coronation of the Virgin – who mysteriously vanished when the regicide Corbet lived at the castle and reappeared when he was executed.

Pass through the door opposite the entry and the high-security atmosphere of the early centuries fades – to be replaced by the elegance of the eighteenth century. Fine plasterwork is seen on the cornice and the ceiling, and over the fireplace an excellent example of the work of the Dublin firm of Booker – gilt and richly carved, this mirror can be dated to 1765. The Small drawing-room and the Large drawing-room contain not only fine furniture, decorated with ormolu and gilt gesso, but also numerous portraits of the great figures from Irish history. The Earl of Clare holds a *bourse* that would have been used to carry the Great Seal of Ireland, and on the table-top underneath the painting there is an actual *bourse*, rich with raised silver and gold-thread embroidery. From another wall look down the great Edmund Burke and a self-portrait of the painter Nathaniel Hone the Elder. These paintings and others like them are part of an inspired idea that emanated from the National Gallery in Dublin: to buy up many of the portraits from the Talbot collection when they came up for sale in 1976 and add to them others, thereby making the castle to all intents and purposes a National Portrait Gallery for Ireland. How well it fulfils this idea. Ranging through the rooms and passages one can trace the faces and sometimes the thoughts of those depicted, their tastes in fashions and many intimate details that give vitality to the study of history.

In the Stairway Hall, which in some ways seems surprisingly small, there hangs one of the two great battle paintings in the castle. This first canvas brings back memories of the French invasions: it shows the Battle of Ballynahinch and was painted in 1798, the year of the invasion, by Thomas Robinson. For the interested eye there is a wealth of detail on uniforms and arms, not least the figure on the extreme right, who is actively waving the Mayo Standard. On the opposite wall, another large canvas shows the Talbot family, the late Lord Milo Talbot with his mother and surviving sister Rose; near it is a small canvas by the miniaturist Samuel Cooper of Richard Cromwell, son of Oliver – surely a generous gesture.

From this hallway you enter the Great Hall, a large place that is not materially altered from what it would have been hundreds of years ago: space, beams, carved heads, two large fireplaces with ornamented back plates, a minstrels' gallery. The 35-foot table is not an old inhabitant of Malahide – it came not so long ago from Powerscourt – but its gleaming patina and strength fit in well. Other items from the past associated with dining are large wine coolers, with massive carved lids and zinc-lined interiors, and Georgian plate buckets. But the whole is dominated by an immense canvas of the Battle of the Boyne, painted by the Dutchman Jan Wyck. It is quite an achievement, for the painter has preserved the essential atmosphere of a battle scene while at the same time presenting recognizable figures such as William III on his everlastingly rearing charger, the artillery in mid-canvas, separate groups from different regiments and other small details. On the eve of the battle a large gathering of the Talbot family

The Great Hall at Malahide, a place for feasting and celebration and sorrow. On the eve of the Battle of the Boyne a large gathering of the Talbots sat down to sup – after the carnage of the next day fourteen of the young men lay stark on the field of war. A large canvas shows Jan Wyck's idea of the battle. Up a small staircase in a corner once lived a four-foot-high lad by the name of Puck, the guardian of the castle – last seen in 1976.

supped at Malahide, and fourteen of the young men who went to battle never returned.

Down at the far end of the hall, on the right, there is a little doorway too small to allow the passage of a normal man. Legend is again our guide and tells us that this was the place of Puck, a little fellow not more than four feet high whose duty in past times was to guard the castle and to warn of approaching danger. The doorway leads to a few winding steps and then a blank wall. One day, for no known reason, he hanged himself. But imaginative minds still seem to see Puck around – the last sighting was 1976, the year of the sale of the treasures of the castle.

A once-private fortress has become a public place; thousands can wander and wonder at the way 'those people' lived, not least in the fine gardens which were remodelled by Lord Milo Talbot between 1948 and 1973. Lord Talbot took advantage of his diplomatic travels to gather rare and fine plants from all over the world. These now flourish in their plenty, for it is reported that his lordship brought back not less than 5,000 specimens. The state of these lovely gardens is a fine compliment to the work of Dublin County Council, who care for them in the most loving way.

*The small drawing-room
(opposite) and the large
drawing-room (below) display
a notable collection of fine
furniture, much of it decorated
with gesso-gilt and ormolu.
Over a fireplace a notable
example of the skill of the
Booker workshop who made
so many fine mirrors; on a
small table under a portrait of
the Earl of Clare rests a
bourse embroidered in gold
and silver thread that
probably once carried the
Great Seal of Ireland.
Around the walls in these
rooms and on the staircase are
portraits of the Talbot family.*

To the east of the castle, and only a few yards from the main building, is the ruin of an old abbey. Doubtful stories suggest that the wretched Corbet allowed the roof to be stripped and that he used it as a shelter for his cattle – truth would be hard to find. But there is one episode of undeniable truth connected with these battered walls, which contain the altar tomb of Maud Plunkett. This lady has a unique distinction. On Whitsun Eve 1329, she married Sir Walter Hussey and immediately after the ceremony her husband was called from the wedding breakfast to a skirmish at Balbriggan, where he was killed. So Maud was a 'Maid, Bride and Widow' in one day, a happening that was celebrated in Gerald Griffin's ballad, 'The bride of Malahide'. Maud was later to marry Sir Richard Talbot of Malahide.

Perhaps the last whisper might come from the grotesque lips of a Sheela-na-gig that is set in the wall high beside the nave of the abbey. By some these weird little figures were looked on as talismans, to others they are either harbingers of evil or of good; this character with the weatherworn features might just be smiling for the future of Malahide – a place originally for war and defence, a place today for pleasure, a study point for the tapestry of the past.

Muckross House *Killarney, Co. Kerry*

Muckross House – all around everything grows greener than anywhere else: the heart of Killarney, mauve-topped mountains, silver-plated lakes, azaleas that grow as high as young oaks. Here rests a house with dozens of chimneys, sharp-pointed gables and so different from all the others – brimming with welcome and with memorials not only of the family who built it but also of the country round about.

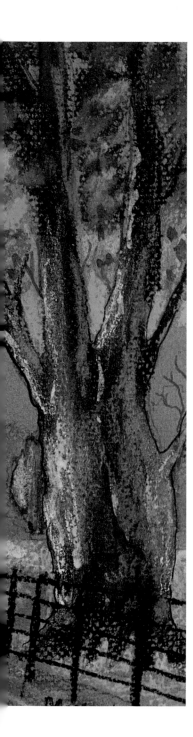

Killarney – *Cill Airne*, 'church of the sloes' – Kerry; tradition has it that St Patrick never came into Kerry, but only looked at it, holding his hands out to it and saying, 'I bless all beyond the Reeks' – the almost mauve, jagged, rugged heights, the Macgillycuddy's Reeks that stand to the west as gale breakers for the gentle beauties of the lakes and their forests and gardens. The peaks up there are the highest in Ireland: Carrauntoohill 3,414 feet, Beenkeragh 3,314 feet and Caher 3,200 feet.

No part of the country has more legends, fairy stories and gossip words than this. There was Fin Mac Cool, who kept his tubs of gold in the lake under Muckross and set his dog Bran to guard them; when an Englishman tried to dive for the treasure Bran seized him. And Ossian, who used to see white horses riding through his fields and mounted one of them which took him to the land of eternal youth. Then one of the most mysterious: John Drake, who took up his abode in the ruins of Muckross Abbey and lived there through all weathers for some ten years; those who claimed to have seen him, state that he was about forty years of age, his hands were small and delicate, his manner tranquil and dignified, and apart from his ordinary clothes he wore nothing but a single blanket bestowed by some kind soul; he never asked alms yet he always had enough to pay for potatoes and fish and to have a halfpenny over to bestow on those who seemed more miserable than himself. The local word was that he had committed a crime which demanded desperate atonement. Some who had braved a walk to the abbey told of how they had heard bitter groans, and angry words and sounds, as though men were engaged in mortal combat. Then one day John Drake disappeared completely – the straw of his bed was damp, his staff and wallet had gone; the wren, the sparrow and the robin peered from the nests he had protected. About ten years later a lady, 'a furriner, by her tongue', came enquiring for John Drake. For days she visited the stone couch where he had lain through the nights; and she wept floods of tears and prayed and gave alms to all who had been kind to him – then she too disappeared.

People were about in the Muckross area from around 2000 BC, the beginning of the Bronze Age there, but Muckross House dates from 1843, built in the Neo-Tudor style for Henry Arthur Herbert, Member of Parliament for Co. Kerry; the architect was William Burn, and it replaced a previous house. Although quite large, it is a compact building with features almost crowded together – sharp pointed gables and a multitude of engaged chimneys sprouting all over the roof. William Burn, an Edinburgh man, made a name for himself as a designer of domestic houses. For Lord Dartrey he built Dartrey House in Co. Monaghan; today this is a ruin, but early photographs show that there was a strong resemblance between the two houses – not only in the chimneys and gables but also in the Tudor-influenced mullions of the windows. Portland stone was shipped from Dorset to Kenmare and then laboriously hauled over the mountains by cart to become dressings and facings and other details. Upstairs there were twenty-five bedrooms – which accounts for some of the sixty-two chimneys, the rest providing flues for a generous number of fireplaces downstairs and in the domestic offices. In 1870 or thereabouts William Atkins of Cork designed the porte-cochère which provides welcome shelter in the late autumn and winter from the driven rain and mist-laden winds.

The first Herbert to hold land in Kerry was Sir William Herbert, who came from Monmouthshire in the Marches between England and Wales; he was granted large areas of land around Castleisland. He had no male issue but his daughter married Lord Herbert of Cherbury; the heir from this union brought to Kerry as his agent his cousin Thomas Herbert, who was the ancestor of the Herberts of Kerry. He had a grandson and heir Edward Herbert, Member of Parliament for Ludlow, who married Frances, daughter of Lord Kenmare. Their daughter Agnes married first Florence McCarthy Mor, a descendant of an earlier Florence who had made trouble with Elizabeth I. When Florence died, Agnes married her cousin Arthur Herbert of Currans and so came back to the Herbert family. The McCarthy estates also passed to the Herberts.

Muckross was held by the Herberts until just before the end of the last century when lack of money caught up with them and trustees were appointed to care for the estate. The head by title of Muckross today is Major General Sir Otway Herbert, who lives in Anglesey – that stronghold of the early druids off the north-west corner of Wales.

Lord Ardilaun, a member of the Guinness family, bought the Muckross estate in 1899 and sold it to Mr and Mrs William Bowers Bourn of California in 1910; they purchased it as a wedding gift for their daughter Maud and her husband Arthur Vincent. When Maud died in 1932 her family presented the house and all of 11,000 acres to the Irish nation as a memorial to her. It was entrusted to the care of the Commissioners of Public Works, who carry out their trust with care and sensitivity. The demesne has been added to and is now known as the Killarney National Park.

Today it is a centre for the traditional crafts – weaving, pottery, bookbinding, basket-making and a practising smithy. There are displays of local geology, plants and animals, and artifacts that give some clues to man's activities in this western part of Ireland. But the house and its contents have much to give – to a degree it has been arranged so as to show how it would have been around the turn of the century, less than a hundred years ago, and it provides some quite startling examples of how taste has changed and how domestic arrangements and utensils have progressed.

In the spacious main hall from which spring the wide stairs there are two examples of the work of local Killarney woodcarvers, in this case the Egan

The staircase hall, with examples of exquisite carving on sideboards by the Egan family. Sturdy stairs with 'barley sugar' balusters.

family of Well Lane. The relief work is quite amazing: some of the figures and rich motifs stand almost free from support; the imagination and sheer skill of the craftsmen seems limitless, and their designs are quite free from the kind of sentimentality that must have been prevalent around them. Out of the hall into the drawing-room which overlooks the sunken garden, and away in one corner hangs a copy of a portrait of that most venerable of long-lived ladies, the Countess of Desmond, who is said to have reached 140 years. Mention is made of her in Raleigh's *History of the World* and in Bacon's *Natural History*. There are also two portraits of Maud Vincent and her husband by John Sargent. Two pleasant Venetian mirrors hang on the walls and there is a games table with some exquisite inlay, the work of another Killarney craftsman.

Although some furnishings have inevitably been removed, the dining-room presents an appearance very much as it was in the late nineteenth century. There is a good mahogany table six feet wide and eighteen feet long, and twelve Chippendale chairs. At one end stands a large walnut sideboard carved in Italy and bearing the Herbert crest. There are just a few

pieces left of the Herbert dinner service with the crest and the family motto – which translated from the Welsh means 'Every man to his taste'.

Mount up to the first floor and it could be the children's room which will attract – here is everything needed for the comfort of the young, scaled down to their size – the kind of furniture for childhood which seems to have passed away from most houses today. Then to the master bedroom, with its huge inlaid Sheraton wardrobe and bed, and through a communicating door to the dressing-room, with a narrow upright washstand used by gentlemen for shaving and the ewer that stands underneath the draining plug of a circular mahogany and marble washstand – a reminder of just how many hired hands would be needed to run a mansion of this size.

The different offices afford many glimpses of the way life was run. Next to the dining-room is the servery, a place that has all but disappeared. Here the kitchen maids would bring up the large bowls of soup, the meat dishes under domed Sheffield-plate covers, and all the etceteras, and here the finer points of serving on to the plates would be demonstrated, probably by a senior footman under the sharp eye of the butler. Down the stairs to the basement on the wall high up can be seen a line of bells for calling the servants to undertake any small task required. Muckross at its peak had twenty-two indoor servants for all the chores – from the cooking, washing

(opposite) The principal
bedroom, with a well-worked
Sheraton-style wardrobe, a
lively 'scrap' screen, drawn-
thread and broderie anglaise
personal linen towels.

(below) The first floor
landing, to the left the great
window of cut and
ornamented glass, more carved
furniture and paintings by a
member of the family. Lively
frieze and Tudor-influenced
ceiling.

up and laundry to the parlourmaid who must be ready on the instant to
appear immaculate in black frock with lace cap and apron.

Other exhibits include a dairy with churns and all the implements needed
for butter-making; in another spot the tools and samples of work of a
monumental sculptor who worked in Killarney from 1912 until 1965; all the
bits and pieces required for harness-making, and also the equipment used in
a printing shop in Killarney during the first half of this century. Killarney is
a fine setting for the Muckross project – a journey back to the turn of the
century.

The setting for the house is almost too beautiful – the mists writhe and
glide around the mountains in and out of vision as the soft breeze blows.
Right in front of the house a great grey-white tongue of what looks like
limestone lies half submerged in the water of the lake, the top covered in
rich green foliage and mosses. Down the wide paths through the woods
there is an atmosphere, a deep feeling of peace.

The sheer extravagance of grasses, mosses, ferns, clinging plants, creepers,
trees small and great, short and tall – vegetation that promises that it has
grown here just like this since the first seed burst forth; the lake water now
duck-egg blue and smiling; the ancient abbey of Muckross, lichened, stained
with the rains, chipped, cracked and opening more every year to the hunger
of the elements – there is no sorrow with the passing years.

Royal Hospital, Kilmainham Dublin

The soil out here not far from the river Liffey has borne many things, yet in a way they have all been contributory to or allied to the final great statement that was inspired by the Duke of Ormonde – the Lord Lieutenant who was granted the Royal Charter from Charles II. The site throughout its history has felt the steps and heard the voices of people concerned with welfare, people who spiritually and bodily have sought to bring relief through good works and selfless dedication.

Probably the first mention of the Kilmainham site comes in the *Annals of the Four Masters*, where there is a reference to a seventh-century monastic settlement. The name Kilmainham is a derivation from Cill Mhaighneann and also has a connection with St Maighne's Church.

The peace of the brothers' work ran possibly for about four centuries and then Strongbow came marching up from the south, where he had landed from the fleet that had brought him and his fierce, well-drilled warriors from Wales. Rivers could be helpful if they were wide and deep enough to sail up, or they could be troublesome if they flowed the wrong way or barred the path of an advance. Coming up to Dublin, Strongbow must have been led to a well-used ford where his men could cross the Liffey. Records mention that in 1174 he granted a priory close to this ford for the Knights Templars (Knights of the Temple of Solomon), the military religious order founded by crusaders in Jerusalem around 1118 to defend the Holy Sepulchre and Christian pilgrims – the order was suppressed in 1312.

About the same year the Templars were replaced by the Knights Hospitallers (full name, Knights of the Hospital of St John of Jerusalem), another military religious order founded during the Crusades (1096–99); it took its name from a hospital and hostel in Jerusalem. The archaic word hospice, in its original meaning, describes well what these worthy orders set out to do: to offer sustenance in a wide sense to travellers and those in need, to provide much that is included in the word home. Sadly, with the suppression of the monasteries in 1541 the doors had to close. Material law may have decreed that their work should cease, but surely the spirit must have continued.

It is likely that the seed for the idea of such an establishment as the Royal Hospital was germinated by Lord Granard in 1675. His official post at that time was Marshal of the Garrisons of Ireland, and he would thus have been faced with the problems that arise for old and infirm soldiers. As their physique degenerated they would find themselves hanging around military establishments, more a nuisance than a help. Slowly the idea grew until in 1679 it received the full blessing of the King and the Duke of Ormonde selflessly donated a site from his intended deer and pleasure park, Phoenix Park. It was that part that lay south of the Liffey – thus the new concept

would rise almost out of the foundations of the earlier ones, although in 1670 any last remaining bits and pieces of the Hospitallers' buildings were demolished.

The architect chosen for this massive project was William Robinson, Surveyor-General since 1661, and the construction was to be financed by a levy on Irish military pay; this was approved by Charles II, and the final costing came out at £23,559. The stipulation was that the Hospital was to offer services in line with those provided by the earlier establishments – for those who 'by reason of Age, Wounds, or other infirmities, since their first coming into Our Army, are grown unfit to be any longer continued in our service'. The interesting point is that similar ideas were passing through the minds of influential people in England and France around this period. In France the scheme for the Invalides was begun in 1670 by Bruant and the great dome was completed by Hardouin-Mansart between 1693 and 1706; in England the Chelsea Hospital came into being from the drawing-board of Sir Christopher Wren between 1682 and 1692. The foundation stone of the Royal Hospital at Kilmainham was laid by the Duke of Ormonde in 1680 and the building was completed by 1686. Over the years there have been many jugglings with these dates, and even suggestions that Wren fathered Kilmainham. But surely nearer the truth is that curious phenomenon whereby creative ideas seem to emerge in practically the same form in a number of different places and through different people, all within the span of a few years.

The basic plan for the Hospital was to be almost a square containing a large inner court. On the north side was to be the dining-hall, a great room 100 feet long by 50 feet wide, originally to be decorated with guns, pikes and swords, and with standards taken from the Spaniards. There was a mention of lime trees being planted round the quadrangle; three sides were arcaded, and at first the fourth was similarly treated except for the central bays of the dining-hall. When the dining-room in the Master's lodge was enlarged by Francis Johnston some arcading went, and the arcade which flanks the chapel has also been closed up.

The main accommodation was provided in the three fully arcaded ranges. The rooms on the upper floors are entered from long corridors running along the inner side of the ranges and overlooking the court. Part of the intention of the enclosed court and arcades was that the veterans would have ample space for leisurely exercise in most weather conditions. An old print probably dating from around the early part of the eighteenth century shows the huge building with the great tower reaching upwards for about 125 feet – its entrance with pilastered Corinthian columns and somewhat heavy pediment. The dimensions of this tower still appear vast and the sheer weight bears down on to the roof of the entrance. Yet the perfection of the proportions of the tower and its mouldings and details give it a magnificence that is in turn transmitted to the whole concept.

One thing that strikes the observer here is the enveloping peace of the place. Whether, coming up a slight hill, you enter through the heavy iron gates guarded by stone pillars holding aloft gutted suits of armour, or whether somehow you can get in through what was at one time the main entrance – the Gothic Revival gateway designed by Francis Johnston – you will find this peace, and even if the not-so-distant traffic cannot be completely silenced its notes are so low that they do not interfere.

What a precious place it must have seemed to those warriors who found their way to the assured welcome. After Boyne some fortunates may have reached it – for the badly wounded a frightful journey by unsprung carts over the potholed roads of 1690. From near and distant places they came to find a home where before many had no home; souls with brave hearts who had soldiered their way round the continents until sabre, shot or years entitled them to work out their days here in the Royal Hospital, Kilmainham.

Bully's Acre lies just inside Johnston's gateway and is Dublin's oldest cemetery. In all it totals nearly four acres and the stones record not only the Hospital's pensioners but also some of the British dead from the 1916 Rising, as well as others – possibly even the bones of the Knights and distant monks: most of the early stones have had their lettering weathered away, but there is one readable from 1652.

The great hall or dining-hall where the pensioners lived out most of their waking hours when indoors looks somewhat similar today to what it did when completed in 1684, although during the nineteenth century quite considerable changes were made, particularly to the ceiling and the panelling – the latter and the doors and architraves being stained a dark brown (a favourite practice of the designers of the period). Later reconstructions have restored the earlier dignity – large canvases in gilt frames hang above the panelling, which has now been repainted to the original stone tint; the portraits include the Duke of Ormonde and Archbishop Marsh. The windows are original, although they now contain twentieth-century stained glass of armorial subjects.

The wonder of Kilmainham lies certainly in the chapel – not only in its size but in the extraordinary quality of the decoration. Probably it is best to look upwards first, as the effect of this fantasy ceiling is to drown out visual memories of the other more refined details. There is nothing in Ireland from the seventeenth century that can come near this masterpiece. Its proportions and shape are quite unexceptional: it is divided into recessed panels and the overall motifs used are plant forms, fruit and flowers, with intermixed sinuous trailing vines – all sounds quite everyday. But no: what is not everyday is the very deep relief the stuccodores used, so deep that in

*(opposite) The Royal
Hospital, Kilmainham –
claimed, and rightly, by many
as the greatest building in
Ireland. Today, after a
wondrous work of
conservation, it stands proudly
to fulfil the next chapter in its
life – as the National Centre
for Culture and the Arts.*

some instances, looked at from below, the forms appear almost free-standing, as if they have no holding support. The more bravura effects were carried out with the use of papier-mâché. It is as though some inspired descendant of Amalthea, daughter of Melisseus, King of Crete, had acquired the magical cornucopia and had wantonly poured forth the riches of the earth's gardens high up there beyond our reach.

Sadly, the names of the plasterworkers are not known. Perhaps they made it all just a little too heavy, for only a few years after the ceiling was completed there were worries about it. By the mid-nineteenth century pieces were falling down, and later in the century there were ominous signs of decay. Drastic action had to be taken. So the gargantuan task of taking casts of it and making an exact replacement was commissioned. How well this was done can be judged today. Could even a sharp eye find fault?

Move to the east end of the chapel and enter another field of masterly craftsmanship: that of supreme chiselwork – in the fluted columns and pilasters with their delicately rendered Corinthian capitals, in the ebullient ovals and swags between them, in the base dado which carries some manifestations of pure genius – the emblems of the lilies, the flower that by tradition is said to have sprung from the repentant tears of Eve as she went forth from the Garden of Paradise. Here the carver has given them such vigour, such a sense of life that they seem almost as though they might be plucked from the panels, living beautiful things – made by James Tabary some time in the 1680s. No, it was not Grinling Gibbons who brought his

In the chapel, fruit, flowers and sinuous vines seem to trail from the ceiling with little visible means of support.

(opposite) The inner court – beneath the arcades the veterans could take gentle exercise in all weathers.

mastery here, although many voices have argued for this. James Tabary was admitted as a freeman in Dublin in September 1682. For all the glory he brought to the woodwork of the Kilmainham chapel it does not appear that he was over rewarded. Notes from a meeting of the governors of Kilmainham for 1687 include this somewhat terse comment: 'Whereas James Tabarict [a variation of spelling for his name] Carver . . . was not allowed the full value of his worke in carveing, frameing and setting up the Altar-peece, Rayle, Pannell and Table in the Chapell . . . it did appeare by the Certificate of Mr Robinson [the architect] . . . that the said Altar-peece . . . was valued at Two hundred and fifty pounds.'

There are some doorways with fine examples of wood-carving in the tympanums. Two unusual compositions show pieces of armour, swords, battleaxes, spears, and one of them a large wheeled cannon. Another has a well-modelled head and rich festoons of flowers and fruit. These were carried out in pine, then treated probably with several coats of lead undercoat, and finished with a stone-like tint.

The glass in the chapel is mostly nineteenth century, showing coats of arms of the various masters; a panel of stained glass behind the reredos was presented by Queen Victoria in commemoration of her visit to Kilmainham in 1851.

The Royal Hospital continued to serve its original purpose until the 1920s, although gradually during the nineteenth century the atmosphere of Kilmainham changed as it became the residence and headquarters of the commander in chief of the army, which post was doubled with the role of Master of the Hospital. In 1930 the complex was handed over to the Free State and after that for a short time it served as a Garda headquarters.

Any building left empty, not occupied with its business of accommodating people, will soon deteriorate. In 1974 the Office of Public Works requested that a study should be made of the Royal Hospital, and a programme of conservation and restoration was eventually started in 1980. The problem for the principal architect, John Costello, was one that might have stopped a lesser man right where he stood: how can you haul back the years, how many tricks of the mason, woodworker and plasterer have now been lost? Any act of genuine restoration, be it ever so humble, must surely be done with the utmost dedication, study, care and expertise – plus one other absolute essential: to succeed fully, it will need to be an expression of love. Wandering round the corridors, through the great rooms, down the arcades, peering up at the stonework dressings, the carefully toned plaster stucco, one can give only one possible answer – John Costello has transfused a great portion of his experience and vigour into the arteries of the Royal Hospital, Kilmainham, making it a rare place and one which is now beginning another career – albeit still on the helping side. It has been designated the National Centre for Culture and the Arts.

The name carries with it a mystique not only because of the great house that it is but also for the treasures it contains. Some would have it that this is the finest house in Ireland. The aftermath of the blood spilt at Boyne on 1 July 1690, when William of Orange ripped apart the intentions of James II, brought peace for some, a time of oppression for others. The some were those persons of wealth and influence; the others were those who bore the weight of the Penal Times. For the some it was a rosy, prosperous period, and within the great demesnes and town houses a splendid life was lived by the members of the Ascendancy. For the others it was hard toil, hedgerow schools, exclusion from the bar, the university and public bodies. The eighteenth century was the full spring tide for the great houses of Ireland. Across the country they came into being: in Co. Fermanagh Castle Coole; out in the west the Browne family built Westport; a few miles north of Port Laoise, Gandon created Emo Court; near Celbridge Mr Conolly – Mr Speaker Conolly – erected Castletown; and in Co. Wicklow Mr Joseph Leeson had the inspiration to build Russborough.

The nearest route is not always the most satisfactory approach to a fine thing. Dublin is a busy bustling city and the roads out to Naas or Tallaght take more than their share of traffic, light and heavy. Be patient and give an extra hour to the trip; take the Bray road after the office men have scorched their way to town and turn right a mile after Bray, then left in Enniskerry and follow the signs for Roundwood, and the breath of rush and tussle is left behind. Turn right before Roundwood and head up to Sallygap. It can be a great place to be on a fine morning, the mountains crowding for airspace. At the Gap is Liffey Head, which reaches 1631 feet but is dwarfed by Mullaghcleevaun, all of 2783 feet to the peak. It is a pastel landscape with that clean blue sky so often to be found in Ireland, with just a few bumps of growing white clouds away to the south. The wind-combed grasses are a pale sage green against the rocks and down in the damp peat valleys are gatherings of chalk-white bog cotton. It is a place of freedom, birds seeking thermals or rising air currents are suddenly exploded upwards. With sight and thought cleared, on to Kilbride and left into Blessington; from here follow the road to Hollywood and keep a lookout as the timber thins on the right-hand side. When it clears there will be Russborough, strung like some great bracelet of classically inspired architectural genius across the landscape, with a total frontage of some 700 feet. Of all the Palladian houses in the country this one seems to have a unique quality; at the same time as the eye takes in the majesty of the design and layout one is also conscious of an atmosphere of home and a feeling of unusual intimacy.

In 1740 Joseph Leeson inherited a large amount of money from his father, who had been a successful brewer in Dublin. The newly rich legatee

Russborough – a treasure by Richard Castle that has a frontage of some 700 feet. From a distance it gives the impression of a gigantic bracelet laid across the landscape of mountains, woods and wide open skies.

Detail of the plasterwork on the wall of the stairwell.

Details of carving on the white marble fireplaces. Subjects chosen from myth and fable.

decided that he needed a great house to mirror his station, which would be further underlined when he was elected Member of Parliament for Rathcormack. He sought out the services of Richard Castle, and what evolved was this splendid place.

The centre block consists of seven bays with two storeys over a basement. It has a central feature of four engaged Corinthian columns with swags between the capitals; the columns rise only with the first storey and carry a rather austere pediment. There is an imposing flight of stone steps up to the front entrance, guarded at each side by imaginatively carved lords of the forest. On each side of the centre block are gently curving colonnades of Doric columns and capitals that connect with wings of two storeys. The spread of Castle's plan continues: high walls lead out from the ends of the wings to Baroque archways surmounted by cupolas, which are themselves connected to smaller pavilions associated with the stables and domestic areas. The architect had not quite finished: walk back out into the park and the final touches to this considerable exercise in symmetry take their place – shrewdly proportioned obelisks add that sense of balance that a lesser eye might have missed.

The façade reacts pleasantly to the sunlight; the silver-grey granite seems to absorb the light and to take on an almost ethereal quality. Apart from the mandatory procession of decorative urns along the parapet and a couple at the top of the steps, the whole building is remarkably free from applied decorative frills and it gains enormously in stature from this economy of detail. Indeed, the entrance gateway sets the scene for what is to come; this is just a very simple arch with lower side entrances to left and right, in plain dressed stone with slightly raised quoins and voussoirs and keystones surmounted with plain pediments.

The building of Russborough started in 1741 and must have taken in its entirety at least ten years. Joseph Leeson made his progress and in 1756 he was created Lord Milltown, four years later Viscount and in 1763 Earl of Milltown and a member of the Privy Council. His lordship had three wives, the last of whom reached the age of 100. During the Rebellion of 1798 the house was first occupied by the rebels and then by English troops who were there for several years; they savaged the roofs, using the timbers for firewood, and did much damage to the outbuildings. The succession lasted until the death of the 6th Earl in 1890, when the property went to his widow and thence to his nephew, Sir Edmund Turton, baronet, who lived in Yorkshire. This gentleman seldom used the house, which then entered a period of neglect, although somehow it escaped the dangers of the period around the Rising and the following Troubles. Eventually Sir Edmund's widow sold the property to a Captain Denis Daly in 1931 and he lovingly sought to return the house to the glories it once had. Lord Milltown had been a great collector and had donated many of his treasures to the National Gallery of Ireland, which establishment allowed the Dalys to retain some of

*The entrance hall – careful,
studied arrangement of
furniture and objects: glorious
chandelier, exquisite porcelain
and bronze figures.*

the works during their tenure. In the latest chapter of its history,
Russborough passed by purchase to Sir Alfred Beit in 1952.

Although the grand design for Russborough must have been Richard
Castle's, he did not live to see the finishing stages – these were carried out
by an associate of his, an amateur or dilettante architect called Francis
Bindon. But it is possible that Castle may have had something to do with
the interior decoration, which certainly in one respect surpasses anything else
done in Ireland. All the principal rooms which lead from one to the other
in the centre block carry quite amazing plasterwork, much of which would
point to the skilled hands of the Francini brothers. The motifs are
bewilderingly various; they seem still to be infused with a restless energy
imparted to them at the time of modelling – and it is freehand modelling,
not falling back on slavish moulding. The Baroque spirit is everywhere, not
only on the ceilings but also in fantasy frames whose oval shapes are
surrounded with billowing plant forms, bunches of fruit and scrolls. These
frames now contain paintings by the Frenchman Vernet that were for a

period removed from the house. It took Sir Alfred Beit some considerable effort to trace them and bring them back to the setting for which they were painted.

In some of the large rooms the plasterwork has a rather odd effect on the scale. One has the feeling that a certain room may not be quite as big as it should be, or that the heavily decorated ceiling is lower in proportion to the room than in fact it is. But the full adventure of the plasterwork is not within any of the principal rooms but on the wall of the staircase: here the modelling has a relief many inches in depth and there is a weight of decorative effects so great it is a wonder that the plaster has not ripped itself from the supporting wall. Pause a while to puzzle out some of the features – not least the head of a voluptuous hound near the bottom. It was of this area that the decorator, Mr Sibthorpe, is supposed to have remarked: 'this stucco represents the ravings of a lunatic, and an Irishman at that!'

Today Russborough lives more fully than ever it did, not only in its own right but the more so because it houses the internationally famous Beit collection of paintings, furniture and precious and rare objects. There can be few great houses that can rival the quality to be seen here. In the Tapestry Room, which holds the finely conserved English State Bed made in London in 1795, there is a delightful early eighteenth-century Soho tapestry by John Vanderbank; inside an exquisite border of flowers an array of eastern moguls, rich with colour, appear in an amazing variety of poses – in a strange carriage mounted on a prancing charger, involved with intricacies in tents, and in aspects of the chase. Throughout most of the rooms to be visited there are great pictures and also lesser objects whose history and associations can none the less fire the imagination. On a table with some other pieces stands a rather ornate microscope with all its bits and pieces and carefully worked case – its one-time owner that proud but ill-fated lady Marie Antoinette, wife of Louis XVI, whose opposition to social reform during the Revolution led to the overthrow of the monarchy and also led her to become the most celebrated victim of the guillotine. Who gave her this instrument, was it a toy, did she ever seriously use it? Of such is the fascination of visiting and exploring places which hold the past.

The view from the windows takes in a fine sweep of the foothills leading up to the Wicklow mountains, and on a calm quiet evening the waters of the Poulaphouca mirror the tantalizing changes of tone and tint as the curtains of the night are drawn across the softening mountain forms. Russborough rests at ease within the demesne – a great place that gives much to the owner and those privileged to visit it.

(above) The dining-room with the unusual mottled grey marble fireplace, a copy of which was made for Sir Alfred Beit's library in his London house. The plasterwork here has not quite the bravura quality of the other rooms and it may have been worked by Irish craftsmen. On the walls hang a series of six paintings by Murillo which illustrate the story of the Prodigal Son. (opposite, left) Detail of a fine Soho tapestry hanging in a principal bedroom; the design was worked from an original by John Vanderbank.

Slane Castle *Slane, Co. Meath*

The name is probably derived from Sláine, who was king of the Firbolgs and who died at Slane and – it is believed – was buried there. Tradition has it that a huge mound was erected over him and was named after him, and that this was the sacred spot where in 433 St Patrick is said to have kindled the first Paschal Fire in Ireland to celebrate the triumph of Christianity over paganism. Whether the Hill of Slane is the burial mound of the Firbolg king must certainly be in doubt: at 529 feet in height, its erection would have presented the followers of Sláine with a truly monumental task. To add to the problem, on the west side of the Hill of Slane there is a rath 27 feet high which is circular in shape and is surrounded by a deep ditch. St Eirc, the first bishop of St Patrick, who died in 514, built himself a hermitage here, and it is likely that there was also a medieval abbey. All of which makes this area around the town of Slane one of those places which brim with legend, word-of-mouth history, recorded history and a fair share of passion, blood and pillage. The Ostmen, the Danes from Dublin, came out here many times to see what more could be wrung from the luckless religious establishments: monks were put to the sword and prisoners herded away. In 1172 the town was subjected to a particularly savage attack from Dermod MacMurrough and a party of the English, the place was sacked and left in flames; in 1175 the English came back once more to pick up any plunder that could be found. The early abbey and the town then appear to have been so dispirited that they fell more and more into decay until 1512, when they were helped to their feet and restored by Sir Christopher Fleming, Lord of Slane.

On the settlement of the English in Meath, Slane became a borough and in the reign of Henry VI ranked as one of the middle class. Since the Fleming family had been engaged in the civil war of 1641, their estates were escheated to the Crown and subsequently became the property of the Right Honorable William Conyngham, ancestor of the Marquess of Conyngham.

The river Boyne flows quietly past the castle, and then towards the town and the long bridge where in 1690 the troops crossed the river to take part in the Battle of the Boyne, when William of Orange defeated James II.

The site of Slane Castle presents many faces. Viewed from the mid-arch of the bridge, with the weirs and slipways of the river in the immediate foreground, the bend of silvery water and the broad parkland, the impression is romantic, almost one of those fairy castles on the Loire. Looked at from closer to and straight on, it has a sense of majesty and promise of splendour; the slight elevation on which it stands gives just the necessary degree of eminence – the battlements are lifted above the ragged profiles of pine trees while the mass of the building conceals itself until one is suddenly clear of the trees and the undergrowth, and the stone mass of

Carved head on the outside wall of the stable block; the treatment shows some influence of early Celtic imagery.

masonry stands boldly there, obscuring with its bulk background, sky and all.

What originally stood on the site is almost impossible to tell – perhaps some form of bretesche on a motte on which could have been built the medieval castle of the Fleming family, and after that an earlier house. On these, and possibly incorporating some of their stonework, was to rise today's pride of Slane.

The 2nd Baron Conyngham commissioned James Wyatt and in 1785 building began; the style that emerged was one of the earliest examples of Gothic Revival in the country. The construction was completed under the direction of Francis Johnston for the 2nd Baron's son, who was later to become the 1st Marquess Conyngham. The symmetrical entrance front façade has more the appearance of some Tudor fastness, with elements of the late Norman. The square towers, which reach little higher than the parapet of the roof, are relieved of sternness by the treatment of the ground-floor windows. On the river front the massive round tower more or less takes over the building – its rotundity seemingly a transplant forcing its way against the squareness of Wyatt's conception. Within this great tower lies the treasure of Slane: the most celebrated Gothic Revival room in the country. A ballroom of quintessential elegance, it rises through two storeys of the tower; integrated with the domed ceiling is truly a fantasy of Gothic tracery, spun out so fine that momentarily it has the appearance of lace – a comfortable chair is needed to enable one to gaze upwards to take in the intricate symmetry and marvel at the way the designer has worked it all out effortlessly to fill the space. This wonder was probably the work of Thomas Hopper, who with James Gandon was called in for consultation. On each side of the fireplace are deep apses which in their turn support more decorative plasterwork – this time verging more towards the fan motif which was such a favourite of Adam, though there is too just a little bit of Gothic influence creeping in. The lower part of the walls is taken up with bookshelves, braced in behind doors that repeat the underlying influence which, although very much Gothic Revival, has a classical purity about it.

Over the fireplace hangs that well-known portrait of King George IV by Sir Thomas Lawrence, which brings out the character of this monarch with all the exuberance and bravura of Lawrence's style. In August 1821 the King stayed at Slane and found himself enchanted by the beauty and ways of Lady Conyngham; the liaison which ensued to some extent dominated his life. Local talk will tell of roadworks to straighten out parts of the road coming in from Dublin so that the royal carriage could make better time. On the opposite side of the ballroom stands rather stiffly a white marble horse carrying a white marble figure of Marcus Aurelius, the Roman

Emperor who – apart from his military accomplishments – is recalled for his *Meditations* propounding the stoic view of life. He and his mount are nineteenth-century copies, somewhat chipped and with pieces missing, but on a sunny late afternoon a blast of strong light flooding in lends them translucence and reflects upwards to the ceiling to produce an almost ethereal sensation, creating knife-edged shadows and an effect as though some giant hand had driven a burin around the design.

There are a number of fine works around the rooms of Slane which came from the royal purse – probably the most outstanding is a massive desk which occupies a bay opposite the fireplace in the drawing-room. It was designed by Henry Holland for George IV, who then gave it to his noble mistress. The ormolu fittings complement the sheer strength of the desk, in particular the lion-heads gripping the handles in their teeth. In this room are some good examples of chairs with embroidered work on backs and seats in the French style of the eighteenth century, which may be of either English or Irish craftsmanship.

The hall, which has four fluted columns with Tuscan capitals and a cornice of mutules (projecting blocks), is a spacious area serving the main reception rooms; a glass light over the entrance door displays armorial bearings. This area and the staircase are the work of Johnston.

Gilt and gessoed chair with embroidered back and seat.

(opposite) Slane Castle – basically the design of James Wyatt, but Johnston, Gandon, Hopper and others were consulted at different times.

Outside and to the left is a slow ramp that connects with the service door for the below-stairs quarters, which today are largely taken up by a restaurant whose quality brings diners from much further afield than just the local town. Away to the left are the stables, reputedly designed by Capability Brown who never actually came to Ireland because – as he said – he was too busy. But perhaps he sent over an assistant, or just the plans – mostly heavy in design with a fortress look about them. On the south side quite interesting warrior heads are set into the wall beside the entrance. There is another piece of inset sculpture in the wall of the yard in front of the service door for the restaurant. This is a life-size figure of a bishop, complete with mitre and robes; his right hand is gloved and an episcopal ring can be clearly made out as the hand is held up in the position of benediction. It is probable that he was originally recumbent on an altar tomb, as behind his head is a pillow and above it a carved canopy, and his feet rest on what is either a hound or a small lion. The date is late fourteenth or early fifteenth century.

The inhabitants of Slane Castle have been full-blooded characters, of strong opinions and ready for action. At the start of the tussle at Boyne in 1690 a father fought on one side and a son on the other, one for King Billy and one for King James. Then as the fortunes of the battle swayed, the one with King James deserted with a fine force of eager men and joined the other side. Soon after that, King James must have been galloping away to the south, stopping among other places at Lismore Castle, before going on to a port that would have a ship for France.

Lady Conyngham was by report a highly controversial lady and would have had an influence on her royal lover. She supported Catholic emancipation and was against the death penalty. Like many other great ladies of her time and later, she lived a full life and a long one, lasting until (opposite) The pride of the castle must be the highly decorative and elegant ballroom; it rises through two storeys of the great tower and displays Gothic Revival craftsmanship at its most refined in the delicacy of the ceiling.

(below) The great round tower, with impressive dressed stonework, windows showing a Perpendicular influence and strong corbelling at the balcony and beneath the battlements.

she was ninety-two; latterly she walked to church every Sunday, supported by George IV's cane. Whatever her early amours with the King, they must have contrasted with the care she lavished on him through the ailments, supposed and real, of his last years.

Walk over the long bridge which straddles the Boyne and turn up the hill that curves round to the left – almost immediately Johnston's fine upstanding gateway comes into view. The arms over the gate are those of the Earl of Conyngham, later to be the first Marquess, impaled with those of his wife, Elizabeth Denison. Over the shield is an earl's coronet and below it the badge of the Order of St Patrick. This entrance is no longer used today, access being by the other gateway off the west road out of the town. Like many of these houses that have been involved on the anvil of history, Slane has taken its hammering, and now – apart from the occasional synthesized beat of pop – gives out a delightful atmosphere of well-earned peace, yet with an eye ever watchful for some new venture to come down that road from Dublin or even perhaps sail up the Boyne.

Tullynally Castle   Castlepollard, Co. Westmeath

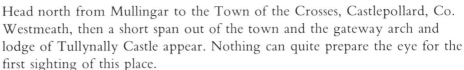

Head north from Mullingar to the Town of the Crosses, Castlepollard, Co. Westmeath, then a short span out of the town and the gateway arch and lodge of Tullynally Castle appear. Nothing can quite prepare the eye for the first sighting of this place.

It has been said that Tullynally is the largest castle in Ireland still lived in as a family home. No one would argue. As the trees clear away to allow a view the size is apparent – turrets tall and short, towers, battlements by the hundred, vast blocks of masonry with a total circumference of nearly a quarter of a mile. Tullynally might be taken for one of those fortified cities like the medieval Carcassone in south-west France. But the embrasures here have never known a crossbolt fired in anger, nor have sentries on the turret tops scanned the distance for approaching cavalry. Look around: there is no protective earthwork, no sign of a moat. Tullynally is one more of those wondrous Gothic Revival exercises in the romantic fashion which exerted their thrall in the late eighteenth and early to mid-nineteenth centuries. The feeling of size here is given strength by the fact that stables, coach houses, domestic offices and a large enclosed inner courtyard are all joined on to the main block.

The present castle and the building before it have been the home of the Pakenhams – later Barons and Earls of Longford – since 1655. Part of the early fortified building survives in the ten-feet-thick masonry walls of the main block. This castle or defended house had been transformed by the early eighteenth century into a two-storey home, and there is a drawing by G. E. Pakenham (the younger brother of the owner at the time), dated 1738, that shows not only the house but also much of the complicated garden system which made great use of water in cascades, canals and other devices; this was later to be put back as a natural landscape.

In 1780 reconstruction and additions were undertaken to the designs of Graham Myers and presumably it was he who put on the third storey.

Between 1801 and 1806 the 2nd Earl of Longford brought in Francis Johnston to begin in a rather gentle fashion the Gothic treatment; this included a battlemented parapet and corner turrets that reached up, looking rather slender against the general mass. The 2nd Earl had two of the generals in the Peninsular War as brothers: Sir Edward Pakenham (who later fell at New Orleans) and Sir Hercules Pakenham. There was also his sister Catherine, who after some considerable parental disapproval was allowed to marry the great Duke of Wellington. It must have been a savage business out in America when Sir Edward commanded the doomed expedition against Andrew Jackson's troops. The slug of lead from some

Tullynally Castle – from a distance it gives the impression of a small fortified town; in fact, the castle covers a greater area than any other in the land.

American musket that is reputed to have laid him low is still preserved. His body was submerged in a barrel of rum to be sent back home, but in the way of transport something went wrong and the word is passed down that the barrel ended up in the West Indies; gossip has it that some locals, realizing what precious spirit the barrel contained, breached the cask and began a celebration – gossip does not state what happened when the level of the rum was lowered and the grisly heart of the matter emerged. In some ways the most unusual member of the family must be Charles Reginald, son of the 2nd Earl. He gave up a brilliant military career to become a monk. As Father Paul Mary he founded a religious order at Mount Argus, Dublin. The Duke of Wellington when he heard this is reputed to have said: 'You have been a damn good soldier – now be a damn good monk.'

In the 1820s the 2nd Earl had an urge for yet more changes and he brought in James Shiel, who contributed to the great hall and added a three-sided bow to the garden front. The house had been called Pakenham Hall, probably from the time of Myers' work; then after Johnston it became Pakenham Hall Castle; and recently Thomas Pakenham, son of the present Earl, has brought back the old Irish name of Tullynally. Around 1840, the 3rd Earl brought in that other stalwart of the Irish architectural scene, Sir Richard Morrison, who designed two wings which make up two sides of a court and serve to join the main block to the stable court; he also erected an imposing castellated gateway. In one of the new wings sumptuous quarters were provided for the Dowager Countess and the other was arranged to give good accommodation for the Earl's forty indoor servants. Morrison further added liberally to the Gothic look with more battlements – some 800 feet of them.

Inside the great hall, which rises through two storeys, there is an impressive sense of space; there is no gallery – it just goes straight up to simple Gothic vaulting. At the base of the walls wood panelling rises to about ten feet and above there are niches containing family crests. Scattered along the panelling are sketches of the building, including one by James Shiel done in 1820 which shows the garden side of the castle very much as it looks today, except for the trees which have grown well up and to a degree have altered the scale. Along with the sketches on the wall are sundry weapons owned by past members of the family. Opposite is a small built-in organ and, intimately in front of it, a large rocking horse that must have been the friend of many generations. Go through a door opposite the main entrance and there is the dining-room as it was remodelled by Shiel into an octagon, occupying the bow to the garden side that he put on. The drawing-room has a refined sense of the vogue for the medieval – just the simplest geometric ceiling with a Gothic alcove. Paintings of sea battles are impressive and point to the family's contribution not only to land but also marine warfare. The library is a fine one – well-cared-for leather bindings fill the shelves to the ceiling.

Move through a betwixt door and down some yards of flagged passages: you come to the below-stairs regions. In the main kitchen there is a wonderful array of glistering copper and brass, rows of fine saucepans for all purposes, jugs and pots – all identified with the coronet of the master of the house. Bygone utensils for the cook include a marmalade cutter and a weird contraption several feet across for taking the buttermilk out of the freshly made butter after it leaves the churn. Down a step or two to the servants' hall and the table is laid with quality white china bearing the sign of Minton.

The most impressive area down here is the large laundry; several girls must have taken all their time to run it – a row of metal-lined troughs with those archaic wavy metal rubbing-boards that must have wrecked dozens of laundry girls' knuckles, and at one end what must be a contender for the world's largest mangle: its width is measured in feet and it could surely apply enough pressure to bend a steel plate for a battleship. High on shelves rest large wicker baskets – no, not for humping the laundry about at Tullynally, but rather for the family to use when in London and to dispatch clothes and suchlike back for the fresh air treatment and loving care of the home service. Across a small passage there is another refinement for the Tullynally laundry – a drying room with a bank of vertical drawers which can be dragged out on guiding rails, each of which is provided with several horizontal boards with ample room for everything from the most minute child's wear up to double sheets.

A letter in the Edgeworth manuscript collection in the National Library in Dublin illuminates aspects of life in the great house. It is dated 1807 and is from Maria Edgeworth to her father, R. L. Edgeworth:

Lord L has finished & furnished his castle which is now a mansion fit for a nobleman of his fortune. The furniture is neither Gothic nor Chinese, nor gaudy, nor frail, nor so fashionable that it will be out of fashion in 6 months but substantially handsome and suitable in all its parts – the library scarlet and black with some red morocco cushioned chairs and some . . . very handsome plain black with white Medusa heads . . . I was desired to estimate these chairs & oh shameful chance! guessed them at a guinea & $\frac{1}{2}$ when their price is seven guineas . . . the immense Hall so well warmed by hot air that the children play in it from morn till night . . . The whole house, every bed chamber, every passage so thoroughly warmed that we never felt any reluctance in going upstairs or from one room to another . . . I hope you anticipate what I am going to say, that now Lord L has made such a comfortable nest he must certainly get some bird with pretty plumage & sweet voice to fill it.

Tullynally was one of the first houses in the British Isles to have central heating; the system here was designed by the inventor Richard Lovell Edgeworth, the brother of Maria the writer of the letter above, who lived quite close at Edgeworthstown. The furnace room, which houses a truly

massive boiler, is well down in the bowels of the castle; it was reached from the outside by a tunnel big enough to accommodate a loaded cart of peat which exited to ground level well clear of the building.

Tullynally Castle has several faces when viewed from outside. If the day is overcast the stonework, the much-battlemented elevations appear strong, massively medieval, but if the day has some warmth to it and the sun plays down on the stone it takes on an atmosphere almost of lightness, of a romantic creation more suited to peaceful pursuits than to the bleak passage of arms which would have attended such a place 500 or more years ago. Walk away in a southerly direction a mile or more, mount a small hill and hope that the clouds will break; if they do the sun lights up a distant Tullynally and makes the stonework gleam with an almost luminous effect – then it does become a fairy castle against the mauves and pale greens of the hills behind.

In literal translation Tullynally means 'Hill of the Swans'. Across the parkland to the south and through the trees can be caught the glitter of a wide expanse of water – Lake Derravaragh. Surely there is more than coincidence in the proximity of the 'Hill of the Swans' to this lake, around which has been spun one of the most moving and sad of all the Irish legends. The Children of Lir were sweet, beautiful beings who aroused the jealousy of a stepmother and found themselves turned into swans on Lake Derravaragh, where it was said that their singing would give sleep to the sick and troubled, and make happy all who heard it. After many years on Derravaragh the Children were banished to distant and inclement places. Centuries later they returned to seek out the palace of their father, King Lir. Then came the sound of a saint's bell and a prayer which restored them to human form – not that of young children but rather of beings hoary with the look of great age. So they passed into some special place where legends live.

The drawing-room – a place for rest and quiet, soft muted cretonnes on easy chairs and sofas, pleasantly decorated ceiling in the geometric manner, canvases of sea battles point to the family's contribution in this area of warfare. (above) One of the most fascinating features of Tullynally is below stairs. Here may be studied a fine array of gleaming copper pans, their lids bearing coronets, Victorian machines for chopping things, and all the necessities for the preparation of a multi-course dinner.

Westport House *Westport, Co. Mayo*

(top) Elizabeth Kelly, daughter of Denis Kelly, a Chief Justice of Jamaica. Painted by Thomas Hudson who taught Sir Joshua Reynolds.

(above) A portrait by Reynolds of the Right Honorable Denis Browne, which displays the artist's distinctive modelling of the face.

Co. Mayo is one of those open places; with Co. Clare, Co. Galway and Co. Kerry, it provides for most people the very essence of Ireland – out here there are more important things than the traffic of commerce, with all its noise and fumes. The west is somewhere that seems to give habitation to much more than the seen things. The unseen finds a habitat in the green lushness of the Killarney lakeland, the broad-scarred bosom of the Burren, the pastel mauve mountains of Galway – and the wide open expanse of Mayo, with the horizon to the west signposted by the looming peaks and perhaps most of all by the sharp, jagged spire of Croagh Patrick. As one drives westwards from Castlebar this symbol of penance seems to be a taunt – always just out of reach. The eye can become so fascinated by the apparently unobtainable quality of the mountain that the descent from the uplands of rock-strewn, peat-bogged, grey-green sheep's pasture is not registered. After the barren, little-inhabited areas are passed through, the sight of the town of Westport comes almost as a passage in a dream – can it have reality or substance? Certainly, for Thackeray it had both. In his *Irish Sketch Book* (1842) he eulogizes the town and many details in it. An eighteenth-century adventure in town planning and construction, it was inspired and largely organized by a most philanthropic patron: the incumbent of Westport House.

During the eighteenth century much of the old town was pulled down and the task of erecting the new was given to James Wyatt, who worked on the great house. It is to him that the present-day inhabitants can express gratitude for the wide streets and pavements, the trees lining the Carrowbeg river through the cenrre, the Mall, the Octagon and many other delightful features.

The site for Westport House itself is about a mile out of town, superbly placed facing away to the west, with Clew Bay speckled with islands and, behind, looming mauve mountains as a backdrop. Woodlands frame the view and ensure seclusion. But John Browne, afterwards the 1st Earl of Altamont, was not the first to think of this as a suitable place for a residence. For Westport House sits on the remains of an earlier building, which in its turn lies on what many believe to be the rough, ragged dungeons of one of the castles of that most celebrated lady of sixteenth-century Ireland, Grace O'Malley: pirate, chieftainess, warrior queen and even at times a mercenary for Queen Elizabeth I.

In the days of this redoubtable character Mayo would have been a wild place indeed – wolves still roamed the land, black eagles flew overhead. The O'Malley tribe held rights by force over the fishing. This produced a rich harvest: cockles, cod, crab, herring, ling, lobsters, oysters, pilchard, scallops and turbot abounded. Large herds of cattle gave them meat and dairy

(top) *Painting by George Moore made around 1760 of Westport and general view, barely recognizable today with the grown-up timbers and town.*

(above) *Painting by the talented Irishman James Arthur O'Connor of Delphi and Lake.*

products. Grace's empire included at the least Hen's Castle in Lough Corrib, Bawn Castle, Kinturk Castle near Castlebar, Renvyle Castle, and Rockfleet Castle, the latter being her headquarters, though – like others with the mind of a tyrant – she liked to keep on the move for security reasons.

There is, however, a more significant connection between her and the masters of Westport House than a few dark slippery dungeons. From her marriage sprang the Mayo line. Her son was created 1st Viscount Mayo in 1627 by Charles I. In 1669 Grace O'Malley's great-great-granddaughter, Maud Bourke, who was born in 1642, married John Browne of Westport. Thus the present Lord Altamont is a direct descendant from that wondrous, fiery woman.

The main mass of the house, as it is seen today, was commissioned by John Browne and begun in 1730 to the designs of the German-born architect Richard Castle. This plan consisted of a long, fairly slim building. Later, in 1778, a further three sides were added, probably to the designs of Thomas Ivory, leaving a court in the centre; at a later date still, the whole was roofed in as one building.

There are two primitive paintings that hang on the main stairway, the work of George Moore in about 1760. One is of the scene looking from the sea and shows a somewhat elaborate system of bridges: at that date no artificial lake had been attempted and thus the rising waves with the incoming tide would have spent themselves against the walls of the house. The other picture looks west out into Clew Bay and more or less repeats the evidence of the first, with Croagh Patrick and Clare Island also visible.

Richard Castle's entrance front on the east side presents an impressive façade. A lengthy flight of stone steps leads up to a rusticated tripartite doorway, with a wide and well-proportioned pediment extending over the door itself and the flanking windows; this contains in the tympanum the arms of the 1st Earl, so the date must be post-1771, the year he received his earldom. Below the pediment are three strikingly carved masks of satyrs. At the roof line, there is a raised section with three square lights which is surmounted by urns: at the corners there once stood two great birds with wings proudly raised – today a solitary bird remains; with only one wing, it seems prepared to fight on in whatever role it can serve its master. At some time, probably in the late nineteenth century, an eager soul searching for more light and encouraged by the prowess of the Victorian glassmakers, with their larger and larger sheets of glass, had the glazing bars removed, thereby to a degree unsettling the balance and composition of the elevation.

The interior of this massive house needed something special, and it was the 3rd Earl, afterwards the 1st Marquess of Sligo, who called in James Wyatt to grapple with the problem. Certainly his finest contribution was

Westport House, a monument to gracious living out in the far west – today easily motored to, yesterday a good blunderbus was needed on the coach against highwaymen.

the large dining-room, with tasteful proportions, finely worked doors and surrounds, and delicate plasterwork using round and oval plaques with classical figures. Wyatt's original drawings for this work still exist and are hanging there.

The table and sideboards display good-quality silver and Waterford glass, together with a notable collection of those most Irish objects, potato rings, including one that still has the container for the precious fruit. This is carved from a piece of bog oak which is by now iron hard, the inside being lined with beaten silver. The invention of motifs by the craftsmen responsible is fascinating, as is their skilled use of the repoussé technique of pushing through the main elements of the design from the back and then finishing from the front with gravers and burnishers.

Westport abounds with little and large things from history that bring the moments alive again. In a small room leading out of the large dining-room, held safely in a glass case, is a worn and threadbare banner. As elsewhere, the historical root leads to France: the year this was made was 1798 and the ladies of Paris worked it with the skill of fine embroideresses at the order of the Directory. When the invasion fleet set out in that year for another go at Albion's back-door, the flag – the Mayo Standard as it is called – was handed to General Humbert, the commanding officer. The landing was made at Kilcummin Bay and the French occupied Killala, from which they were driven with considerable slaughter by General Trench, commanding the King's forces; then, after some more bloodshed and turmoil, the Standard was delivered to the safekeeping of the masters of Westport.

Upstairs in a glass case rests a cannon ball made by the family to be used at the siege of Limerick, whose walls proved tougher than James II's French General Lauzun supposed when he claimed that they could be razed with roasted apples. On the same shelf, under a glass dome, rests a strange-looking mass of creamy white paste. This is a lump of bog-butter discovered some time ago in a family peat-bog; it remains today in a static, non-putrid condition, pointing to the extraordinary preservative qualities of the bog. In another glass cupboard, exquisite Meissen figures jostle with a pedlar doll standing about eight inches tall and displaying a tray of enticing wares in miniature: tiny packets of herbs, spools of thread, sparkling trinkets.

Most families of distinction have one member who stands out in originality above the rest. The Brownes of Westport do not fail in this respect. In 1788 was born Howe Peter Browne, who was to become the 2nd Marquess of Sligo and to live to the full – and more – everyone's idea of a Regency 'buck'. He came to life with a golden spoon in his mouth, inheriting 200,000 acres of farms, moors and bogs, as well as valuable sugar plantations in Jamaica. He was a friend of George IV, who was godfather to his eldest son, an associate of Lord Byron and De Quincey, a patron for the poor mutts who battered each other to insensibility with rough bare *(opposite, above) Two close-up details from a painting by James Arthur O'Connor of Westport harbour; his style is almost that of a miniaturist.*

(below) A sensitive and well-modelled woman and child by the French sculptor Dalou that stands at the west end of the Long Gallery.

(below) The rear of the house looks to the west across a man-encouraged lake – elegant steps and balustrades and, just out of sight, a rough Greek sarcophagus.

knuckles, and his horse Waxy won the Derby in 1811. Here was a man who showed his skill with the reins by driving his coach from London to Holyhead, a distance of 270 miles, in 35 hours, a feat which won him a wager of 1,000 guineas. In 1815 he tried to rescue by sea his friend Murat, one of Napolean's generals, from Naples; the scheme went wrong and Murat was shot. His extravagances were notorious: when his father died in Lisbon the 2nd Marquess spent £10,000 just to charter a boat to bring back the body.

Doubtless his most famous escapade came in 1811 when the idea of treasure-hunting struck him. He chartered a brig and set sail for Greece; quite by chance, or so it seems, he saw his friend and co-student from Cambridge, Byron, lying on the beach at Phaleron Bay. For a time the two journeyed together, but parted when the Marquess felt led to excavate at

Mycenae. This was not going to be a scientific 'dig', but rather raw looting. He ended up with numerous items of Greek antiquity, including the celebrated columns from the doorway to the Treasury of Atreus. These massive objects, with the rest, were loaded into his ship – the latter derided by Byron, who wrote in a letter to a friend: 'Sligo has a brig with 50 men who won't work, 12 guns that refuse to go off, and sails that cut every wind except a contrary one . . . He has en suite a painter, a captain, a gentleman mis-interpreter (who boxes with the painter), besides sundry English varlets.'

The Marquess set sail, but had doubts about the skill of his men to navigate safely back home, so he boldly stopped a passing British warship and bribed two sailors to join him to oversee the navigation and safety of his vessel: not the kind of act – even from a Marquess – that would be calculated to amuse the Admiralty or others in high places. On his arrival, he was arrested and tried at the Old Bailey, sent to Newgate prison for four months and fined £5,000. But that was not quite the end of the story. During the trial his mother was so impressed with the way the judge, Sir William Scott, handled her son, and Sir William was so impressed by the pleading of his mother, that a love-affair blossomed between them. The day the 2nd Marquess came out of prison, his mother took the judge as her second husband.

The two columns from the Treasury lay in the cellars of Westport for the best part of a century, until in 1906 they were identified by the 6th Marquess, who presented them to the British Museum; copies were made, which today stand fixed to the south side of Westport. Another visible sign of this exploit of the 2nd Marquess is a rough Greek sarcophagus that lies slightly askew in a meadow in front of the west side of the house – unlabelled, it must seem a curious object to those who come upon it.

The family did much during the terrible famine years of the nineteenth century. The 3rd Marquess spread his money to help where he could, reducing himself by so doing almost to a pauper. The conditions 'out west' were typified by those prevailing in the town at Westport, where there was a breakdown of the system and of normal life. The migrations started and at least forty-nine per cent of the people left either for Britain or for the long sail to the New World.

Wander round the large rooms, the intimate sitting-rooms, the bedrooms, some with gargantuan, heavily carved furniture in the German baronial hall style, down into the basement, where the battle for existence goes on. Here, with courage, the faithful retainers dispense good cups of tea and old-fashioned cakes, rare books are for the purchasing, children find fun places, and for the inquiring ones there are always the Grace O'Malley dungeons that smell convincingly damp and are cold to the touch.

The entrance hall, which is also the main exit, carries obligatory paintings of horses and their attendants on its walls, but also a good collection of that great Irish painter, James Arthur O'Connor (*c*.1792–1841). O'Connor was the son of a Dublin printseller and engraver, and appears to have been self-taught. His small canvases record in a simple and convincing manner the scenes of his day. In particular, there is a view of Westport Quay, hanging halfway up the large, centrally placed, marble staircase. It sets down, almost with the fine-quality detail of a miniature, the whole scene, from which can be gleaned the types of vessels, the costumes, the carts and other equipment of the port – described thus by Thackeray in his memoirs: 'There was a long handsome pier, and one solitary cutter alongside it, which may or may not be there now. As for the warehouses they are enormous, and might accommodate, I should think, not only the trade of Westport, but of Manchester too.' The gentlemen of the family did much, both with ideas and funds, to encourage industry associated with textiles and other materials; they tried to make Westport the principal port for the whole of the west of Ireland. The plans failed, leaving the mute evidence of these huge warehouses, still today largely empty and with broken windows staring a little sadly down the Carrowbeg, whose waters become sluggish as they reach the sea.

There is a particular object that catches the eye as one enters the hall. In a large niche in the wall, halfway up those marble stairs, stands a slightly over life-size figure of an angel, carved with delicacy from pure white marble; the angel stands there with one hand outstretched and it is said that whenever the young children of the family returned home they would run up the steps and reach for the welcoming hand. Perhaps they understood

(above) Massive carved cupboard with a relief of several inches. Probably German.

(left) Equally massive carved eagle support for a sideboard.

better than most a striking piece of symbolism on the head of the angel. From the top the representation of a flame springs upward; religious symbolism suggests that it represents the presence of the Holy Spirit.

Down the entrance steps and into a vehicle of our own time, slowly to gather speed down the drive, past the placid waters of the man-made lake, with brightly coloured rowing-boats, past the serried ranks of horse-drawn caravans . . . after nearly a mile one can pause by a bridge and wistfully look back at Westport House: in the evening's slanting rays of the sun, it appears as a pale cliff across the reaches of the water, casting long reflections over the surface that is pierced by the broken branches and tree-trunks which have fallen with countless winter winds.

Afterword

Castles, mansions, houses that in their design reflect architectural skills – these are not just private assets for a period of history or a single owner, they are an essential part of any country's artistic legacy. They are much more than personal heirlooms to be handed down: these buildings from past centuries have been the keeping places of the work of painters, those skilled in drawing, print-makers, sculptors and the whole range of great craftsmen who have worked with fine woods, precious metals, jewels, glass, ceramics, textiles, base metals, alloys and other materials.

It is sometimes overlooked that the keeping places themselves are just as important as the objects they protect – that the sturdy walls of stone and brick are not impervious to the forces which can wreak damage to the works of art within. The process may be considerably slower, but the end result can be the same – destruction. The noble dwellings have often in their history had to meet not only the forces of natural elements, water and the power of winds, but also in the earlier centuries had to contend with the blast of powder, the tearing impact of cannon balls and slighting by the conqueror. Add to these, accidental and intentional fire, dilapidations unchecked because of failing family finances, and the toll of the great places that have been shuffled from the landscape becomes sad reading.

Acts of creative expression by the legion of architects, artists and craftsmen that are one with every period of history are invaluable artefacts not just for that period but often even more for the times that follow. It is an inescapable fact that if one page from an illuminated manuscript is lost through lack of care or a painting is consumed by fire, if a fine piece of Venetian glass splinters across a tiled floor or a notable piece of architecture deteriorates to the point of passing, at that moment the rich and splendid tapestry that is the background and support of the progress of us all is thereby diminished.

Spend a period searching through records and books concerned with the works of the artists of the past and the total loss exceeds many times what might have been thought possible. Armies under avaricious commanders march on treasure houses and seize priceless gold and silver plate, only to consign it to the furnace to produce bullion worth a fraction of the original pieces. Acts of greed or ignorance? No matter – the treasures are lost. Tears shed over the description of precious things that have gone cannot hide the fact that the next generation has been robbed before it is born. All too often fashion can be the elusive culprit – a design, a technique, a particular use of a material can be labelled overnight as 'old hat' and consigned to some limbo. Who should make the deific decision that a genuine creative act is no longer worthy of preservation – perhaps for no better reason than that the maker of the decision suffers from limited vision?

The noble dwellings mentioned here harbour a great deal more than lovely and beautiful things. To visit them is to be able to participate even for just a short time in an atmosphere that will stay with the consciousness – it will be an enrichment drawn from the total environment.

The skills of masons, carpenters, metalworkers – those who have created with the talent of their hands the fabric for living. Combine with these the often thrilling passage of history, the facts of those who braved, those who achieved, those who gave. It can be an uplifting experience to walk round Lismore Castle and realize that your steps could be following those of Sir Walter Raleigh; or to stand looking through the windows at Lissadell and hear the voice of W. B. Yeats; or to cross the park at Birr Castle and stand beside the 'leviathan' and let the eye follow that of the 3rd Earl as it searched through the immensities of deep space; or to trundle in imagination down the avenue of limes in a fine coach and to walk up the steps to spend an afternoon with Lady Louisa Conolly in the great gallery at Castletown. All this and far far more was theirs, but it is also ours. Too many have already fallen, their only memorial a faded photograph or painting.

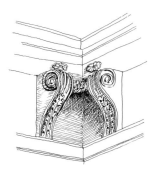

A sign set up by the Forestry Commission of Northern Ireland at Belleek, Co. Fermanagh, informs us:

The first castle was built here by Sir Edward Blennerhassett in 1612. The castle and the estate were sold to the Caldwell family in 1662.

The castle was extensively improved by Sir James Caldwell. Writing in 1778 to his son John who was in Canada, Sir James tells of having spent £16,000 on Castle Caldwell. Two large walled gardens with fish ponds were constructed and the lands which extended to 700 acres were improved.

Sir John Caldwell inherited the estate after the death of his father in 1784. During the last decade of the eighteenth century Sir John also carried out extensive modifications to the castle and a museum was added to the east wing with six new rooms above it.

The museum contained some rare Irish antiquities, items from abroad and a large collection of stuffed birds and animals from other countries.

The fortunes of the estate declined during the latter half of the nineteenth century. The contents of the castle were auctioned in 1876 and from this date it rapidly declined into a ruin.

The ruins of Castle Caldwell

Further Reading

Adams, C. L. *Castles of Ireland* London 1904

Atkinson, A. *Ireland in the Nineteenth Century* Dublin 1815

Automobile Association, The *Touring Guide to Ireland* London 1976

Bagshawe, W. H. G. *The Bagshawes of Ford* 1886

Barrington, Jonah *Personal Sketches of his Own Times* London 1827–32

Bence-Jones, Mark *Burke's Guide to Country Houses (Ireland)* London 1978

Bourniquel, Camille *Ireland* London 1960

Bowden, C. T. *A Tour through Ireland in 1790* 1791

Boylan, Lena *The Early History of Castletown* Dublin 1967

Breffney, Brian de *Castles of Ireland* London 1977

Breffney, Brian de and Rosemary ffolliott *The Houses of Ireland* London 1975

Craig, Maurice *Dublin 1660–1860* Dublin and London 1969

Craig, Maurice *The Architecture of Ireland* London 1982

Craig, Maurice and The Knight of Glin *Ireland Observed* Cork 1970

Cromwell, T. K. *Excursions through Ireland*, 3 vols 1820

Curran, C. P. *Dublin Decorative Plasterwork of the 17th and 18th centuries* London and New York 1967

Curties, Edmund *A History of Ireland* London 1936

Eager, Alan R. *A Guide to Irish Bibliographical Material* London 1964

Fitzgerald, Brian *The Geraldines* London 1951

Fraser, James A. *A Handbook for Travellers in Ireland* Dublin 1844

Gaughan, J. Anthony *The Knights of Glin* Dublin 1978

Guinness, Desmond and Ryan, William *Irish Houses and Castles* London 1971

Hall, Mr and Mrs S. C. *Ireland: Its Scenery, Character, Etc.* London 1841

Harbison, Peter; Potterton, Homan and Sheehy, Jeanne *Irish Art and Architecture* London 1978

Inglis, Brian *The Story of Ireland* London 1960

Killanin, Lord and Duignan, Michael V. *Shell Guide to Ireland* London 1962

Leask, H. G. *Irish Castles and Castellated Houses* Dundalk 1941

Lecky, William Hartpole *A History of Ireland in the 18th Century*, 5 vols London 1892

Lewis, Samuel *Topographical Dictionary of Ireland*, 2 vols London 1837

Luckombe, Philip *A Tour Through Ireland* Dublin 1780

McParland, Edward *James Gandon* London 1985

O'Brien, Máire and Conor Cruise *A Concise History of Ireland* Rev. ed. London 1984

Pococke, Richard *Pococke's Tour in Ireland in 1752* Dublin and London 1891

Sadler, T. V. and Dickinson, P. L. *Georgian Mansions in Ireland* Dublin 1915

Sligo, Marquess of *Westport House and the Brownes* Ashbourne, Derbyshire 1981

Stafford, Thomas *Pacata Hibernia* London 1633, reprinted Dublin 1810

Summerson, John *Architecture in Britain 1530–1830* London 1953

Tocnaye, de la *Ramble through Ireland by a French Emigrant* Cork 1798

Trotter, John Bernard *Walks Through Ireland in 1814 & 1817* London 1819

Twiss, Richard *A Tour in Ireland in 1775* London 1776

Weld, Isaac *Illustrations of the Scenery of Killarney and the Surrounding Country* London 1812

Wright, Rev G. N. *Scenes of Ireland* London 1834

Young, Arthur *A Tour in Ireland* London 1780

Acknowledgments

The author wishes particularly to thank Anne Crookshank for her unstinted help with queries, and further to express his gratitude to the owners and administrators of the castles and houses concerned, who have all given considerable and willing assistance with information, as well as gracious permission to draw, paint and photograph wherever he wished. He would like to include here the Producer of the Radio Telefís Eireann series, Denis O'Grady; also Sheila Carden, Production Assistant; Simon Weafer, Cameraman; Breffni Byrne, Cameraman; Liam McDonagh, Electrical Supervisor; Pat Johns, Sound Recordist; Bryan Day, Film Editor; and Brian Lynch, Dubbing Mixer.

Besides the above, he would like to thank the following for their cooperation: Bord Fáilte, The Office of Public Works, The National Trust of Northern Ireland and the Historic Irish Tourist Houses and Gardens Association. Thanks, too, to the many others who lent a hand in passing.

The author and Thames and Hudson gratefully acknowledge additional illustrations supplied by: Bord Fáilte Eireann; The Office of Public Works; National Trust of Northern Ireland; Bryan Mills; Richard Hammonds, Hereford (for taking the transparencies of the paintings).

Index

6.15.87 24 95 H&I Ac# 33571